Contextualization

Meanings, Methods, and Models

David J. Hesselgrave
and
Edward Rommen

Foreword by
George W. Peters

APOLLOS
Leicester, England

Copyright 1989 by
Baker Book House

APOLLOS is an imprint of Inter-Varsity Press
38 De Montfort Street, Leicester LE1 7GP, England

Printed in the United States of America

British Library Cataloguing in Publication Data

Hesselgrave, David J.
    Contextualization.
    1. Christianity. Communication. Cross-cultural
    I. Title   II. Rommen, Edward, *1947–*
    261

    ISBN 0-85111-413-X

Unless noted otherwise, the Scripture quotations are from the Holy Bible, New International Version, Copyright © 1973, 1978, 1984 International Bible Society. Used by permission of Zondervan Bible Publishers. The other versions cited are the New American Standard Bible (NASB) and the King James Version (KJV).

An edited version of "Contextualization and Epistemology" from *Hermeneutics, Inerrancy and the Bible* by Earl D. Radmacher and Robert D. Preus is copyright © 1984 by the Zondervan Publishing House and is used by permission. An edited version of "Authentic Contextualization: Taking Truth Out of the Top Drawer and Placing It on the Lower Shelf," from *A Journal of Christian Studies* 5, nos. 1 and 2 (Winter 1985–86): 79–96, appears with the permission of Lincoln Christian Seminary and the journal editors.

To
Donald A. McGavran
and the memory of
J. Herbert Kane
and
George W. Peters

Contents

Foreword

The missiological world is full of such concepts as indigenization, communication, conceptualization, incarnation, enculturation, and last but not least contextualization. Words such as these are crowding the vocabulary of missiology. Sometimes, like clouds floating in the sky, they neither permit the sun to break through and warm the people nor allow rain to refresh the parched fields. Such concepts are widely used and hotly debated in missiological circles because standard definitions are hard to come by. It seems that every author ascribes to them his or her own meaning. The concepts involved desperately need to be articulated even though they are, so far, perhaps more felt than clearly defined.

It is to be expected that well-qualified, Bible-believing, scientifically and theologically trained missiologists in the School of World Mission and Evangelism of Trinity Evangelical Divinity School would tackle this situation and seek to bring some clarity into the most used (perhaps also the most misused, misunderstood, and debated) concept of contextualization. Drs. Hesselgrave and Rommen deserve to be congratulated for the work they have done. I believe this book is the most comprehensive treatise on the subject produced by evangelical scholars. It clearly draws the line between legitimate and nonlegitimate—between biblical and liberal—contextualization.

The application of the principle of "continuum" must not be interpreted as though there is only a quantitative difference between approaches and as though an inner relationship exists in the various methods and models of contextualization. Rather, we must see the polarity to which the presuppositions of the various contextualizers lead. The presuppositions concerning the Word of God *written* have created the unbridgeable gulf between the conservative and the liberal approaches.

This document gives clear evidence that the authors have spared no effort to acquaint themselves with representative literature related to the subject of contextualization and that they have mastered the subject. Now, in a competent manner, they evaluate the contemporary meanings and practice of contextualization. Their respect for the Bible as the infallible Word of God written provides a firm foundation, and thus the work constitutes a safe guide through the wilderness of ideas about contextualization for all who strive to remain true to the Bible message in contextualizing its message for every nation.

This book gives every evidence of being a scholarly treatise, and such it is. It is not written for entertainment but in order to clarify issues and to serve missionaries and all who are reaching for ways to make the message of God relevant to our age and to people of various worldviews, cultures, and psychologies. At the same time it is a staunch defense of the position of those who believe that contextualization can be done without whittling away the sharp edge of the biblical gospel. The gospel is relevant to all ages, cultures, and peoples; but its communication must be contextualized in order for it to be experienced as the living message of God.

No book has ever been written that answered all the questions that can be asked. Neither does this one. The authors, however, approach the subject with a broad perspective—the historical, psychological, sociological, anthropological, theological, and practical points of view required to clarify the various meanings and methods of contextualization. Examples and diagrams illuminate and assist our understanding of the meaning and practice of contextualization. It should be kept in mind that Dr. Hesselgrave is one of the most widely recognized authorities in cross-cultural communication. His expertise shines throughout this book. Dr. Rommen is becoming an authority in practical contextualization, holding two doctorates in closely related fields.

I thank the Lord for this work, and I thank the authors for taking the time and expending the energy required in preparation of this study. It will serve well the evangelical constituency and all others who search for the truth in contextualization. I heartily recommend this book to my co-workers.

George W. Peters

Preface

Undergirding this book is a simple thesis: namely, contextualization is more than a neologism, it is a necessity. Of course, this thesis rests on certain presuppositions. First, it is imperative that the Great Commission be fulfilled and the world be evangelized. Second, however world evangelization is defined, at the very least it entails an understandable hearing of the gospel. Third, if the gospel is to be understood, contextualization must be true to the complete authority and unadulterated message of the Bible on the one hand, and it must be related to the cultural, linguistic, and religious background of the respondents on the other.

Numerous books and articles on contextualization are available; however, works that are evangelical are comparatively few. Moreover, to our knowledge there is no single volume that undertakes to do exactly what we have attempted here—namely, to explain and evaluate a variety of contextualization meanings, methods, and models from an evangelical perspective. Obviously, this attempt entails certain risks. We recognize that there is much more to be said on the topics we deal with here. Also, important contextualization proposals necessarily have been omitted. But our hope is that the proposals we have selected are sufficiently representative and the evaluations sufficiently comprehensive that theorists and practitioners alike will be enabled to grasp the essentials of an evangelical perspective on this "new" and important subject in a helpful way. Specifically, it is our hope that in some small way this book will contribute to the tasks of distinguishing between aberrant and valid contextualization attempts, of reinforcing proposals that are scripturally sound and culturally viable, and of contextualizing the gospel in ways that will contribute to "Great Commission mission" around the world.

It is only right and proper to acknowledge the contributions of numerous individuals and organizations that have made this volume possible. The encouragement and support of Trinity Evangelical Divinity School, and the liberal sabbatical policy of the board of education of that institution, have provided incentives and opportunities that have resulted in this volume. Fellow faculty members and students at Trinity Evangelical Divinity School—School of World Mission and Evangelism have played an important role. The officers and editors of Baker Book House have been most supportive and helpful. Our secretaries, Mrs. Judy Tetour and Miss Linda Walters, have provided valuable assistance. We would be remiss if we failed to mention our wives, Gertrude Hesselgrave and Ainee Rommen, without whose constant and consistent support endeavors such as this would be all but impossible. Finally, there are two "trios" of offspring—Dennis, Ronald, and Sheryl on the Hesselgrave side, and Tim, Crystal, and Becky on the Rommen side—who have enriched our personal lives and, in a variety of ways, have contributed to all of our missionary and missiological endeavors.

In the interests of clarity and simplicity, we have followed traditional English usage and have often used the masculine pronoun without regard to gender.

Some time ago we inquired of each other as to whom we should dedicate this book. We decided that it should be dedicated to three pioneering missiologists who have made signal contributions to the discipline of missiology during the last generation: J. Herbert Kane, Donald A. McGavran, and George W. Peters. Since that decision was made, two of the three, Professors Kane and Peters, have gone to their eternal reward. That fact changes the text of the dedication, but it does not change the intent, which is to recognize and honor, however inadequately, the persons and contributions of three premier men of missions to whom we, and all who would take interest in this book, owe a debt that can never be fully repaid.

David J. Hesselgrave
Edward Rommen
Deerfield, Illinois

The Historical Background of Contextualization

Introduction to Part 1

The missionary's ultimate goal in communication has always been to present the supracultural message of the gospel in culturally relevant terms. There are two potential hazards which must be assiduously avoided in this endeavor: (1) the perception of the communicator's own cultural heritage as an integral element of the gospel, and (2) a syncretistic inclusion of elements from the receptor culture which would alter or eliminate aspects of the message upon which the integrity of the gospel depends. Thus, missionaries of all ages have had to come to grips with not only their own enculturation, but also the customs, languages, and belief systems of the world's peoples. At times this has involved deliberate adaptation of the message to the cultural givens of the listeners—a kind of truth encounter in which Christian advocates seek to take advantage of common points of reference. At other times this activity has involved them in some form of power encounter in which it becomes necessary for them to circumvent or even overcome barriers inherent in the receiving cultures. All of this is done in order to communicate the gospel in a more understandable, culturally relevant form, that is, to contextualize it.

The brief historical survey that follows is not intended to present a complete history of contextualization in biblical and subsequent times, but rather to demonstrate the universality of the problems which make some sort of contextualization necessary and to provide some insight into the many attempts at contextualization (and related activities) which have been a part of the expansion of Christianity. Our overview will take us from the epochs covered by the biblical texts to the eras of the early, medieval, and post-Reformation church.

Reflections from the Old and New Testaments

In 2 Kings 18 we have the account of Sennacherib's siege of Jerusalem. After exacting an enormous amount of tribute (vv. 14–16) Sennacherib was emboldened by Hezekiah's apparent weakness and demanded the complete surrender of the city. At one point in the confrontation an Assyrian delegation approached the gates of the city in order to negotiate a surrender. Being well trained, the diplomats knew the Hebrew language, and the field commander began to describe the negative consequences which would be meted out on the city if the Jews did not surrender. The Assyrian's boasting was an attempt to undermine Hezekiah's confidence. According to the Assyrian all such confidence would be in vain since neither Egypt, nor Judah's God, nor Hezekiah's own army would be able to defend the city. He even offered Hezekiah two thousand horses, knowing that the king would not be able to raise that many riders. This boasting apparently began to have an effect on the Jerusalemites. Not wanting their people—many of whom had gathered on the wall—to hear this discouraging conversation, Hezekiah's ambassadors asked the Assyrian commander to continue his speech in

Aramaic. Not to be outdone, he refused and began to address the people on the wall in Hebrew.[1]

What is obviously involved in this incident are attempts to capitalize on the linguistic difference in order to achieve specific goals. The ambassadors of both Hezekiah and Sennacherib sought to achieve an advantage by using the language of their opponents. But does this constitute an example of contextualization? Hardly, at least not in the modern, missionary sense of that word. What, then, can we expect to find in Scripture that bridges differences of language and culture to effect God's purposes rather than human designs?

Our understanding of and approach to contextualization as it occurs in the Bible will depend in part upon our ability to discover active and deliberate attempts to communicate cross-culturally a specific religious message of clearly definable content. The results of this inquiry will, of course, vary with the two Testaments.

Obstacles to Contextualization in the Old Testament

In the case of the Old Testament we are hard-pressed to find examples of cross-cultural communication of a specifically religious message. However, there seems to be no lack of intercultural encounter. Consider the following examples in various areas: politics (Josh. 9; 1 Kings 15:16–22), religion (Judg. 6:31–32; 1 Kings 18:1–40; Zeph. 1:4–8), trade (2 Chron. 8:17–18; 9:21; Ezek. 27:12–25), and art (Ezek. 23:11–21).

An example of conscious and deliberate adaptation which comes somewhat closer to the modern understanding of contextualization is recorded in Jeremiah's letter to the Babylonian exiles (Jer. 29). The prophet urges them to live normal lives and wait patiently for the Lord's deliverance. Jeremiah's admonition to build homes, plant gardens, and eat what they produce is an appeal to normal living. But there is more here; he urges the exiles to "seek the peace and prosperity of the city" (v. 7). The term "seek" (dāraš) should, in this case, be taken in the sense of "working toward something or on behalf of someone" (as in Deut. 11:12 ["cares for"]; 23:6; Ezra 9:12). Thus, to seek the peace

---

1. According to C. F. Keil, "'aramim was the language spoken in Syria, Babylonia and probably also in the province of Assyria and may possibly have been Rabshakeh's [the field commander's] mother-tongue, even if the court language of the Assyrian Kings was an Aryan dialect. With the close affinity between the Aramaean and the Hebrew, the latter could not be unknown to Rabshakeh, so that he made use of it, just as the Aramaean language was intelligible to the ministers of Hezekiah, whereas the people in Jerusalem understood only yhudit, Jewish, i.e. the Hebrew language spoken in the kingdom of Judah" (The Books of the Kings [Grand Rapids: Eerdmans, 1950], 439).

(well-being) of the city "was no doubt to promote it by their efforts, to be careful in preserving it."[2]

Jeremiah's admonitions, then, were intended to encourage and to enable the Jews to contribute actively to the general well-being of Babylon. Although there is no mention of the communication of a specific message, the charge to "pray to the LORD for it [the city]" does imply that their activity was based, at least in part, on the Jews' unique covenant relationship with God. Therefore, making a positive contribution to the culture and life of Babylon involved more than overcoming cultural barriers. It meant living out the faith in a culturally understandable, appropriate manner. Still, living out one's faith is one thing. Proclaiming it is quite another.

All too often well-meaning students of the biblical text have been deceived into thinking that they can conclusively demonstrate the existence of a vibrant missionary movement in the Old Testament by pointing to a few isolated proof-texts, for example, Jonah or the Servant Songs (Isa. 42:1; 49:5). Others maintain that all such attempts to establish a clearly conceived concept of mission or even the beginnings of mission in the sense of an active sending (a going out to the heathen) in the Old Testament have failed. Does this latter argument mean that we should agree with those who emphasize its exclusive nature and abandon our search for a missionary dimension in the Old Testament? That would be as one-sided as the proof-text approach.

A more balanced approach has been proposed by Johannes Blauw, who suggests that the theology of mission should not be grounded on the narrow basis of a few proof-texts, but rather on the broad sweep of the biblical testimony taken as a unified whole.[3] When the Old Testament material is examined in this way, the student is suddenly confronted with a wealth of information which is directly related to Israel's missionary responsibility. That they had a responsibility even for "strangers" (non-Israelites who had taken up residence in Israel) can be seen clearly in the fact that these "foreigners" were to be subject to many of the same religious regulations as were the Jews themselves (Exod. 12:19; Num. 15:15–16). This applied specifically to the Sabbath (Exod. 20:10), the Day of Atonement (Lev. 16:29), Passover (Num. 9:14; Exod. 12:48), circumcision (Exod. 12:48), sacrifices (Lev. 17:8–9), and worship (2 Chron. 6:32–33). One of the most explicit statements is given in Deuteronomy 31:12, which charges Israel with teaching the

2. John Calvin, *The Book of the Prophet Jeremiah and the Lamentations* (Edinburgh: Calvin Translation Society, 1852), 420 n. 1.

3. Johannes Blauw, *The Missionary Nature of the Church* (New York: McGraw-Hill, 1962).

"aliens" so that they too may come to know the greatness of God. But if God's chosen people had a responsibility to communicate cross-culturally, and if that activity of necessity would have involved them in at least some form of contextualization, why do we find so little if any contextualization in the Old Testament? Several reasons might be suggested.

First, we should take note of the fact that God explicitly prohibited Israel from entering political and religious covenants with certain peoples (Exod. 23:20–33; 34:10–16). For example, upon entering Canaan Israel was required to drive out all other peoples in what amounted to a move towards some form of cultural exclusivism. The purpose, of course, was to preserve Israel's unique relationship to God and its spiritual purity. Thus, rather than encouraging accommodation or adaptation to the religious givens of the new environment, God demanded that Israel cut down and utterly destroy the Canaanite Asherah poles (Exod. 34:13). This may have helped preserve Israel's covenantal fidelity, but it was hardly conducive to contextualization as we have come to know it.

Interestingly, Israel not only failed to implement God's design and eliminate this threat (Judg. 1:27–33), but even entered into a covenant with one of these peoples—the Gibeonites (Josh. 9). As a result the chosen people were forced to live with an intense pressure which wafted them back and forth between open rebellion against God and what in some cases amounted to a necessary but exaggerated isolationism, fighting for their very existence. In either case the possibility of a healthy adaptation to cultural differences was severely restricted.

Second, the process of contextualization was hindered by the lack of a clearly defined message. Since the very essence of the gospel depends on the death and resurrection of our Lord, the message which was to have been communicated during the Old Testament period was not as well defined as was the case after Christ's resurrection. George W. Peters goes a step further and asserts:

It must be realized that there is no real gospel message—good news—for the Gentiles before the cross and resurrection of Christ. In his cardinal and redemptive acts of incarnation—sin-bearing, death and resurrection—Christ identified Himself with mankind. In His life, culture and earthly ministry He identified Himself with Israel as predicted in the Old Testament.[4]

4. George W. Peters, A Biblical Theology of Missions (Chicago: Moody, 1972), 52.

Third, because of its ethnocentric orientation the Old Testament covenant community appears largely to have ignored any missionary responsibility it may have had. The Jews do not seem to have been actively engaged in a ministry of proclamation. Thus, in spite of being surrounded by a multitude of different ethnic groupings, contact with them was seldom if ever characterized by an attempt to communicate a religious message. This conclusion is based, in part, on the account of Jonah's reluctance to become actively involved in a missionary venture and, after being forced to do so, his obvious unwillingness to share with a people other than his own the benefits of a covenant relationship. It would seem that this case was typical of the way in which Israel misunderstood and misapplied their own election, interpreting it exclusively in terms of privilege rather than responsibility. Thus the account of Jonah's experience serves not so much as evidence of direct missionary activity as resounding condemnation of Israel's ethnocentrism.

As we have pointed out, the Old Testament does afford us with examples of intercultural encounters in which one group seeks to gain some advantage by adapting to and using cultural differences. However, since those early attempts at intercultural adaptation seldom involved a religious message and were often initiated by non-Israelites, we should probably not refer to them as contextualization, but rather as nascent attempts at overcoming cultural barriers.

Contextualization in the New Testament

When we turn our attention to the New Testament, we face a radically altered set of circumstances for our discussion of contextualization. First, Christ's coming and the completion of his salvific work provided focus for the message. After the Easter events listeners were not simply being invited to marginal participation in Israel's covenant relationship with Yahweh, but were being offered a practical and realizable path to personal salvation—*sola gratia, in Christo, per fidem*. Second, the New Testament documents are not primarily descriptive. That is, they are not only an account of the missionary expansion of the church, but also the very instruments used in that outreach. In other words, we are dealing with documents which owe their very existence to the already operative missionary program. For these reasons it becomes somewhat easier to isolate examples of contextualization which are more closely aligned with situations faced in our modern multicultured world and which involve not only an attempt to gain some advantage by adapting to and using cultural differences, but also the deliberate, conscious communication of a clearly definable religious message (content).

Possible Approaches

There are a number of ways in which we can look at the contextualizing activity reflected in the New Testament. First, we can focus our attention on specific reports of individual believers who, faced with obstacles to contextualization, sought to develop ways and means of overcoming them. This is not to say that every situation is neatly delineated. In fact the New Testament accounts give clear evidence of the tension involved in the early believers' struggle to make the transition to other cultures. For that reason it is not surprising to find examples of cross-cultural encounters similar to those found in the Old Testament (including a few cases of apparent failure). We find encounters in the areas of politics (Acts 16:19–40), religion and philosophy (Acts 17:16–34), magic (Acts 13:4–12), and economics (Acts 19:23–41).

Second, we can concentrate on the fruits of a contextualizing literary activity which led to the creation of the New Testament documents themselves. Each of the four Gospels, for example, reflects the cultural orientation of its author and is clearly addressed to a particular audience. Matthew's Jewish orientation is reflected in his emphasis on messianic prophecy, kingship, the divine titles of Jesus, and the Aramaisms which characterize his Jewish-Greek language. Luke, on the other hand, reflects a distinctly Hellenistic mind-set. This can be seen in his use of what has been described as good Koine Greek with a rich and varied vocabulary enhanced by numerous Semitisms. The comprehensive range of Luke's Gospel with its emphasis on the universal implications of the gospel gives it a unique appeal.[5]

Third, we can highlight the concerted effort on the part of early church leaders to establish a basis for the ongoing contextualization of the gospel by working systematically to eliminate a number of obstacles both within and without the church. For some the prospect of a missionary outreach which went beyond or even by-passed the traditional Jewish institutions was unthinkable. As a result many of the early believers resisted reaching out to the Gentiles. This not only threatened to stifle the expansion of the church, but led to serious contention within the church. Peter and Paul, for example, are reported to have struggled with issues (Gal. 2:11–16) such as those which were resolved at the Jerusalem Council (Acts 15). However, God in his mercy prodded and directed the early church, as in the case of Peter's ministry to Cornelius (Acts 10). It becomes apparent that the contextualizing activity of the New Testament believers was not simply a

5. Merrill C. Tenney, *New Testament Times* (Grand Rapids: Eerdmans, 1965), 229–30.

matter of a voluntary or spontaneous response to cultural differences, but rather a matter of God's pushing them to destroy the barrier between Jews and the Gentile world.

Examples

Consider, as an example of New Testament contextualization, Paul's approach to the linguistic and cultural problems at Lystra (Acts 14:8–20). This city was situated in remote mountainous country. Although it was colonized by Augustus in A.D. 6 and was connected to Pisidian Antioch by a military road, it was not on a major trade route. Therefore its indigenous culture was left relatively unaffected by Roman influence.[6] Luke tells us that after witnessing the miraculous healing of a lame man, the Lystran crowd became agitated and began shouting in their Lycaonian dialect. Obviously these people were "not the aristocracy of Lystra, the Roman colonists, whose language was Latin . . . but the native inhabitants (the *incolae*). Their language was one of the many languages which had been spoken in Asia Minor since ancient times."[7] It seems safe to assume that the very exacting author Luke would have included this fact only if it bore significance for the interpretation of the event. From what followed the miracle it would appear that the apostles did not, at least initially, understand what was being said.

In addition to the language problem the apostles seem to have been unaware of the particular legend which in all likelihood prompted the crowd's reaction. As recorded by Ovid in his *Metamorphoses* (8.626 ff.), an elderly couple, Philemon and Baucis, slaughtered their last goose to feed Zeus and Hermes after these gods, wandering about in human form, had been rebuffed by many of the people of that region. As a result, the inhospitable citizens were punished and the couple was rewarded. Against this backdrop it is not hard to understand the people's reaction. They were not about to make the same mistake again; identifying Paul and Barnabas as gods, they immediately began preparations for a collective expression of homage.

If our interpretation is correct, we have here not only an example of language-related difficulties, but also a failure to take into account cultural differences (the Lystrans' beliefs in classical legends). Both factors were at the heart of the rather significant misunderstanding. Once the apostles realized what was happening, they responded with a contextualized message (Acts 14:15–17). Beginning with their listen-

6. Donald Guthrie, *New Testament Introduction* (Chicago: Inter-Varsity, 1965), 109–10.

7. F. F. Bruce, *The Acts of the Apostles: The Greek Text with Introduction and Commentary* (Grand Rapids: Eerdmans, 1952), 281.

ers' frame of reference (polytheism), Paul and Barnabas urged them to turn from empty and useless idols to the living God who had already been revealed to them in nature. Although natural revelation gives true knowledge of God, it is not gospel; thus the final step in the apostles' argument was that God sent his Son for our salvation. The pattern developed as a result of this encounter was subsequently used by Paul with those who had no prior exposure to biblical revelation (see Acts 17:16–31).

A second case of New Testament contextualization illustrates the degree to which the early church resolved the issue of cross-cultural application of specific elements of the gospel message (or what they thought to be such). In Acts 15 Luke gives a detailed account of the Jerusalem Council. According to him, the whole debate was triggered by the claim of certain Judaizers[8] that an individual could not be genuinely converted unless circumcised according to the custom of Moses (15:1). What appears to have been at stake is the question of what part of the Jewish religious tradition was an integral, and therefore a supraculturally valid, part of the gospel. From the Jewish perspective the circumcision requirement seemed quite reasonable. In a time of great missionary expansion the Jews may have feared that the ethical quality and the traditional distinctives of Christianity would be compromised by the tremendous influx of new converts.[9] The demand for circumcision may well have been voiced in order to limit that flow and preserve the old traditions. In addition, there was a growing problem within the church with regard to fellowship between Jewish and Gentile Christians, especially at common meals. A circumcised Jew found it all but impossible to sit down at the same table with an uncircumcised Gentile, even if both were believers.

In order to resolve the issue the apostles were called upon to decide what aspects of the Christian message as it was then being presented would have to be considered binding for all believers regardless of their religioethnic background. Peter, Paul, and Barnabas opened the debate with reports of what God had done in and through them, all of which led to the conclusion that God had already made a decision to allow the incorporation of Gentiles into the Christian community without prior relationship to Israel and its institutions (15:7–12). James took this to its logical conclusion. According to him God had redefined the people of God and had already begun to gather a new people for himself from among all nations (v. 14). It thus became apparent that salvation de-

---

8. These individuals were converted Pharisees. See v. 5.

9. F. F. Bruce, *The Book of Acts*, vol. 5, *The New International Commentary on the New Testament* (Grand Rapids: Eerdmans, 1966), 311.

pended on the individual's relationship to God rather than to the traditions and institutions of any particular ethnic group. The regulations that the Jerusalem Council did require were designed to facilitate fellowship among the various factions of believers by encouraging at least a minimum of ritual cleanness.[10] But the gospel is restricted to those elements which have been revealed by God to have salvific import. Anything else is open to negotiation in order to maintain the unity of the church.

In this chapter we have attempted to show that certain obstacles to contextualization have always confronted any attempt to communicate the gospel cross-culturally. During the Old Testament period intercultural encounters occasioned efforts to use cultural differences to gain some advantage. This was done by both non-Israelites as well as Israel, and only rarely did it involve a specifically religious message. The transition to contextualization as we know it today did not begin until the New Testament era. With the completion of Christ's work of salvation and the resultant gospel, early believers began the process of establishing a basis and specific strategies for overcoming intercultural obstacles. Once those initial steps were taken, the task was passed on to subsequent generations of believers.

10. The four categories mentioned in Acts 15:20 correspond to regulations in Old Testament law against the pollution of idols (Lev. 19:4; cf. 1 Cor. 10:20–21), fornication (Lev. 18:6–18), eating that which has been strangled, and eating blood (Lev. 17:10–14). These are obviously issues of dietary or ritual cleanness and not primarily ethical matters. That omission seems to have been considered by some early interpreters. Accordingly, variant readings (mostly in the "D" or "western" group of texts) of the admonition in 15:20 include the prohibitions against idolatry, fornication, and murder, and a negative formulation of the Golden Rule (see Didache 1:2).

2

Reflections from the History
of the Church and Its Missions

The Early Church

Background

Most important for an understanding of the postapostolic church's mission are the two ways in which the sociocultural situation of the early church differed from the situation today. First, mission work was done within the framework of one relatively homogeneous geopolitical matrix. The church seems to have considered its primary responsibility to have been fulfilled when the outer perimeters of the Roman Empire had been reached. Thus the missionary task was carried out within a limited and clearly defined geographic area which was already saturated with Roman culture. For this reason the early missionaries were not seen primarily as the representatives of a specific culture. Of course, there can be no doubt about the cultural differences which characterized the Mediterranean basin, for example, in the area of education. However, wherever the missionaries went they could assume a relatively high degree of Roman influence. The early missionaries cleared no jungle, established no settlements. They entered no place which had not already been visited by Roman legionaries and merchants. They traveled on roads built by Roman soldiers. Everywhere they went they encountered not only the same external structures, but also the same fundamental mind-set, the collective Roman psyche. It can be said that the early Christian mission brought only religion and that only within the Roman Empire.[1]

Second, while missionary outreach of the early church gives the appearance of an organized effort, the church's mission was not organized; that is, there were no sending agencies comparable to today's missionary society. One could hardly expect otherwise. The ecclesiastical structures developed as the church expanded. Thus the early church's response to the challenges presented by the world cannot be separated from its inner politics and the tension that developed between successive generations of believers as they sought to determine the future of the young church. It would seem, then, that the intraecclesiastical search for adequate structures together with the threats from non-Christian opponents conspired to force the active, organized pursuit of *propagatio fidei* into a subordinate position.

The early church expanded, albeit in an apparently haphazard, unorganized way, without any evident strategy. Yet it did so in a remarkably consistent and determined manner which was never interrupted even by the most severe of setbacks. This phenomenon is best explained by the fact that most of this missionary activity was being carried out by lay people rather than by professional missionaries. At the beginning of the second century the church does seem to have had some professional missionaries, that is, individuals who devoted all of their time to the proclamation of the gospel and the planting of new churches. However, workers of this type soon became a rarity. Expansion of the church was normally carried on from person to person and from church to church through the diaconate, the works of Christian philosophers, signs and wonders, and martyrdom.

That state of affairs led to missionary activity which differed from our own in at least two ways. First, for the early church the two operations which we refer to as foreign and home missions were identical. Even after the limitations of traditional Judaism had been overcome (Acts 15), the missionary proclamation remained observably domestic. The believers carried the gospel "not to foreign lands, but to their own countrymen. They presented it not in some foreign language, which had first to be learned, but rather in their own mother tongue."[2] It

---

1. Karl Holl, "Die Missionsmethode der alten und die der mittelalterlichen Kirche," in *Kirchengeschichte als Missionsgeschichte*, vol. 1, *Die alte kirche*, ed. H. Frohnes and U. Knorr (Munich: Kaiser, 1974), 3ff.

2. Hans von Soden, "Die christliche Mission in Altertum und Gegenwart," in *Kirchengeschichte als Missionsgeschichte*, 1:22–31.

would seem, then, that the second generation of missionaries did not have to face the same set of contextualization problems we encounter today.

Second, the degree to which the church was familiar with, and a part of, its immediate cultural environment brought not so much the difficulty of adaptation, but the danger of assimilation. Being a Greek to the Greek was as easy for Paul and his immediate successors as it is difficult for our missionaries to identify with those to whom they minister. Thus the most pressing task of the early missionaries was to maintain their integrity, identity, and unique character.

Methods

In terms of the overall strategy for implementing their commission the early church seems to have continued in Paul's footsteps. Their general strategy was simple: "Mission moves first of all through the Roman Empire in order to cover it so to speak with a wide network of stations from which the more detailed work of reaching the surrounding area could be directed."[3] However, when we inquire into specific methods, we meet with the unexpected. Institutions and methods taken for granted in modern missions, for example, the professional missionary and the evangelistic sermon, were by all appearances practically unknown.

The office of professional missionary began to disappear after the beginning of the second century and seems to be almost unknown by the third century. Support for this conclusion comes from a letter Bishop Cornelius wrote to a colleague in A.D. 252. According to Cornelius, the Roman church had one bishop, forty-six presbyters, seven deacons, seven subdeacons, forty-two acolytes, and fifty-two exorcists, lectors, and guards.[4] Obviously none of these titles describes an office which could be classified as missionary in the modern sense of that term.

True, this had not always been the case. Apostles in the sense of full-time commissioned itinerant evangelists are mentioned in Didache 11:3–6: "Concerning Apostles and Prophets: act according to the Law of the Gospel. Every Apostle who comes to you should stay only one day and if necessary two. But if he stays three days, he is a false prophet. If the Apostle goes he should receive nothing but bread, until he stays overnight again. If he takes money, he is a false prophet." Eusebius also speaks of these professional missionaries:

3. Holl, "Missionsmethode," 5.
4. Eusebius, *Ecclesiastical History* 6.43.11.

Among those who were celebrated in these times was also Quadratus, who, report holds, was distinguished along with the daughters of Philip by a gift of prophecy, and many others besides were known at this time, who take first rank in the apostolic succession. And these, being pious disciples of such great men, built in every place upon the foundations of the churches already established everywhere by the Apostles, spreading the Gospel more and more, and scattering the saving seeds of the kingdom of heaven far and wide throughout the whole world. Indeed, most of the disciples of that time, struck in soul by the divine Logos with an ardent love of philosophy, first fulfilled the Savior's command and distributed their goods among the needy, and then, entering upon long journeys, performed the work of evangelists, being eager to preach everywhere to those who had not yet the work of faith and to pass on the writing of the divine Gospels. As soon as they had only laid the foundations of the faith in some foreign lands, they appointed others as pastors and entrusted to them the nurture of those who had recently been brought in, but they themselves went on to other lands and peoples with the grace and cooperation of God, for a great many marvelous miracles of the divine Spirit were still being worked by them at that time, so that whole multitudes of men at the first hearing eagerly received within their souls the religion of the Creator of the universe.[5]

This fits into the pattern known (only?) to the generation of Christians who had had contact with the Twelve. But by Eusebius's time (ca. 320) that type of missionary or evangelist no longer existed. The term *apostle* was still being used but, following a trend which had already been initiated in the New Testament, was used exclusively to identify the Twelve. And whenever they were mentioned, it was usually in reference to the stability or legitimacy of the church rather than to its expansion.[6]

In light of this development it is not surprising to discover that the major force for expansion was the one-on-one activity of individual lay Christians, as we have said, and that contextualization for these early Christians entailed not so much a concerted effort to overcome sociocultural barriers, but rather an attempt to demonstrate that they were able to take their proper place in the empire and more than any other group able to make a unique positive contribution to the stability and moral fiber of society. This included personal evangelism as well as good works.

5. Ibid., 3.37.2ff.
6. Tertullian's criterion for the legitimacy of a church was its ability to trace its origins to the apostolic churches. In his *Prescription Against Heretics* 21 he writes, "We hold communion with the apostolic churches because our doctrine is in no respect different from theirs. This is our witness of truth."

Various reports of conversion are among the evidences of this activity. Tertullian, for example, quotes an opponent of the faith as saying, "A good man is Gaius Seius, only that he is a Christian." Another is reported to have said, "I am astonished that a wise man like Lucius should have suddenly become a Christian."[7]

A second evidence consists of descriptions of personal witness. According to ancient accounts the Christians were well known for their ministry of friendship evangelism. One of Christianity's chief opponents, Celsus, complained:

> We see, indeed, in private houses workers in wool and leather, and fullers, and persons of the most uninstructed and rustic character, not venturing to utter a word in the presence of their elders and wiser masters; but when they get hold of the children privately, and certain women as ignorant as themselves, they pour forth wonderful statements, to the effect that they ought not to give heed to their father and to their teachers, but should obey them; that the former are foolish and stupid, and neither know nor can perform anything that is really good, being preoccupied with empty trifles; that they alone know how men ought to live, and that, if the children obey them, they will both be happy themselves, and will make their home happy also.[8]

In spite of the rather negative tone of this report, there can be no doubt that the Christians were spreading the gospel by word of mouth in their places of work and education. Origen's answer to Celsus focuses on the fact that as a result of this activity, men and women turned from an undisciplined life of perversion.

A third evidence is the reports of moral excellence. It was the moral excellence of lives thus changed which was a major drawing power. In fact, this may have been the most important aspect of early Christian witness. That Christians were the most upstanding citizens was one of the prime arguments of the apologists. For example, Aristides, writing to Hadrian (reigned 117–138) in about the year 125, bases part of his defense of the Christians on the obviously different quality of their character:

> But the Christians, O King, while they went about and made search, have found the truth. . . . Wherefore they do not commit adultery nor fornication, nor bear false witness, nor embezzle what is held in pledge, nor covet what is not theirs. They honor father and mother, and show kindness to those near to them; and whenever they are judges, they judge

7. Tertullian, *Apologeticus* 3.1.
8. Origen, *Contra Celsum* 3.55.

uprightly. They do not worship idols [made] in the image of man; and whatsoever they would not that others should do unto them, they do not to others; and of the food which is consecrated to idols they do not eat, for they are pure. And their oppressors they appease [lit., comfort] and make them their friends; they do good to their enemies; and their women, O King, are pure as virgins and their daughters are modest; and their men keep themselves from every unlawful union and from all uncleanness, in the hope of a recompense to come in the other world. Further, if one or another of them have bondmen and bondwomen or children, through love towards them they persuade them to become Christians, and when they have done so, they call them brethren without distinction. They do not worship strange gods, and they go their way in all modesty and cheerfulness.[9]

Aristides goes on to tell how Christians took care of strangers and supplied the needs of the poor and the imprisoned. Churches were even reported to have arranged for the burial of the poor. It seems that contextualization took the form of discerning and responding to the moral and physical needs of the world around them.

Another institution of modern missions which seems to have been missing in the early church is the evangelistic sermon. This type of public oration faded out after about 250. There were, of course, exceptions; for example, Gregory Thaumaturgus ("wonder worker") is reported to have conducted itinerant evangelistic expeditions throughout Pontus and Cappadocia between 243 and 272. But, in general, apologetic disputations seem to have taken the place of this type of sermon and became a major area for contextualization attempts.

One of the more interesting lines of investigation pursued by the early apologists was the perceived affinity between the work of certain secular philosophers and Christian thought. This led to a number of attempts at contextualization which range from simple affirmation of the ancient philosophers' ability to discover the truth to an incorporation of the philosophers' findings into Christian theological treatises. An example of the former is the reference to Socrates in Justin Martyr's *Second Apology:*

Our doctrines, then, appear to be greater than all human teaching; because Christ, who appeared for our sakes, became the whole rational being, both body, and reason, and soul. For whatever either lawgivers or philosophers uttered well, they elaborated by finding and contemplating

9. Aristides, *Apology* 15 (Syriac text). It is also reported by some opponents of Christianity that the Christians took care of not only their own poor, but those who belonged to no community.

some part of the Word. . . . And Socrates, who was more zealous in this direction than all of them . . . exhorted [the Athenian officials] to become acquainted with the God who was to them unknown, by means of the investigation of reason, saying that it is neither easy to find the Father and Maker of all, nor, having found Him, is it safe to declare Him to all. But these things our Christ did through His own power. For no one trusted in Socrates so as to die for this doctrine, but in Christ, who was partially known even to Socrates.[10]

At the other end of the continuum is a more refined methodology by means of which the apologists sought to bring together their biblical and philosophical understandings of God. Against the biblical background God was conceived of as the true and living God, good to humankind, compassionate, and long-suffering. Thus he was the Father and Maker of all. But because of the influence of philosophical speculation the apologists tended to reject the immanence of God. In the Platonic and Aristotelian tradition they focused on God as eternally immutable and the source of all existence. God was above the universe and therefore not really located in time and space. This emphasis on transcendence prevented Justin from expressing adequately the biblical concept of God, for he "could not formulate the divine indwelling in intellectual terms."[11]

According to some scholars, the apologists developed the Logos doctrine in order to describe satisfactorily the divine indwelling, the incarnation. In John's Gospel this term is used in the explanation of how God himself was involved in human life and in the world (John 1:1–14). For the apologists, however, the Logos seems to have been conceived of as hovering between God and the world. The Logos was one with God and yet not God. With the help of this idea the early Christian writers were able to affirm a relationship between God and the world and at the same time hang on to their desire to isolate God from any immediate intercourse with the world. This seems to be the tenor of Justin's concept of the "spermatic word":

I confess that I both boast and with all my strength strive to be found a Christian; not because the teachings of Plato are different from those of Christ, but because they are not in all respects similar, as neither are those of the others, Stoics, and poets, and historians. For each man spoke well in proportion to the share he had of the spermatic word, seeing what was related to it. . . . For next to God, we worship and love the Word who

10. Justin Martyr, *Second Apology* 10.
11. James Pan, "Contextualization: A Methodological Enquiry with Examples from the History of Theology," *South East Asia Journal of Theology* 21/22 (1980/81): 51–53.

is from the unbegotten and ineffable God. . . . For all the writers were able to see realities darkly through the sowing of the implanted word that was in them. For the seed and imitation imparted according to capacity is one thing, and quite another is the thing itself, of which there is the participation and imitation according to the grace which is from Him.[12]

In a more explicit statement Justin describes the functional relationship between the Father and the Word. After giving several examples of divine theophanies in the Old Testament Justin writes:

You must not imagine that the unbegotten God Himself came down or went up from any place. For the ineffable Father and Lord of all neither has come to any place, nor walks, nor sleeps, nor rises up, but remains in His own place, wherever that is. . . . How, then, could He talk with any one, or be seen by any one, or appear on the smallest portion of the earth? . . . [They saw] Him who was according to His will His Son, being God, and the Angel . . . and they call Him the Word, because He carries tidings from the Father to men.[13]

All of this may well have helped the apologists resolve some of their own intellectual tensions. In the process the Word of God was kept at "a safe distance from intercourse with man for the sake of maintaining the Platonic transcendence in all its bareness."[14] Thus it would seem that the philosophical predisposition of the authors had a profound effect on their understanding and formulation of biblical truth. In any case, the motivation for and outcomes of contextualization were not entirely in accord with what is being proposed today.

The Middle Ages

Background

Following the collapse of the Roman Empire the Middle Ages (ca. 500–1200) took on the basic form of an agrarian society. Among this era's most prominent characteristics for our purposes are the emergence of the nobility, the institutionalizing of Christianity, and the preservation of Latin antiquities.

The nobility which emerged as a result of the agrarian, feudal structure of society had a profound effect on the way in which the gospel was introduced and accepted. This was especially true of the Germanic tribes that played such an important role in the spread of Christianity

12. Justin Martyr, *Second Apology* 13.
13. Justin Martyr, *Dialogue with Trypho* 126–28.
14. Pan, "Contextualization," 55.

during this era. In fact, it would not be an exaggeration to suggest that the real initiative for missionary outreach often came, not from the religious community, but rather from kings and monarchs.

Take, for example, the case of Ansgar. His biographer, Rimbert, describes how King Ludwig the Pious of Germany began searching (ca. 830) for a man who was committed to God and would be willing to assist a Danish king, who had recently been converted at Ludwig's court, with the task of reaching Denmark with the gospel. The response of the religious community was anything but encouraging. "They refused and said that they knew of no one who was possessed of so great devotion as to be willing to undertake this dangerous journey for the name of Christ."[15]

Christianity had become extremely institutionalized by this time and understood itself primarily in terms of sacramental Catholicity. It should also be pointed out, however, that for centuries the church provided educational and literary resources and produced the educated classes. The decline of general or public education had led to widespread illiteracy throughout continental Europe. It could not be assumed that even kings and nobles would be able to read and write. It is said of Charlemagne, for example, that he tried to learn to write, but that having begun his efforts late in life, he "met with little success."[16] Thus the clergy with their monastery libraries were among the few literate individuals who were in a position to preserve and advance the cultural heritage passed on to them from the Greco-Roman societies.

Among literates the missionaries stood out as having been exceptionally well trained. Columban (ca. 540–615), for example, is reported to have sweated through the study of grammar, rhetoric, geometry, and the Holy Scriptures, at several Irish monasteries. It was only after he had received what may have been the best education available in Europe, and after having established himself as an able writer, that he at age forty-five left for his mission to the kingdom of the Franks.[17] This may help explain why he and other medieval missionaries were able to interact so freely with kings, on occasion themselves assuming the role of statesmen, establishing schools, and even providing biblical translations and liturgies. It should be pointed out that what these keepers of traditions preserved was not the old traditions in their entirety, but rather the fruits of the latter phase of ancient civilization, that is, Latin antiquities.

15. Charles Robinson, *Anskar: Apostle of the North*, translated from Rimbert's *Vita Anskarii* (London: SPG, 1921), 39.

16. Einhard, *Vita Caroli Magni* 22–27.

17. James Thayer Addison, *The Medieval Missionary* (Philadelphia: Porcupine, 1976), 5.

The proverb *Graeca non leguntur* ("no one reads Greek") took on great significance, especially in light of the Gnostic tradition and the growing tension with Byzantine Christianity. As a result the Greek New Testament attracted only scant attention, and little care was given to the maintenance and preservation of the ancient manuscripts.

Hans-Dietrich Kahl suggests that the medieval milieu was further complicated by two triangular sets of relationships. On the one hand, there were the geopolitical realms of the Old World (the Latin Occident), the European East (including the Slavic countries), and the Islamic Orient. On the other hand, within Europe itself another three-cornered relationship developed between Rome, Constantinople, and the "empire without emperor" north of the Alps.[18]

Case Studies

In light of our missiological interest, two paths of expansion stand out: (1) the course of missionary outreach north of the Alps into Germany and Scandinavia, and (2) the encounter with Islam. Both provide examples of how Christian missionaries sought to come to grips with multicultural situations. In each case the approach taken seems to have been openly confrontational, as vigorous and aggressive as that of those to whom they sought to minister.

1. *Outreach north of the Alps.* Bishop Ansgar of Hamburg, the apostle of the north, was publicly commissioned by Pope Gregory IV in 831. This commission entailed authority to evangelize the neighboring races of the Swedes and Danes, as well as the Slavs and the other peoples that inhabited the regions of the north.

This, however, was anything but an easy undertaking. Not only would the missionaries have to brave the Viking threat and hostile local leaders; they would also face strong competition from indigenous religious traditions. The inhabitants of Birka, Ansgar's first station in Sweden, were wont to cast lots in an effort to ascertain the will of the gods with regard to any major decision.[19] This practice provided Ansgar and his colleagues with an opening for contextualization, an opportu-

---

18. Hans-Dietrich Kahl, "Die ersten Jahrhunderte des missionsgeschichtlichen Mittelalters. Bausteine für eine Phänomenologie bis ca. 1050," in *Kirchengeschichte als Missionsgeschichte*, vol. 2a, *Die Kirche des frühen Mittelalters*, ed. Knut Schäferdiek (Munich: Kaiser, 1978), 13–18.

19. "In casting lots the Danes were accustomed to cut a branch from a fruit-bearing tree from which they broke off a number of small sticks. Having cut certain marks on these, they placed them on a spread-out cloth. The priest then picked up three of these sticks and, in accordance with the marks that he found on them, answered 'yes' or 'no' to the question addressed to him" (Robinson, *Anskar*, 68).

nity to demonstrate the superiority of the Christian faith by presenting it within a conceptual framework well understood by his listeners.

A disgruntled Swedish king, with the help of his Danish allies, had attacked Birka. Having no way of defending themselves and no hope of securing refuge, and having had their first offer of tribute in exchange for peace (one hundred pounds of silver) rejected, the inhabitants "exhorted one another to make vows and offer greater sacrifices to their own gods." At that, Herigar, Ansgar's fellow missionary, vented his anger:

> Your vows and sacrifices to idols are accursed by God. How long will ye serve devils and injure and impoverish yourselves by your useless vows? You have made many offerings and more vows and have given a hundred pounds of silver. What benefit has it been to you? . . . If you desire to make vows, vow and perform your vows to the Lord God omnipotent, who reigns in heaven, and whom I serve. . . . If ye seek His help with your whole heart, ye shall perceive that His omnipotent power will not fail you.[20]

As it turned out, the people of Birka accepted Herigar's advice. Unbeknown to them their attackers were at that very moment casting lots, seeking to ascertain from their gods whether it "would be possible to accomplish their purpose without endangering their own welfare." What they found out was that their "god would not permit this place to be ravaged by them." As a result they broke off the attack, and Birka was spared.

This demonstration of God's response to the missionaries' faith provided an opportunity to proclaim the gospel in a way which was effectively related to the socioreligious matrix.

> Alas, wretched people, . . . ye now understand that it is useless to seek for help from demons who cannot succor those who are in trouble. Accept the faith of my Lord Jesus Christ, whom ye have proved to be the true God and who in His compassion has brought solace to you who have no refuge from sorrow. . . . Worship the true God who rules all things in heaven and earth, submit yourselves to Him, adore His almighty power.[21]

2. *Encounter with Islam.* South of the Alps there was the encounter with Islam. Constantine of Thessalonica has gone down into the annals of history as the apostle of the Slavic peoples. Indeed he did introduce Christianity into that region around A.D. 870, and he even reduced

20. Ibid., 67–68.
21. Ibid., 69.

their language to writing, creating the Slavic alphabet, in order to teach and provide them with the Scriptures and a liturgy in their own tongue. But in addition to this he was actively involved in the encounter with Islam. His biographer reports that at the age of twenty-four he was asked by the Byzantine emperor to go into Muslim territory and defend the Christian teachings of the Trinity. All of this was occasioned by an open challenge:

> Afterward the Hagarites, who were called Saracens, blasphemed the single Deity of the Holy Trinity, saying: "Assuming that God is one, how can you Christians further divide Him into three, saying He is Father, Son and Spirit? If you can explain clearly, send us men who can speak of this and convince us. Then send us a man who can speak with us and convince us."[22]

So it came about that Constantine, who had already proven himself to be a capable defender of the faith, was called upon to go and meet the challenge. During a meal one of the Saracens, all of whom were well versed in scholarship, geometry, astronomy, and other sciences, tested Constantine:

> Philosopher, perceive you the wondrous miracle, how the Prophet Mohammed brought us joyful tidings from God and converted numerous peoples; and how we all keep his law without transgression in any way? But in keeping Christ's law, you act and do whatever pleases each of you, one this, another that.

Constantine answered:

> Our God is like the depths of the sea. Thus did the Prophet speak of Him: "And who shall declare His generation? for He was cut off out of the land of the living." For the sake of this search many descend into these depths. And with His help, the strong in mind swim across and return, receiving a wealth of understanding. But of the weak in mind, some drown like those attempting to cross in rotten ships, while others flounder in impotent idleness, barely breathing from exhaustion. However, your sea is deceitful and self-serving so that everyone, great and small, can leap across. For it is not beyond human means but something you can easily do.[23]

22. Marvin Kantor and Richard S. White, trans., *The Vita of Constantine and the Vita of Methodius* (Ann Arbor: University of Michigan, 1976), 13.
   23. Ibid., 15.

Of course, Constantine was not limited to sarcasm. He was sufficiently well versed in the Koran to be able to answer the Muslims'
charges on their own terms. At one point the Muslims ridiculed his
belief in the Trinity by suggesting that since Christians are so fond of
gods, they should give wives to them in order to increase their number
even more. Constantine's answer included a quotation from the Koran:

> Speak no such despicable blasphemy. For well have we learned from the
> prophets, fathers and teachers to glorify the Trinity, the Father, the Word
> and the Spirit, three hypostases in one being. And the Word became flesh
> in the Virgin and was born for the sake of our salvation, as your prophet
> Mohammed bore witness when he wrote the following: "We sent our
> spirit to the Virgin, having consented that She give birth." For this reason
> I make the Trinity known to you.[24]

Like Constantine other missionaries resorted to two basic methods
in their attempt to deal with the challenge of Islam: (1) confrontation
based on rhetorical and philosophical skill, and (2) acquisition and
utilization of a thorough knowledge of their protagonists' scriptures
and thought patterns.

Pietism

The reader may wonder why we jump from the Middle Ages to the
seventeenth century, by-passing the Reformation. The basic reason is
that mission does not seem to have played a major role in the life of the
Reformation churches. This may have been due in part to the fact that
the Reformers were preoccupied with the task of establishing their
own structures, fending off the opposition (the Counter Reformation),
and generally fighting for their own survival. On the other hand, some
of their theological—and in particular their ecclesiological—positions
were not all that conducive to a worldwide missionary vision. For
example, John Calvin, although he allows for the occasional need for
apostles and evangelists, sees them as "extraordinary, because it [this
office] has no place in churches duly constituted."[25] In any case, Protestant missionary activity did not begin until after the Thirty Years' War
and the onset of the Pietists' missionary endeavors.

The first Protestant missionaries, Bartholomew Ziegenbalg and
Heinrich Plütschau, were sent to India in 1705 through the combined
efforts of the Danish king and the University of Halle, which was under

---

24. Ibid., 17.
25. John Calvin, *Institutes of the Christian Religion*, 4.3.4–5.

the leadership of August Francke. For those early missionaries the proclamation of the Good News was the very essence of the missionary task. This conviction inevitably led to the concrete question, "How can we proclaim to another, that which has taken possession of our hearts?"[26] That question was being asked by men and women whose knowledge of the host culture's language was minimal at best, and who had little if any theological training which could have helped them deal with the challenges of cross-cultural ministry. One of the greatest short-comings in missionary training at that time was the instructors' lack of cross-cultural experience. Augustus Spangenberg spoke of a theologian who was teaching missionaries, but "had in his whole life never even seen a heathen, not to mention converted one."[27]

Given these shortcomings, it is quite understandable that the early Protestant missionaries adopted methods which were patterned after European models. One of their basic tools was Johann Freylinghausen's outline of systematic theology, which had become standard fare for missionaries trained at Halle. An evangelistic approach reflecting this work has been described in some of the early reports from East India:

> If one seeks to help these miserable people, one must literally preach idolatry out of them and destroy their large catalogue of gods, before one can bring them to the one eternal God. Once they have believed on the one God, it is necessary to drill into them His attributes, to show them the moral decay in which we humans by nature languish, the necessity of rising out of that decay, and to commend to them with flexibility and seriousness the means of grace in Jesus Christ.[28]

From this it can readily be seen that a purely logical or theological path to the heathen's heart was being followed.

It did not take long for the missionaries themselves to discover the inadequacies of this method. On the one hand, their approach to preach-ing introduced the very specialized language or vocabulary of one seg-ment of European Christianity which, even when accurately trans-lated, often remained unintelligible. On the other hand, they realized that this approach tended to ignore the physical and social needs of their listeners. For example, on August 15, 1718, Ziegenbalg wrote to his mission leadership that if they were going to attain their primary goal, conversion, they would have to begin addressing the desperate

26. Karl Müller, *200 Jahre Brüdermission* (Herrnhut: Verlag der Missionsbuchhand-lung, 1931), 1:301.
27. Ibid., 1:302.
28. As quoted ibid., 1:301.

social and physical needs of those among whom they ministered.[29] As a result, the missionaries in India began to explore additional avenues of ministry including homes for orphans and schools.

As they gathered experience, both the active missionaries and the leadership of the pietistic Moravian movement began to make some adjustments; that is, they initiated attempts at contextualization. For example, Count Nikolaus von Zinzendorf advised his missionaries on Greenland not to use the terms *lamb* and *sacrifice* since there were no lambs on Greenland and Greenland religion knew no sacrifices. He was convinced that by using terms which were outside the conceptual framework of the listeners, the process of communication would be complicated and bear undesirable fruit. "If we are not careful," said Zinzendorf, "we will, with the passing of time, have them reciting the Psalms in Latin." What the Moravian leader advocated was an accommodation to the unique nature of each culture, even if that meant searching for new terms: "The brothers [working] among the heathen will sometimes have to think: Dear Paul! As you spoke such and so in your day, so [today] I speak thus and so. If a needle is the greatest need of the heathen, then we should call the Savior a needle."[30] It would seem, then, that the very first generation of Protestant missionaries was not only aware of the problems in cross-cultural ministry, but also creatively engaged in searching for ways to improve the cultural relevance of their message, though both the methods and the results often left something to be desired.

This brief survey of the historical records has revealed the not so surprising fact that throughout the ages believers have, with varying degrees of success, struggled with the implications of a multicultural world. The missionary activity of the early postapostolic church consisted largely of one-on-one lay witnessing and apologetic disputations. In the Middle Ages well-educated missionaries sent out by the nobility took an aggressive, confrontational approach. The early Protestant missionaries began with European models but later searched for creative ways of making their message more relevant to the native culture. We can say, then, that there were various attempts at contextualization, although the attitudes, approaches, and activities we have described do not strictly correspond with what that term connotes today.

29. Arno Lehman, *Es begann in Tranquebar* (Berlin: Evangelische Verlagsanstalt, 1955), 136.
30. Müller, *200 Jahre*, 1:307.

3

What Is New?

"So God created man in his own image . . . male and female he created them. God blessed them and said to them, 'Be fruitful and increase in number; fill the earth and subdue it. Rule. . . .' " (Gen. 1:27–28).

In a real sense, contextualization, culture, and theology all have a simultaneous beginning. Along with the shafts of light that broke through the foliage of Eden on the first morning of human life, the silence was broken by the voice of God. Communication commenced between God and man. In embryonic form all that we speak about in this book was there. Since that morning men and women have wrestled, not just with the problems of knowing God and subduing earth, but also with communicating what they have learned about divine will and their own environment. Ever since Eden and especially since Babel, men and women have fallen prey to miscommunication and misunderstanding. Despite attempts to break through those barriers—crowned humanly by the rhetoricians' inventions at Alexandria, Athens, and Rome, and divinely by God's interventions at Bethlehem and on Pentecost—they remain. In fact they are as forbidding today as they have been throughout the millennia of human existence.

There have been remarkable breakthroughs by men such as Gregory Thaumaturgus, Constantine of Thessalonica, Ansgar, and Ziegenbalg who crossed cultural barriers to win both educated and uneducated pagans to faith in Christ and fellowship in his church. But on a broader scale it has remained for those of more recent times to arrive at an enlarged concept of context and a deepened understanding of culture. A new word was needed to denote the ways in which we adjust messages to cultural contexts and go about the doing of theology itself. That new word is *contextualization.*

"In the Beginning"

The Third Mandate Program of the Theological Education Fund

Whatever may have been the occasion of the first use of the term *contextualization,* it made its public debut in the publication *Ministry in Context: The Third Mandate Programme of the Theological Education Fund (1970–77).*[1] The Theological Education Fund (TEF) was launched by the International Missionary Council (IMC) at its Ghana assembly in 1957–58. The new TEF was also given its first ("advance") mandate, which resulted in the extending of funds, textbooks, and library facilities to certain theological schools in the Third World.

In 1961 in New Delhi the IMC joined the World Council of Churches (WCC) and became the Division of World Mission and Evangelism (DWME) of that body. At the initial meeting (1963) of the DWME at Mexico City the life of the TEF was extended through a second ("re-think") mandate (1965–70). The intent was to enhance the kind of Third World theological education that would lead to "a real encounter between the student and the Gospel in terms of his own forms of thought and culture, and to a living dialogue between the church and its environment."[2]

In 1969 a new advisory group to the TEF was formed. Headed by W. A. Visser't Hooft, this group recommended that a third ("reform") mandate be adopted, that a period of study and consultation be scheduled for 1970 to 1972, and that funding activities be carried out from 1972 to 1977. These recommendations were approved by a meeting of the DWME in 1969.

The chairman of the TEF during the period of the third mandate was Karekin Sarkissian, a prelate of the Armenian Orthodox Church. In March 1971 Shoki Coe (Taiwan) was named director of a "new and colorful TEF team" which included associate directors Aharon Sapsezian (Brazil), James Bergquist (United States), Ivy Chou (Malaysia), and Desmond Tutu (South Africa). The expediters of this third mandate

---

1. *Ministry in Context: The Third Mandate Programme of the Theological Education Fund (1970–77)* (Bromley, England: Theological Education Fund, 1972).
    2. Ibid., 13.

were commissioned "to help the churches reform the training for the Christian ministry (including the ordained ministry and other forms of Christian leadership in church and world) by providing selective and temporary assistance and consultative services to institutions for theological education and other centers of training."[3] As stated in the official documents, "the determinant goal of its work is that the Gospel be expressed and ministry undertaken in response to (a) the widespread crisis of faith, (b) the issues of social justice and human development, (c) the dialectic between local cultural and religious situations and a universal technological civilization."[4]

The first meeting of the new TEF committee was held in Kampala, Uganda, in July 1971 and the second in Bromley, England, in July 1972. At the first meeting the staff received directions as to how to pursue studies already in progress. The second meeting resulted in general agreement on issues and guidelines for their implementation.

The foregoing history makes it evident that contextualization is rooted in dissatisfaction with traditional models of theological education, but that is only part of the story.

Concurrent Discussions in the World Council of Churches

Before the 1961 WCC meeting in New Delhi the influence of men like Karl Barth and Hendrik Kraemer as well as the influence of the Eastern Orthodox Church had resulted in a renewed emphasis on the Bible and biblical theology in WCC circles. In 1961 the phrase *according to the Scriptures* was added to the WCC official doctrinal statement. Almost overnight, however, questions concerning the unity, authority, and relevance of Scripture came to occupy center stage in WCC discussions. The conclusions of two important WCC-related meetings in 1971 revealed that the ecumenical movement was moving in a new direction on these questions, a direction that reinforced and gave impetus to the TEF and its third mandate program.

One of the 1971 meetings was the consultation on dogmatic or contextual theology in Bossey, Switzerland. In an October 1970 circular letter the chairman of the consultation (and director of the Ecumenical Institute of the WCC), Nikos A. Nissiotis, had noted that the rise of a new technological society had the effect of leading to "a kind of 'contextual or experiential' theology which gives preference, as the point of departure for systematic theological thinking, to the contemporary historical scene over against the biblical tradition and confessional statements constructed on the basis of biblical texts, taken as a whole and

3. Ibid., 17.
4. Ibid., 17–18.

thus used uncritically."[5] Both Nissiotis's letter and the subsequent Bossey meeting raised serious questions as to whether contemporary theology can be based on its own premises alone or should also be based on premises from the "experimental realm of thought and action of the environment of which theology is part and for which it exists."[6]

Perhaps a more important meeting in 1971 was that of the Faith and Order Commission (WCC) in Louvain, Belgium. Those gathered at Louvain considered the reports of regional study groups established to respond to what WCC leaders viewed as escalating crises in the church and society. First, the mood of society was antiauthoritarian, and consequently the authority of the Bible could no longer be assumed. Second, historical-critical methodology yielded alleged contradictions in the Bible which made it difficult to decide which biblical statements could be assumed to be authoritative and which could not. Third, the distance between the ancient text and the modern context caused Christians to question the relevance of the Bible.[7]

In response to these issues and the regional reports, the Louvain meeting published a statement which charted the course that the WCC has subsequently taken. The statement represented an attempt to find a kind of middle ground. On the one hand it rejected the fundamentalist and evangelical position that the Bible is historically accurate and fully authoritative because it is the inspired Word of God.[8] On the other hand it discouraged the idea that the Bible is somehow our contemporary and that the historical character of Scripture is of no concern whatsoever. The Louvain position was that by the authority of the Bible "we mean that it makes the Word of God audible and is therefore able to lead men to faith."[9]

In this view, the historical character of the Bible is important because it has preserved the witness upon which the church was founded. The inspiration of the Bible cannot be assumed, but it can be experienced since through it God's claim upon us is made compelling. The works of great preachers and theologians can be thought of as similarly inspired when their interpretations effect this experiential encounter. The perceived contradictions of the Bible result from diverse interpretations of God's actions in history on the part of Bible writers and can be

5. Quoted in Bruce C. E. Fleming, *Contextualization of Theology: An Evangelical Assessment* (Pasadena, Calif.: William Carey Library, 1980), 6.

6. Ibid., 6–7.

7. William J. Larkin, Jr., *Culture and Biblical Hermeneutics: Interpreting and Applying the Authoritative Word in a Relativistic Age* (Grand Rapids: Baker, 1988), chap. 9.

8. "The Authority of the Bible—the [Louvain] Report," *Ecumenical Review* 23, 4 (October 1971): 434.

9. Ibid., 426.

sorted out by determining which interpretataion accords best with
God's "saving event." The distance between the biblical text and the
modern interpreter is to be overcome *dynamically* by allowing the
Bible to pose questions which the interpreter must answer in accordance with his understanding of the biblical witness and of the ways in
which God is working today.[10]

It is apparent, then, that contextualization came to be most systematically defined and promoted by the TEF (subsequently reorganized as
the Programme of Theological Education), and support for the conciliar
meaning and method of contextualization enjoyed wide support within
World Council circles early on.

A New Word for an Old Enterprise?

So, what is new? Were Nissiotis, Coe, and their colleagues in the
WCC simply attaching a new term to the ageless endeavor we have
already surveyed? A reading of the official documents of the TEF shows
that this was not their understanding:

> The third mandate's strong emphasis on renewal and reform in theo-
> logical education appears to focus upon a central concept, contextuality,
> the capacity to respond meaningfully to the Gospel within the frame-
> work of one's own situation. Contextualization is not simply a fad or
> catch-word but a theological necessity demanded by the incarnational
> nature of the Word. What does the term imply?
>
> It means all that is implied in the familiar term "indigenization" and
> yet seeks to press beyond. Contextualization has to do with how we
> assess the peculiarity of Third World contexts. Indigenization tends to be
> used in the sense of responding to the Gospel in terms of a traditional
> culture. Contextualization, while not ignoring this, takes into account
> the process of secularity, technology, and the struggle for human justice,
> which characterize the historical moment of nations in the Third World.
>
> Yet a careful distinction must be made between authentic and false
> forms of contextualization. False contextualization yields to uncritical
> accommodation, a form of culture faith. Authentic contextualization is
> always prophetic, arising always out of a genuine encounter between
> God's Word and His world, and moves toward the purpose of challenging
> and changing the situation through rootedness in and commitment to a
> given historical moment.
>
> It is therefore clear that contextualization is a dynamic not a static
> process. It recognizes the continually changing nature of every human

---

10. Larkin, *Culture and Biblical Hermeneutics*, chap. 9.

situation and of the possibility for change, thus opening the way for the future.

The agenda of a Third World contextualizing theology will have priorities of its own. It may have to express its self-determination by uninhibitedly opting for a "theology of change," or by recognizing unmistakable theological significance in such issues as justice, liberation, dialogue with people of other faiths and ideologies, economic power, etc.

Yet contextualization does not imply the fragmented isolation of peoples and cultures. While within each diverse cultural situation people must struggle to regain their own identity and to become subjects of their own history, there remains an inter-dependence of contexts. Contextualization thereby means that the possibilities for renewal must first of all be sensed locally and situationally, yet always within the framework of contemporary inter-dependence which binds both to the problems of the past and present and to the possibilities for the future.

Finally, contextualization, while it stresses our local and situational concerns, draws its basic power from the Gospel which is for all people. Thus contextualization contributes ultimately to the solidarity of all people in subordination to a common Lord.

If, then, contextualization becomes a chief characteristic of authentic theological reflection, a request for support submitted to the TEF will be judged to have potential for renewal when:

1. There is evidence of contextualization in *mission*.
2. There is evidence of contextualization in *theological approach*.
3. There is evidence of contextualization in *educational method*.
4. There is evidence of contextualization in *structure*.[11]

Now we are prepared to answer the question: What is new? Contextualization is a new word—a technical neologism. It may also signal a new (or renewed) sensitivity to the need for adaptation to cultural context. To its originators it involved a new point of departure and a new approach to theologizing and to theological education: namely, praxis or involvement in the struggle for justice within the existential situation in which men and women find themselves today. As such it goes well beyond the concept of indigenization which Henry Venn, Rufus Anderson, and their successors defined in terms of an autonomous (self-supporting, self-governing, and self-propagating) church. It also goes beyond the Roman Catholic notion of accommodation defined by Louis J. Luzbetak as "the respectful, prudent, scientifically and theologically sound adjustment of the Church to the native culture in attitude, outward behavior, and practical apostolic approach."[12]

11. *Ministry in Context*, 20–21.
12. Louis J. Luzbetak, *The Church and Cultures* (Techny, Ill.: Divine Word, 1970), 341.

"Words Mean What I Say They Mean"

The early proponents of contextualization were most successful in persuading others to adopt their word *contextualization* (though as we will see some objected), but they were less successful in persuading others to adopt their meaning and method.

Opposition to the Word "Contextualization"

In the late 1970s James O. Buswell III and Bruce C. E. Fleming both took exception to the notion that conservative evangelicals should adopt the new term. Buswell argued that the terms *indigenous, indigeneity*, and *indigenization* are not outmoded, static, and closed to the future as some have alleged. Not only that, they are less abstract, less technical, and better understood than are *contextualization* and kindred terms.[13] Fleming concluded that the word was already so tainted by liberal presuppositions and so tarnished with misunderstanding and confusion that it should be laid to rest forthwith. He proposed the term *context-indigenization*.[14] Neither alternative was adopted by many missiologists.

New Meanings for a New Word

Most conservative evangelicals were already enamored with the word *contextualization*. They chose to adopt and redefine it where they rejected the meaning prescribed by the TEF initiators. They agreed that the new definition should reveal a sensitivity to context and a fidelity to Scripture. But when it came to definitional nuances they parted company, as a small sampling of some early proposals will reveal:

1. "We understand the term to mean making concepts or ideals relevant in a given situation" (Byang H. Kato).[15]
2. "[Contextualization is] the translation of the unchanging content of the Gospel of the kingdom into verbal form meaningful to the peoples in their separate culture and within their particular existential situations" (Bruce J. Nicholls).[16]
3. "Contextualization properly applied means to discover *the legitimate implications* of the gospel in a given situation. It goes deeper than application. Application I can make or need not

13. James O. Buswell III, "Contextualization: Theory, Tradition, and Method," in *Theology and Mission*, ed. David J. Hesselgrave (Grand Rapids: Baker, 1978), 93–94.
14. Fleming, *Contextualization*, 60–67.
15. Byang H. Kato, "The Gospel, Cultural Context, and Religious Syncretism," in *Let the Earth Hear His Voice*, ed. J. D. Douglas (Minneapolis: World Wide, 1975), 1217.
16. Bruce J. Nicholls, "Theological Education and Evangelization," ibid., 647.

make without doing injustice to the text. Implication is *de-manded* by a proper exegesis of the text" (George W. Peters).[17]

The complexity of the problem of definition for evangelicals is also evident in Harvie M. Conn's criticism of his fellow evangelicals. He chastises them for confining contextualization to matters relating to the effective communication of the gospel to peoples of other cultures. Conn understands that evangelicals fear that the existentialist approach to theologizing espoused by the ecumenical movement will erode biblical authority. But in their fear, Conn says, evangelicals throw the baby out with the bathwater. Would-be evangelical contextualizers need to recognize their own culture-boundedness; they ought to wrestle with the relationship between the biblical text and their own cultural context. They must allow Scripture to judge their own enculturated interpretations and lifestyles. For Conn contextualization is the process of *conscientization* of the whole people of God to the hermeneutical claims of the gospel.[18]

The broad sweep of evangelical literature on the subject reveals a consensus that, whether in the East or the West, Christians do have a primary obligation to allow Scripture to interpret Scripture, to let the text speak from within its own context, and to permit it to sit in judgment upon them and their own culture. Some might even agree that due to influences from the Western intellectual tradition and other factors, this process is as difficult as Conn insists that it is. Most would prefer to call this process *decontextualization* and think of it as the contextualizers' attempt to free themselves from the interpretational biases of their own culture insofar as is possible before attempting to adapt the biblical message to the understandings and needs of other cultural contexts. For some, Conn's *conscientization* definition borrows too much from the TEF understanding.

The Heart of the Problem

There is really nothing wrong in prescribing preferred meanings to existing words provided one does not adopt an Alice-in-Wonderland approach that insists that "words mean what I say they mean." To offer a stipulated definition is like offering an invitation to have a cup of coffee. It is up to others to accept or reject the offer.

17. George W. Peters, "Issues Confronting Evangelical Missions," in *Evangelical Missions Tomorrow*, ed. Wade T. Coggins and E. L. Frizen, Jr. (Pasadena, Calif.: William Carey Library, 1977), 169.

18. Harvie Conn, "Contextualization: A New Dimension for Cross-Cultural Hermeneutics," *Evangelical Missions Quarterly* 14 (January 1978): 44–45.

This brings us to the heart of the problem for evangelicals. There is not yet a commonly accepted definition of the word *contextualization*, but only a series of proposals, all of them vying for acceptance. It is imperative, then, that evangelicals understand both the meanings and the methods, stated or implied, in the various stipulated definitions. It is not incumbent upon them to agree on the precise wording of a definition, but it is essential that they agree on the criteria necessary for an authentic biblical contextualization, that they be able to distinguish between defensible and aberrant proposals, and that they actually contextualize the gospel and theology in ways that will commend themselves both to God and to their hearers.

Though an activity that can be thought of as contextualization is as old as the missionary enterprise, the term itself—and initial meanings, methods, and models—arose from within relatively recent conciliar Protestant circles. By and large, conservative evangelicals have adopted the term but have experienced difficulty analyzing existing contextualizations and in constructing their own model. Since both the word and the endeavor will be important aspects of theologizing and missionizing in the future, it is incumbent upon evangelicals to give careful attention to the meanings, methods, and models of contextualization.

Contemporary Understandings of and Approaches to Contextualization

Introduction to Part 2

History—whether sacred or profane, ancient or modern—testifies that some sort of contextualization is necessary if we are effectively to cross cultural barriers with the gospel. But what sort of contextualization does the Bible enjoin? What sort does it proscribe? What kind will the missionary/theologian's preunderstandings dictate? What kind will his abilities allow? What kind of contextualization will clarify the gospel for people in a respondent culture? To what kind of contextualization will they respond?

If better informed in the social sciences than their predecessors, contemporary contextualizers are not more unified. Indeed, as one examines proposals coming from the schools, churches, and missions around the world one is tempted to conclude that a consensus is not only lacking; it is unattainable! As we shall see later, in part 3, unity is impossible unless some radical shift in the epistemological and theological commitments of many contextualizers is forthcoming. At any rate, it is essential that we examine some of the more significant proposals emanating from the various cultural and geographical segments of the world church. Only as we do so will we be prepared to understand, compare, and evaluate current contextualization proposals and, in the end, to attempt the kind of contextualization that pleases God, conforms to his Word, communicates to the world, and commends itself to the body of Christ.

With that in mind we proceed to an overview of some of the proposals from the world church. Readers should be warned, however, that, though we speak of contextualized African theology or Asian theology, there are great differences among proposals offered from within these wide geographical areas. Therefore there is a sense in which we should think rather of African theologies, Asian theologies, and so on.

Readers should also take note of the fact that in part 2 we do not undertake an evaluation of contextualization understandings and proposals. Some of the more salient of the proposals put forward here will be examined in part 3. In this section we attempt only a very brief overview of contextualization discussions in various parts of the world and an introduction to models proposed by some selected contextualizers.

4

Europe
Jürgen Moltmann

The Role of European Theology

Throughout history European theologians and philosophers have exercised consistent and often decisive influence on the course of theological debate. Who, it might be asked, has not heard of Rudolf Bultmann and his attempt to contextualize theology by reinterpreting (demythologizing) it for modern man? What student of theology has not been challenged by the works of Friedrich Schleiermacher, Karl Barth, Wolfhart Pannenberg, and a host of other German theologians?

But in spite of our familiarity with these thinkers, their contribution to the recent discussion and practice of contextualization is not so obvious. For example, are European theologians the originators, refiners, or guardians of what has now become known as liberation theology? Many are not sure. The same question could be posed with regard to an array of theological ideas associated with Continental and, in particular, German theology. The answers to these questions, however, depend on how one delineates European theology's overall position among and impact on world theologies and how the theological expressions of various cultures relate to one another in general, and German theology in particular.

Karl Rahner, one of the few systematic theologians to address such questions, recently attempted such a description.[1] Rahner suggests that self-reflection is one of the most important tasks of every scientific endeavor. As he sees it, this must include an investigation of the historical, cultural, and societal factors out of which a particular discipline has arisen. This task remains manageable as long as the developments under consideration are the products of one more or less homogeneous sociocultural context. However, once such scientific activity is simultaneously pursued in several distantly related contexts, the nature of self-reflection is radically altered and becomes increasingly complex.

Systematic theology has traditionally been the exclusive domain of the heirs to the Greco-Roman tradition in the cultures of Europe and, to a lesser degree, in North America. But now that churches have been established in almost every region of the world, theologizing is no longer limited to one cultural context. A vast number of potentially different types of theology do, or certainly will, coinhabit our world. Moreover, this state of affairs cannot be viewed with indifference since each regional theology is partially responsible for the truth and the unity of the faith of the worldwide church; that is, each theology should be pursued and practiced as a service to all other theologies.

What then does this mean for European theology? According to Rahner, European theology should function as theological guardian, mediator, protector, and, of course, recipient.

First, European theology can be viewed as the guardian of tradition. Although we must now view the world in the light of multiple churches and theologies, it remains an incontestable fact that Europe and its theology occupies the place of an older daughter. For reasons known only to God Europe was reached with the gospel earlier than the younger churches, and for centuries European believers have been struggling through theological issues, producing documents, and testing structures. This experience is as much the normative and historical heritage of the entire Christian community as it is of the European church itself. Thus, present-day European theology preserves the normative past of Christian theology for all people. This includes the fundamental texts and creeds as well as the critical, exegetical, and systematic tools needed for theology's tasks. European theology is as much in need of critical self-examination as every other theology, but, as compared with the younger theologies, its experience and skills put it in a better position to accomplish this task.

Second, European theology can serve as mediator between other the-

1. Karl Rahner, "Aspekte Europäischer Theologie," in *Schriften zur Theologie* (Zürich: Benzinger, 1983), 15:84–103.

ologies and as coordinator of the many theological models now being developed. In literary activity and the number of its professors, finances, and institutions, European theology remains the most scientific and intensely practiced theology in the world. Being the source of missionary outreach and the progenitor of numerous younger churches, as well as the educator of many Third World theologians, Europe's theological community is eminently suited to be mediator and coordinator. There may come a day when African or Asian theologies will assume this role.

Third, European theology provides protection from the dangers threatening other theologies. The very task of having to inculturate theology exposes Third World theologians to several dangers. The mentality of those non-Christian cultures could, for example, influence the theologian and lure him to reject as European fundamental and non-negotiable elements of the gospel. Since European theologians have already struggled through similar issues, European theology can provide practical help to prevent syncretistic patterns from damaging the whole church.

Fourth, European theology is itself called upon to remain teachable. By engaging in open dialogue with the other theologies it is itself enriched and challenged to reconsider issues thought to have been resolved. The anthropological concept of soul migration (transmigration of souls from one body to another in reincarnation), for example, received scant treatment in the older European texts. Today this subject has become so important in Asian culture that European theologians are being forced to reexamine it, that is, to apply with renewed rigor and exactness the theological tools accumulated throughout its own history. The same principle applies to such issues as prayer, mysticism, and spirituality. Thus, by example, European theologians can demonstrate what each culture must do for itself.

The kind of self-examination called for by Rahner has been reflected in the work of a number of European theologians, in particular those in Germany. Ernst Käsemann, for example, accused modern European theology of emphasizing conversion only to forget its implications for daily living and thus to mislead both the masses and students of theology.[2] In spite of the advantages of existing amid the "Christian" societies of Europe, Käsemann charges, the church has become the captive of its own cultural matrix and is in need of revolutionary rediscovery of freedom.

Another scholar in the forefront of this process of self-evaluation is Johann Baptist Metz. According to this well-known Catholic, the church in Europe has entered a time of crisis precipitated by its failure

2. Ernst Käsemann, *Der Ruf der Freiheit* (Tübingen: J. C. B. Mohr, 1972).

to relate its own tradition and faith to its societal environment. His answer to this challenge is a theological model, "political theology," which he understands to be "a critical corrective over against the extreme tendency toward privatisation in contemporary theology" and at the same time "the positive attempt to formulate the eschatological message under the conditions of modern society."[3]

Jürgen Moltmann, the theologian we have chosen for consideration in this chapter, exemplifies the attitude, skill, and orientation referred to by Rahner. His now-famous work, *A Theology of Hope*, reflects the kind of exacting theological investigation which we have come to associate with European scholarship. Of possibly greater import, however, is his expressed willingness to reflect critically on his own tradition and culture and thus remain teachable. For those reasons his ideas have had a great impact on Third World theologies of liberation.

Jürgen Moltmann: A Theology of Hope

In 1964, long before the prominence of Gustavo Gutiérrez and Latin American liberation theology, Jürgen Moltmann published *A Theology of Hope*. It was conceived as an examination of the basis and the consequences of Christian eschatology. According to Moltmann, eschatology had become nothing more than the sterile teaching of death and dying, rather than the living, vital hope which is supposed to rise out of the inherent contradiction between present and future. End-time events such as the second coming, the last judgment, and the resurrection of the dead were relegated to some future last day, divorced from our experience and thus robbed of their critical, guiding hope which has an impact on the present. As a result, eschatology developed as a kind of appendix to theology, taking up a barren existence at the end of systematic theology. Eschatology, however, was never intended to be the end of anything, but rather the beginning. It is in its essence the doctrine of a living hope in the future.

> The eschatological is not one element of Christianity, but it is the medium of Christian faith as such, the key in which everything in it is set, the glow that suffuses everything here in the dawn of an expected new day. For Christian faith lives from the raising of the crucified Christ, and strains after the promises of the universal future of Christ. Eschatology is

---

3. Johann Baptist Metz, *Zur Theologie der Welt* (Mainz: Grünewald, 1973); "Christentum in Politik," in *Jenseits bürgerlicher Religion* (Munich: Kaiser, 1980), 94–112; "Politische Theologie des Subjekts als theologische Kritik der bürgerlichen Religion," in *Glaube in Geschichte und Gesellschaft* (Mainz: Grünewald, 1980), 29–42.

the passionate suffering and passionate longing kindled by the Messiah. Hence eschatology cannot really be only a part of Christian doctrine. Rather, the eschatological outlook is characteristic of all Christian proclamation, of every Christian existence and of the whole Church.[4]

To live as a Christian, then, is to live in the expectation of the coming kingdom of God. The very nature of the church is determined by its hope. It is no longer living for and to itself but rather in the expectation of the coming kingdom. For that reason its primary role in this world is the proclamation or announcement of the kingdom's coming. To awaken hope in men and women is the missionary responsibility of the church.[5]

The mission of the church, according to Moltmann, is participation in the liberating sending of Jesus. Whenever we, who are poor, blind, and captive, hear the Word we begin to celebrate the feast of liberation. In some cases (e.g., the Crusades or colonial missions) we have gone too far. In other cases we have not gone far enough, reducing missions to the development of financial assistance rather than preaching the liberating Word. The message of the coming One is liberating as long as it does not threaten men and women with the repression of eternal punishment. The legitimization of the Christian message depends on the "other side of proclamation," that is, socialization, humanization, and Christianity's calling in society. The church has been called out to "creative discipleship" and simply cannot accept the obvious wrongs of society and its evil structures. Rather, it awakens hope by practicing a present eschatology which in the expectation of God's coming kingdom criticizes and changes society.[6]

Vital hope, then, springs out of an inner theological contradiction as well as an open opposition to sinful surroundings. Since our faith binds us to Christ and opens up the future in Christ, hope should be the constant companion of faith. According to Moltmann, this is the hope which offers the believer and the church the basis for contextualized theology, namely, a theology able and willing to aggressively confront its political environment with a view toward the reformation of society.

The Hermeneutic of Hope

In order for this biblical hope to be properly interpreted and applied to our world, a melting of the historical and contemporary horizons has

---

4. Jürgen Moltmann, *A Theology of Hope* (New York: Harper and Row, 1967), 16.
5. Ibid., 283–85.
6. Ibid., 329–35. Compare Moltmann, "Gott kommt und der Mensch wird frei" (address given at Ökomenisches Treffen, Hamburg, 20–22 Sept. 1974), 21ff.

to be achieved. Texts which come to us from our past should not be examined simply in terms of experiential possibilities offered within that particular situation. These past messages need to be interpreted in their historical context—how their writers understood their own past, as well as their hope for the future. Only when the future horizon of the historical text is melted into the present horizon of the interpreter can the texts be understood and their truth applied.[7]

> The text can be understood only in the context of the comprehensive history which joins the past with the present—and indeed not merely with the present that today exists, but with the future horizon of present possibilities, because the meaning of the present becomes clear only in the light of the future.

> Only a conception of the course of history which does in fact join the past situation with the present and with its future horizon can provide the comprehensive horizon in which the limited present horizon of the expositor and the historical horizon of the text blend together.[8]

The way in which this relationship between then and now is worked out can be seen in several of Moltmann's basic theses.[9]

1. *The context and the text.* The context for a theology of hope is determined by a sensitivity to the possibilities of an open future. According to Moltmann, we are in debt to the 1960s, when there was an awakening in many areas of life, a breaking away from apathy, and a developing of the willingness to work toward a new future. This general forward-looking attitude accounts for the rapid development of theologies of hope. The historical perspective is provided by the text of the Bible. A theology of hope is an interpretation of the future horizon of biblical promises which guides today's concept of mission.

2. *The God of hope.* Christian theology speaks of God historically and eschatologically. Just what is history? Romans 4 and Hebrews 11:8–19 give us the example of Abraham, father of the faith. His life exemplifies what an individual experiences when he follows the God of hope. Abraham's life shows us that history means exodus. The same thing can be seen in the liberation of the Israelites from Egypt. Yet this life also involves an eschatological promise. It is the new future which rises out of the creative possibilities of God. This is not a legalistic

---

7. Moltmann, *Theology of Hope,* 272–79.

8. Moltmann quotes from Wolfhart Pannenberg, "Hermeneutik und Universalgeschichte," *Zeitschrift für Theologie und Kirche* 60 (1963): 116.

9. Jürgen Moltmann, "Einführung in die 'Theologie der Hoffnung,' " in *Das Experiment Hoffnung* (Munich: Kaiser, 1974), 64–81.

dogma but the hope of fulfilment which is open to the unexpected. In the final analysis hope is God himself. If we follow biblical usage and speak of the God of hope we will begin to emphasize the future as the existence of God's possibilities which at present, of course, can be seen only as that which is to come. If one understands God as the coming One and the power of the future, God becomes the basis for liberation. He lifts man above that which exists and frees him from the structures of this world and its society. God's future is not a dimension of his eternal existence, but rather it is his movement toward us. So we have no need of extrapolating the future from the present. Rather, we anticipate the future in the present (*futurus* as opposed to *adventus*).[10]

3. *The Messiah of hope.* Jesus' preaching is eschatological anticipation. He is doing today what is to come tomorrow, primarily in providing hope and grace for the unrighteous, not as judgment but rather as joy. This is offensive to some. The poor Jesus anticipates the kingdom of God among the poor; the justice of God comes among those with no legal rights; the glory of God is realized among the sick and leprous. In that service we see the cross of Christ as the sign of God's hope on earth for all who live in the shadow of that cross.

4. *The fellowship of hope.* The church is made up of a pilgrim people since it has no final resting place on earth. The front line of the exodus is not emigration but liberation because in the present struggle with the powers of the past and with fear and hope, we are moving out of the past into God's future.

Political Theology

For Moltmann all of this involves the return to an existential hermeneutic which concentrates on reflection upon life itself rather than upon vague and abstract theories. To be of practical value, this hermeneutic will have to be developed into a realistic political hermeneutic. According to Moltmann this represents the third in a series of theological models: (1) the medieval theology of love; (2) the Reformation theology of faith; and (3) the political theology of the modern era.

Political theology represents an attempt to relate theology (faith) to society in general. Moltmann is initially interested in his own society and focuses on several aspects of post-war German culture: (1) the political environment after the war, which left the country without a real capital, divided and cut off from its own history, and (2) the religious climate, essentially a form of civil religion like that envisioned

---

10. Moltmann points out that the German term *future* does not do justice to the Latin concept, which makes a distinction between the *futurum*—that which will be— and the *adventus*—that which is to come (*Das Experiment*, 73–74).

by Jean-Jacques Rousseau, in which Christianity was an involuntary part of a life devoid of decisions and community.

Several attempts have been made to adapt the gospel to that environment: (1) Rudolf Bultmann's demythologizing approach, which leaves one with no absolute standards; (2) Wolfhart Pannenberg's universal historical theology, which seeks to provide objective orientation and reasons for faith, but is for that reason too narrow and tends to support European prominence over other cultures and religions; (3) Trutz Rendtorff's theory of Christianity in which everything is to be integrated in the church, after which it becomes difficult to know what is Christian since modern European culture is equated with Christianity; and (4) evangelical apocalypse, which demands opposition to evil but operates in the "empty rooms of society, which are ignored by the ruling consciousness."[11]

Moltmann's alternative is political theology, which is best understood as the field, the milieu, the context, and the stage on which Christian theology is to be done during this modern era. Looking to the cross as the crux of Christ's struggle with the public powers of his day, political theology directs the cross as an instrument or a symbol of criticism against what Moltmann calls political religion, the symbolic integration of a people and the unity of religion and society or civil religion. It leads to a number of modern idols which oppress and subjugate people under a tyranny of arrogance and fear. Political religion is the focal point of political theology's criticism. Two fundamental assumptions underlie this criticism. The first is that the Old Testament's ban on idol worship includes those forces which alienate and dehumanize men today. The second is that the theology of the cross represents the radical application of the Old Testament ban on idol worship in demythologization, in natural theology with its profanization of God, and, in political theology through the fundamental democratization of power structures.[12]

It is the Christian belief in a *Deus crucifixus* which liberates men from their idol worship. Since the church (the community of believers) cannot identify itself with those idols (power structures), it must form its own fellowship. Having been liberated, the church is no longer in need of self-confirmation; it has nothing to prove, and it can and must open itself to the poor and oppressed. It cannot remain politically neutral. It must take a stand which works toward the democratization and

11. Jürgen Moltmann, *Politische Theologie—Politische Ethik* (Munich: Kaiser, 1984), 21–26.

12. Ibid., 58.

the liberation of the oppressed. Hope is not only an open future but also a future for the hopeless.

Jürgen Moltmann's response to the insipidity of post-war Christianity in Europe is his attempt to contextualize the Christian doctrine of eschatology. The resultant theology of hope emphasizes an active, present openness to the future, the implications of which lead directly to his political theology. Political theology is best summarized in terms of the cross, which is political criticism as well as hope for a politics of freedom. It is his remembrance of the crucified One which forces Moltmann to embrace a political theology.[13]

13. Ibid., 69.

5

Anglo-America
Bruce J. Nicholls and Charles H. Kraft

The Contextualization Debate

The Theological Education Fund (TEF) contextualization proposal gave expression and impetus to a profound change that was already taking place in the churches of the English-speaking world, especially in Britain and America. World War II was the coup de grâce to Anglo-American ecclesiastical and cultural provincialism, at least at the leadership level. Missiologists, theologians, and other scholars came to appreciate that even though there is but one Bible, one Mediator, and one gospel (Alas, not all were committed to that proposition!), nevertheless Christians of various cultures have their own ways of going about the task of understanding and communicating the Christian message.

Some of the pace-setters in the process of change were those most intimately involved in making the Scriptures and the gospel available to people of other cultures—linguists such as Kenneth Pike of Wycliffe Bible Translators' Summer Institute of Linguistics and Eugene A. Nida of the United Bible Societies and the American Bible Society; anthropologist-linguists such as William Smalley and Jacob Loewen who were involved with the journal *Practical Anthropology*; the missionary-author Don Richardson, and others. Books such as *Mes-*

sage and Mission, Peace Child, Christianity in Culture, and *Communicating Christ Cross-Culturally* became common fare in Bible colleges and seminaries.[1]

Meanwhile, fueled by a new sensitivity to the roles of culture and resurgent non-Christian religions, church scholars across the theological spectrum shifted their sights. Paul Tillich announced that if he had his life to live over he would not write a systematic theology but a theology based on the history of religion. George McAfee Brown contributed *Theology in a New Key.*[2] Wilfred Cantwell Smith capped off his theological inclusivism with *Towards a World Theology.*[3] After some teaching experiences in Africa, conservative theologian Morris A. Inch authored *Doing Theology across Cultures* and then *Making the Good News Relevant.*[4] Of course theologians were by no means alone in confronting cultural issues. New Testament scholars, specialists in Christian education, teachers of psychology and counseling— over the years an increasing number of Christian educators found themselves encountering cultural questions as they attempted to relate to foreign students, ethnic minorities, and new arrivals to the Western world.

One of the by-products of this process has been what might be called the contextualization debate in the English-speaking church. We would expect that long-held and diverse theological commitments would yield very different understandings of contextualization. Accordingly, Bruce C. E. Fleming's *Contextualization of Theology,* Bruce J. Nicholls's *Contextualization,* Donald A. Carson's *Biblical Interpretation and the Church,* William J. Larkin's *Culture and Biblical Hermeneutics,* and other works reflect various aspects of the liberal-conservative debate.[5]

1. Eugene A. Nida, *Message and Mission: The Communication of the Christian Faith* (New York: Harper, 1960; New York: Harper and Row, 1969); Don Richardson, *Peace Child* (Glendale, Calif.: Regal, 1974); Charles H. Kraft, *Christianity in Culture: A Study in Dynamic Biblical Theologizing in Cross-Cultural Perspective* (Maryknoll, N.Y.: Orbis, 1979); David J. Hesselgrave, *Communicating Christ Cross-Culturally: An Introduction to Missionary Communication* (Grand Rapids: Zondervan, 1978).

2. George McAfee Brown, *Theology in a New Key: Responding to Liberation Themes* (Philadelphia: Westminster, 1981).

3. Wilfred Cantwell Smith, *Towards a World Theology: Faith and the Comparative History of Religion* (Philadelphia: Westminster, 1981).

4. Morris A. Inch, *Doing Theology across Cultures* (Grand Rapids: Baker, 1982); *Making the Good News Relevant: Keeping the Gospel Distinctive in Any Culture* (Nashville: Thomas Nelson, 1986).

5. Bruce C. E. Fleming, *Contextualization of Theology: An Evangelical Assessment* (Pasadena, Calif.: William Carey Library, 1980); Bruce J. Nicholls, *Contextualization: A Theology of Gospel and Culture* (Downers Grove: Inter-Varsity, 1979); Donald A. Carson, ed., *Biblical Interpretation and the Church: The Problems of Contextualization*

But sides in this debate have not been drawn simply on the basis of classical theological differences. Most of the thirty-three theologians, anthropologists, linguists, missionaries, and pastors who met at Willowbank, Bermuda, in 1978 to study issues relating to the gospel and culture were considered evangelicals. The papers and conclusions of that meeting were edited by John R. W. Stott and Robert T. Coote.[6] A perusal of those volumes reveals significant disagreements on very basic contextualization issues despite the evangelical consensus of the participants. A short time after the journal *Gospel in Context* was launched, funding was withdrawn by its conservative sponsor on the ground that it was not contributing to clear evangelical outcomes. Especially after the publication of Charles H. Kraft's magnum opus, *Christianity in Culture*, his approach was taken to task by his older colleague at Fuller Theological Seminary, Donald A. McGavran, and then by various other scholars, including Inch and Edward N. Gross.[7] Influenced by Kraft, Phil Parshall made a number of somewhat tentative proposals for a contextualized approach to Muslims,[8] the more radical of which occasioned criticism from fellow evangelicals.

The jury is still out on contextualization in the Anglo-American Christian community, and no consensus is likely to be reached for some time. Within the ecumenical orbit title after title reflects a preoccupation with liberation theology themes and interreligious dialogue. Within the conservative camp, there is a continuing effort to tap the resources of the behavioral sciences to traverse cultural boundaries more successfully. Charles R. Taber believes that though culture and language are imperfect tools for understanding God's ways, "God has sanctified them by using them fully in the Incarnation of his Son and in the inspiration of the Bible."[9] Harvie M. Conn encourages an expansion of the trialogue between theology, anthropology, and mission.[10]

(Nashville: Thomas Nelson, 1985); William J. Larkin, Jr., *Culture and Biblical Hermeneutics: Interpreting and Applying the Authoritative Word in a Relativistic Age* (Grand Rapids: Baker, 1988).

6. John R. W. Stott and Robert T. Coote, eds., *Gospel and Culture* (Pasadena, Calif.: William Carey Library, 1979); the volume later was reedited and republished: John R. W. Stott and Robert T. Coote, eds., *Down to Earth: Studies in Christianity and Culture* (Grand Rapids: Eerdmans, 1980).

7. Donald A. McGavran, *The Clash Between Christianity and Culture* (Washington, D.C.: Canon, 1974); Edward N. Gross, *Is Charles Kraft an Evangelical? A Critique of "Christianity in Culture"* (Collingswood, N.J.: Christian Beacon, 1985).

8. Phil Parshall, *New Paths in Muslim Evangelism: Evangelical Approaches to Contextualization* (Grand Rapids: Baker, 1980).

9. Charles R. Taber, "Hermeneutics and Culture: An Anthropological Perspective," in *Gospel and Culture*, 129–30.

10. Harvie M. Conn, *Eternal Word and Changing Worlds: Theology, Anthropology, and Mission in Trialogue* (Grand Rapids: Zondervan, 1984).

John Jefferson Davis opens the door to an exploration of the potential of historical-cultural hermeneutics.[11]

Two prominent writers who have taken very different positions and have not shifted ground in contextualization discussions are the New Zealander Bruce J. Nicholls and the American Charles H. Kraft. To an overview of their positions and approaches we now turn.

Bruce J. Nicholls: Dogmatic Theology and Relational Centers

As a long-time missionary to India with the Bible and Medical Missionary Fellowship, Bruce J. Nicholls speaks to contextualization issues as a missionary-missiologist. At the same time, as executive secretary of the World Evangelical Fellowship Theological Commission and secretary to the Theological Research and Communication Institute in New Delhi, he brings theological concern and acumen to the discussion on contextualization. Theological concern may seem to overtake and even surpass missiological interests in Nicholls's writings. If this is the case it is because he has a profound conviction that if contextualization reveals itself to be theologically suspect, it will inevitably be missiologically unacceptable as well. With Archbishop William Temple, who contributed much to relating the twentieth-century church to its society, he is convinced that theology is the queen of the sciences and that all of our problems are basically theological.

Most of Nicholls's many important contributions to missions-related literature come as monographs in journals, special series, or larger works. His writings on contextualization are no exception. Perhaps as significant as any are the two monographs chosen as a basis for this study—one presented at the Willowbank Consultation on Gospel and Culture[12] and the other in the Outreach and Identity series of the World Evangelical Theological Commission, *Contextualization: A Theology of the Gospel and Culture*. A perusal of these two monographs reveals that from very early on in the discussion on contextualization, Nicholls entertained two primary concerns. First, he was deeply disturbed by the contextualization approach proposed and promoted by the TEF third mandate leaders Shoki Coe and Aharon Sapsezian. Second, he desired to develop an approach that would be more biblically defensible and missiologically sound.

11. John Jefferson Davis, "Contextualization and the Nature of Theology," in *The Necessity of Systematic Theology*, 2d ed. (Grand Rapids: Baker, 1980), 184–85.

12. Bruce J. Nicholls, "Towards a Theology of Gospel and Culture," in *Gospel and Culture*, 69–82, or *Down to Earth*, 49–62.

The Wider Debate

Nicholls does not hesitate to point out that differences in definitions, departure points, and the directions taken in contextualization grow out of a long-standing theological debate. Especially since the Uppsala convention (1968), theology has become more and more secularized in World Council circles. The line between the church and the world has blurred. Ecumenical mission has come to be understood in terms of "the salvation of history and the world rather than of the church."[13] The unity of the church has come to be a sign of the unity of mankind and the world. Since men and women of all faiths, cultures, and ideologies are searching for world community, it has become incumbent upon Christians to engage in dialogue with them, understand them, and learn from them so that all together might progress toward unity and truth. In all of this, universalism tends to be assumed and conversion downplayed if not disparaged.

At the same time evangelicals, while becoming increasingly concerned about the broader ramifications of the gospel, have nevertheless maintained that any understanding of contextualization which is separated from the proclamation of the gospel and the indigenization of the church is unacceptable. Biblical authority, limitarianism, Great Commission mission, world evangelization, the necessity of conversion— such are the points of departure for the church's mission to the world and they must be the foundation for any discussion of contextualization of the gospel.

Nicholls does not lose sight of the fact that this ongoing debate between ecumenists and evangelicals is the backdrop against which the most fundamental of contextualization disagreements must be understood. Not all differences stem from this wider debate, but, apart from an appreciation of the fact that initial contextualization proposals emanated from ecumenical presuppositions, confusion is inevitable.

Alternatives in Contextualization

Utilizing G. Linwood Barney's model of culture, Nicholls views culture in various layers (see fig. 1). The surface layers build on the deeper layers so that values are based on worldview and give rise to institutions such as law, marriage, education, and so on. Religion, therefore, influences all layers but, when genuinely held, always involves the deepest layer of culture: ideology, cosmology, and worldview.

In the view of many the world is a closed system. Culture describes

13. Ibid., 22.

Figure 1
The Layers of Culture

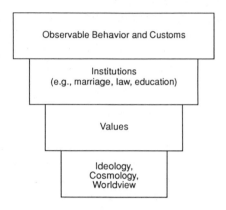

Based on a discussion by G. Linwood Barney, "The
Supracultural and the Cultural Implications for Frontier
Missions," in *The Gospel and Frontier Peoples* (Pasadena,
Calif.: William Carey Library, 1973), 49–50.

all there is. Even religion is a human product and can be completely subsumed under the category of culture. From a Christian point of view, however, the world is the arena of a great battle between the forces of God and Satan. Though the eventual outcome is assured by virtue of the sovereignty of God, ultimate triumph does not mitigate the present struggle. Humanity, as the creation of God, reflects the *imago Dei* but, as a result of the fall, it also reflects a sinful nature. Culture, as the product of human life, is good, but it is also tainted by sin. Supracultural messages and phenomena invade the world, but they emanate from both God and Satan and therefore are sometimes divine, sometimes demonic. It is into this kind of world that the church is called to be the instrument of God and that the Christian gospel is to be contextualized and communicated. As a result the church is faced with various sets of alternatives.

1. *Two levels of contextualization—cultural and theological.* Anthropologists and sociologists largely concern themselves with "cultural level" contextualization. They operate in the more visible surface layers of culture that have to do with institutions, artifacts, and observable behavior. Their approach is phenomenological and their product is ethnotheology. Theologians, on the other hand, primarily operate in the deeper layers of culture that have to do with worldview, cosmology, and moral and ethical values. It is not without reason that Nicholls takes special note that the two groups are therefore suspicious of each

other.[14] Anthropologists and sociologists can be expected to be most unhappy with this sort of analysis, but it is a key to understanding Nicholls's view of contextualization.

2. *Two approaches to contextualization—existential and dogmatic.* The imposition of Western theologies on Third World churches by missionaries and nationals alike often has a devastating effect because national Christians have been discouraged from theologizing within their own cultures. If theology is to be relevant within a given cultural situation it must be contextualized. But, speaking in general terms, Nicholls believes that task may be approached either existentially or dogmatically.

The ecumenical approach to contextualization is basically existential. Two basic principles interact with each other in this approach: (1) the relativity of text and context, and (2) the pursuit of truth via the dialectical method. Theologizing of this sort cannot result in a perfect or an absolute theology because it is a human endeavor. Nicholls points to Daniel von Allman of Switzerland and S. Wesley Ariarajah of Sri Lanka as proponents of this kind of contextualization.

With Ernst Käsemann, Rudolf Bultmann, and others, von Allman views the gospel as the preaching of and reflection on the Christ event. In the New Testament the Aramaic preaching tradition comes to be expressed in the cultural forms of Hellenistic Judaism. The preaching tradition is expressed first in worship and ultimately in theology. Paul's sometimes successful and sometimes unsuccessful efforts to correct and adapt this Hellenized gospel become a model for contextualization efforts today because theologies must always go through this same process.

Ariarajah believes that all religious traditions have their "story" of God, the world, and the destiny of humankind. These various stories reflect both the religious experience of Christians, Hindus, Buddhists, and others, and the activity of God as he leads all to a common community and destiny. By laying aside any notion that "our story is the only true story" we are enabled to engage in a true dialogue with those of other faiths, a dialogue that enhances this process toward unity.

Nicholls eschews this kind of theologizing and embraces an alternative approach which "begins with an authoritative biblical theology whose dogmatic understanding is contextualized in a given situation."[15] It can, therefore, be termed dogmatic contextualization. Comparing his dogmatic assumptions with those who follow the existential approach, however, Nicholls makes the somewhat vague determina-

14. Ibid., 24.
15. Ibid.

tion that the two views are "not irreconcilable alternatives, but the starting point for doing theology will determine the end product."[16]

3. *Two dangers in approaching the task of contextualization—the fear of irrelevance if contextualization is not attempted, and the fear of compromise and syncretism if it is taken too far.* There is a need to use existing cultural forms that can be baptized and pressed into the service of Christ if the gospel is not denied in the process. Unless this is done it is likely that only the surface layers of culture will be changed. But since by definition contextualization appropriates indigenous linguistic and cultural forms, it always risks cultural and religious syncretism. The only viable choice in the face of these two dangers is a contextualization that is true to both indigenous culture and the authority of Scripture.

The Nature of Biblical and Dogmatic Theology

1. *Understanding our preunderstandings.* Preunderstandings or precommitments largely determine how we view the authority, interpretation, and use of Scripture. Three types of factors play important roles in the formation of preunderstandings: first, ideological factors that reflect one's worldview and value system; second, a cultural element comprised of the influence of society's institutions and customs; and, third, the supracultural element which involves either acceptance of Christ and his lordship or rejection of Christ in favor of humanism, Marxist atheism, or false religions.

The overriding elements are supracultural. Mahatma Gandhi was influenced by the gospel but could not accept the lordship of Christ. His understanding of the Bible was determined by a Hindu monistic worldview. Martin Luther's radical conversion to Christ, on the other hand, resulted in an entirely new understanding of the authority already resident in sacred Scripture by virtue of its inspiration.

Cultural factors are nevertheless important. It would be idealistic to think that any theologian, be he Asian, African, Latin American, or Western, could free himself from the influences of his native culture or of the cultural influences inherent in his theological training.

The ideological position of an Asian theologian such as Ariarajah—impregnated with Hindu mysticism as it is—plays a significant role in his view of the Bible. Or, to turn to the Western world, the ideological positions of men such as Adolf von Harnack, Friedrich Schleiermacher, Søren Kierkegaard, and Bultmann (and Ernst Fuchs and Gerhard Ebeling associated with the new hermeneutic) effectively eliminate the

16. Ibid.

verbal and propositional elements of revelation in the category *Word of God.*

2. *Understanding the authority of the Bible.* Evangelicals are grateful for insights into the role of the interpreter's experience in his understanding and use of the Bible. But they are concerned about theologians who move away from the objective authority of the Bible as they tend toward subjective approaches based on an experience of God which they attempt to make relevant to others. God the Holy Spirit controlled the processes of revelation and inscripturation. Therefore the Bible has an authority that precedes and transcends our subjective experience of it. Though the words used to describe that authority—words such as "infallible," "inerrant," and "autographs"—may indeed be rooted in historical circumstances, "behind them stand supra-cultural verities which are inherent in the Word of God itself."[17] With Augustine, evangelicals believe that "what Scripture says God says."

The Bible manifests rationality, perspicuity, and unity as correlates of its inspiration. Scripture, therefore, can be understood in its own terms. Scripture interprets Scripture.

As for cultural elements, Nicholls says, "God the Holy Spirit overshadowed cultural forms through which he revealed his word in such a manner that these cultural forms conveyed what God intended to be revealed. God was not at the mercy of human culture. He controlled the use of it for his particular purpose of revelation."[18]

3. *Understanding the Bible's cultural conditioning.* The overruling providence of God makes an inseparable bond between content and form in the Bible. In the Old Testament era God chose to reveal his Word to Israel. As a result, the culture of Israel uniquely reflected a divine-human interaction unlike anything in surrounding cultures. In fact, the Old Testament record shows that through patriarchs, judges, and prophets the Lord constantly led his people in a struggle against false contextualization and syncretism to preserve them from a paganizing conditioning by other cultures. In this process he used some cultural forms such as circumcision for his purposes while rejecting others such as idolatry.

Providentially, Hebrew culture preserved the uniqueness of the divine message, and ultimately Jesus Christ was born as a Jew. It is an affront to God to speak of a black Christ or a Hindu Christ, or to think that he could have been born as a woman. The New Testament writers wrote from within a Hebrew cultural framework, but in view of the divine purpose to reach all nations, they adopted and transformed some

17. Ibid., 43.
18. Ibid., 74.

Hellenistic and pagan forms while totally rejecting others. The word *erōs* (sensual love) was rejected; *mythos* (myth) and *daimōn* (demon) were used only in a negative sense; *kyrios* (lord), *logos* (word), and *sōtēr* (savior) were used in a way consistent with Hebrew usage; *mystērion* (mystery) and *metamorphōsis* (transformation or transfiguration) were given entirely new meanings. Thus the Bible offers models for the contextualization process.

4. *Understanding and interpreting the Bible.* Finally, a careful study of the Scriptures themselves reveals sound hermeneutical principles for their interpretation. Nicholls mentions four of them:[19]

   a. The lifestyle principle of faith commitment. The first requirement for understanding the Word of God is to live the life of faith.

   b. The objective-subjective principle of distancing from and identification with the text. The right use of linguistic tools and historical method (the grammatico-historical method) makes possible the discovery of the *sensus literalis* or literal and natural meaning of the text, that is, what the writer *said* as distinguished from his *intention*, which involves the use of the much more speculative historical-critical method. Yet in distancing and identification the interpreter stands back and allows the text to correct his own preunderstandings and his understandings of other passages. For example, it has been proposed that the concept of God as Father is inappropriate for a matrilineal society, and therefore alternative language and symbols should be used. But Nicholls says that rather than semiabsolutizing his native or respondent culture, the interpreter/exegete should carefully explain the biblical concept of God as Father in the matrilineal society.

   c. The body-life principle of the believing community. The biblical notion of the priesthood of believers means that the hermeneutical task is not a purely private one. It is to be done within the framework of the believing community.

   d. The mission-in-the-world principle. The distinctions between the kingdom of God and the kingdom of Satan and the church and the world must be maintained. When the world rather than the church is the center of God's activity and when the mission is secularized so that the salvation of all of history is asserted—as it is in liberation theology—biblical theology is truncated.

From Biblical Theology to Contextualized Theology—The Process

Unlike dogmatic biblical theology, all contextualized theologies are incomplete and relative. Nevertheless, they are necessary. By adher-

19. Nicholls, *Contextualization*, 48–52.

ence to certain principles these theologies can be made to progress toward a closer approximation to the biblical formulation. Nicholls's treatment of the contextualization process is primarily suggestive and somewhat repetitive.

1. *The starting point must always be found "within the circle of faith-commitment to God's revelation in Christ."*[20] Common ground may be found in various cultures as was the case when Paul preached in Athens, but culture does not provide the beginning point.

2. *Contextualization should concern itself with "relational centers."* History reveals that God the Holy Spirit guides in such a way that the givens of biblical theology are applied to specific historical and cultural contexts. Luther's treatment of justification by faith was sorely needed by the medieval church. John Wesley's emphasis on the experiences of the love and grace of God spoke to the deepest needs of the oppressed classes in eighteenth-century England. Numerous similar examples could be given, but it is important to note that these same theological emphases are needed today, though they will be contextualized differently. Lutheranism's justification by faith needs a restatement in Indian theology. The relational center of the covenant in Reformed theology is especially appropriate in Islamic cultures. The liberating power of the Holy Spirit as emphasized in the Pentecostal movement has great significance in Latin America.

3. *The inseparable but distinct work of the Creator-Savior must be maintained.* When the distinction between creation and redemption is blurred as it is in some contextualized theologies, confusion results. In the Bible these two lines of God's activity meet in the incarnation, the death, and the resurrection of Jesus Christ. This must be insisted upon.

4. *Authentic contextualization recognizes the alienation of man in culture.* The biblical contextualizer studies the cultural context and the questions it poses. But the process of theologizing is a one-way process in which culture as the product of people created by God and yet alienated from God is judged. That which is contrary to God's Word is to be destroyed. That which is true to God's Word is to be recreated. For example, the Indian concept of *karma* can become a cultural bridge in communicating the gospel to Hindus, but only if the biblical idea of sowing and reaping is maintained while the idea of *karma* as an absolute principle divorced from the Lawgiver is destroyed.

5. *It should not be forgotten that both universals and variables are to be found in the indigenous church.* Universals lead to formal correspondence among all churches. Cultural variables lead to dynamic equivalence. Unless a proper tension is maintained between the two,

20. Ibid., 55.

there can be no true contextualization of the church. Churches progress toward conformity in their attitudes toward slavery and polygamy, for example, as they conform to Christ and his will. Other attitudes, such as the obligation to render worship, are "convertible" but will retain something of their cultural heritage and therefore contribute to diversity among churches.

According to Nicholls, then, contextualization of the gospel is both possible and necessary. But true contextualization is *dogmatic*. It begins with biblical theology. And it results in a judgment upon all of culture—some of which it rejects and some of which it recreates to the glory of God.

Charles H. Kraft: Dynamic-Equivalence Transculturation

One of the most controversial American contributors to contextualization thinking and literature is Fuller Theological Seminary's Charles H. Kraft. Criticism and controversy notwithstanding, there can be no question that Kraft has influenced many missions people on both the theological left and the theological right. No one can lay just claim to being versed in Anglo-American contextualization without having thought through the issues Kraft has raised. The seminal *Christianity in Culture: A Study in Dynamic Biblical Theologizing in Cross-Cultural Perspective* forms the primary source for this review of his thinking, though we will draw from other writings as well.

Kraft does not make great use of the term *contextualization* in *Christianity and Culture*. We suggest two possible reasons for this. First, Kraft does not agree with the Louvain report that one can overcome the distance between the biblical text and the modern interpreter if this theologizing begins with interpreting God's action in the contemporary historical context. Since many early contextualizers took this approach Kraft may want to distance himself from them. Second, Kraft is concerned with the whole gamut of the process of divine communication to humanity—including revelation, interpretation, translation, and application—and therefore he uses a variety of words to describe various aspects of the communication and contextualization processes.

Preunderstandings and Commitments

Most of Kraft's conclusions flow quite naturally from his preunderstandings. Concerning those preunderstandings he is explicit and forthright.

1. *The cultural and the supracultural.* Kraft takes a high view of culture. All peoples share the same basic needs but they attempt to organize and meet those needs by developing worldviews and devising

behavioral patterns that make up their culture. No one sees reality as it really is. Reality is filtered through the worldview provided by one's culture. God not only has ordained culture, but also is at work in the various cultures and endeavors to transform them and bring them ever closer to his reality and ideal. He accepts subideal aspects as starting points in this process. Christians, and particularly Christian missionaries, have the responsibility to withhold premature judgment, to understand the culture of receptors, and to work in their cultural framework with a view to transforming people and culture with God. In this regard Kraft agrees with the second solution to the distance problem mentioned in the Louvain report, which asserted that the supracultural message of the Bible can speak directly to anyone in any era if it is set free from the historically conditioned forms in which it is clothed.[21]

2. *Communication and culture.* Kraft draws from communication theory, especially as it is described by the general semanticists.[22] Meaning is not in words or things but in persons who have content in mind and express it in a code (usually language). Meaning also is "that which the receiver of a message contructs in his head and responds to."[23] Even the many common reconstructions and responses among human beings reflect a variety of cultural orientations, perceived needs, and personal preferences.

Several conclusions follow from this. First, all communication is proximate; communicators operate within a range of meaning. Second, cultural conditioning plays a vital role in this process. Correspondence of meanings between source and receptor depends upon "the extent of agreement between communicator and receptor concerning what the cultural symbols signify."[24] Third, written communication such as that of the Bible presents additional problems; not only is the receptor separated from the writers by culture and language, but also he cannot verify meanings with them.

3. *General and special revelation.* Kraft agrees with theologians who distinguish between general and special revelation. However, he thinks they err when they regard the difference between the two as the revelational information communicated rather than the purpose or function of that information. That which brings a proper response to God is

---

21. Ellen Flessemann-van Leer, ed., *The Bible: Its Authority and Interpretation in the Ecumenical Movement* (Geneva: World Council of Churches, 1980), 6–7, 61–74.

22. Charles H. Kraft, *Communication Theory for Christian Witness* (Nashville: Abingdon, 1983).

23. Charles H. Kraft, "Interpreting in Cultural Context," *Journal of the Evangelical Theological Society* 21 (December 1978): 359.

24. Ibid.

revelatory.[25] General revelation includes information which is sufficient even for salvation. But it is so general and predictable that it does not attract attention. Special revelation does not so much add new information as it adds to the stimulus and results in perception of the revelation.

Revelation, then, is not just past tense; it has a continuing dimension. The notions that revelation ceased with the writing of the last book of the Bible and that subsequently God only enlightens and illumines are false. Every time a person makes a discovery of divine truth such as Peter experienced when he said to Jesus, "You are the Christ, the Son of the living God," revelation occurs.[26]

4. *The "inspired classic casebook."* For Kraft the Bible is indeed a unique book but not in the senses often proposed. It is not, for example, unique in the traditional evangelical sense of being verbal propositional revelation—a view that he considers static and closed-minded. Kraft does not believe that "as soon as the last New Testament document was committed to writing [God] totally changed in his method of operation to such an extent that he now limits himself to the written record."[27] No more Bible books are being written because they are not needed, but revelation is still occurring in a dynamic process by which God communicates not only information but himself by providing stimuli to which people respond. By a proper use of the materials of general and special revelation, especially the Scriptures, we can participate in this ongoing process.

To do so, however, requires a proper understanding of what the Bible is. The Bible is inspired, but inspiration attaches more to its meanings than to its words. It is inerrant, not in its whole extent but only where intended teachings are concerned. It contains supracultural truths, but they "float on a cultural ocean" because of the culture-specific nature of the Bible messages.[28] The Bible is the Word of God only in a potential sense. When used incorrectly it is not the Word of God.[29]

In times past certain events occurred in which people of the cultures of Scripture perceived that it was God who was speaking to them. They recorded the most significant of these communication events, and then the Holy Spirit guided in the process of selection and collection of those that are included in the Bible. Of course, those that are included deal with problems of the cultures of Bible times in ways that were

---

25. Kraft, *Christianity in Culture*, 183.
26. Ibid., 163–64.
27. Ibid., 212, 396.
28. Ibid., 131.
29. Ibid., 221.

meaningful to those people. They may not be readily understood today and they may not speak to issues of our cultures today. It is important, then, that we understand not only the message of the Bible but also the method of the Bible so that we too can be instrumental in occasioning similar revelatory events. The Bible is primarily an inspired casebook which provides us with models and methods designed to guide our communication.[30] At the same time it is a yardstick by which we can measure how well we are doing.[31] And it is a tether which prevents us from going too far in this risk-taking venture.[32]

Paradigm and Process

To carry out the tasks associated with this continuing revelatory process—such as interpretation, translation, and application—a paradigm shift is required. We must adopt a cross-cultural perspective in the place of our monocultural one. We must rely more on tools provided by the behavioral sciences, especially anthropology and linguistics.

1. *The dynamic-equivalence model.* Kraft builds upon the dynamic-equivalence translation model of Nida and others. Dynamic equivalence, he says, goes far beyond the formal word-by-word equivalence model where "the focus of understanding is on the surface-level linguistic forms through which the message is conveyed."[33] It involves a more complex and demanding set of procedures which Kraft puts in diagrammatic form (see fig. 2).

Kraft's concerted focus on response and effect seems to go beyond Nida, who describes a dynamic-equivalent translation as being the "closest natural equivalence to the source-language message" and then places considerable emphasis on the three terms *closest, natural,* and *equivalence.*[34] Perhaps Kraft's approach should be termed *impact translation.* In any case, he proceeds to use the dynamic-equivalence paradigm as a model for all contextualization-related activities. In Nida's approach these activities can be subsumed under the tasks of correctly interpreting Scripture and effectively communicating its message within the context of another culture.[35]

2. *Hermeneutics—interpreting Scripture.* According to Kraft, the problems of interpreting Scripture include two errors which are espe-

30. Ibid., 198.
31. Ibid., 187.
32. Ibid., 191.
33. Ibid., 264.
34. Eugene A. Nida, *Towards a Science of Translating: With Special Reference to Principles and Procedures Involved in Bible Translating* (Leiden: E. J. Brill, 1964), 166–71.
35. Nida, *Message and Mission.*

Figure 2
Dynamic-Equivalence Translation Procedure

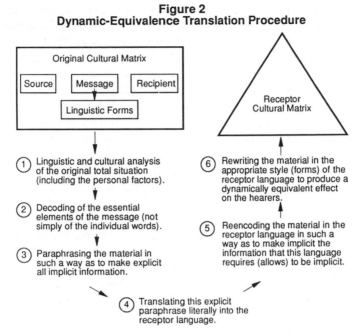

Original Cultural Matrix

Source | Message | Recipient

Linguistic Forms

Receptor
Cultural Matrix

(1) Linguistic and cultural analysis of the original total situation (including the personal factors).

(2) Decoding of the essential elements of the message (not simply of the individual words).

(3) Paraphrasing the material in such a way as to make explicit all implicit information.

(6) Rewriting the material in the appropriate style (forms) of the receptor language to produce a dynamically equivalent effect on the hearers.

(5) Reencoding the material in the receptor language in such a way as to make implicit the information that this language requires (allows) to be implicit.

(4) Translating this explicit paraphrase literally into the receptor language.

Charles H. Kraft, *Christianity in Culture* (Maryknoll, N.Y.: Orbis; Exter: Paternoster, 1979), 275. Used by permission.

cially common. First, we tend to interpret Scripture in the light of our own cultural conditioning. The Bible, however, has come to us in forms provided by Hebrew, Aramaic, and Greek cultures. Many of the assumptions implicit in biblical communication events are not mentioned in the text. For example, the Gospel of John does not mention the significance of the Samaritan woman being at the well at midday or the necessity to go to her "husband" before making a decision. Apart from understanding the cultural implications assumed in the passage, interpretation is incomplete or erroneous. As a matter of fact, it was Bultmann's desire for a contemporary cultural interpretation that led to his demythologizing of Scripture. To make our Western monocultural interpretation the basis for applying the biblical message to either our own contemporary culture or a Third World culture is disastrous.

Second, we err when we rely on the principle of the plain meaning of Scripture to solve difficult problems in interpretation. The Bible uses symbols with which we may be familiar but which our culture interprets differently from the writers. The plain meaning in such cases can be most misleading. By way of illustration, our culturally-conditioned interpretational reflexes prevent us from understanding that in Hebrew culture plural marriage was not primarily a sexual matter, that Jesus was not impolite in the way he addressed his mother at the temple and at the feast, and that the "faith that was once for all entrusted to the saints" mentioned in Jude 1:3 was not a system of doctrine, but a relationship to God. Similarly their interpretational reflexes cause Nigerians to misinterpret Psalm 23 because in their culture only the very young or the insane tend sheep; the Sawis of New Guinea admire the treachery of Judas because of their value system; and the Chinese interpret the dragon of Revelation in a positive light because of their symbol system.

When the original language is similar to ours, or when a statement represents something of a cultural universal, or when an experience common to all of mankind is referred to, we may do fairly well in understanding Scripture. Otherwise we do not. Since anthropologists and linguists understand culture and usually are bicultural themselves, they have better tools for analysis than do historians and philologists. These tools are needed to distinguish between cultural form and cultural meaning and between culture universals and culture specifics. The use of such tools in interpretation results in ethnolinguistic or culturolinguistic hermeneutics.[36]

3. *Transculturation—communicating God's Word into receptor cultures. Transculturation* signifies to culture what *translation* signifies to language. When it comes to translating the Bible and then moving on to communicating and theologizing for a different culture, Kraft returns to the dynamic-equivalence paradigm.

From Kraft's point of view, interpreters, translators, and theologizers are faced with an ironic state of affairs. The universals or generalized statements of Scripture come closest to expressing the supracultural will of God and are easiest to interpret and translate; yet generalized abstract statements lack the stimulation and impact necessary if receptors are to pay attention and receive them as God's Word. Culture-specific forms and symbols present the greatest obstacle to translation and transculturation, but at the same time stimulate revelation.

Obviously this poses a dilemma for Christian communicators in a post-Christian Western world which is chronologically and informationally A.D. as well as in the Third World, much of which is chronologically A.D. but informationally B.C. In neither case does the primary problem have to do with providing additional information. Even those who have never heard the gospel have enough information to be saved if they would but respond to the information they have. We must go with the gospel, as Kraft says, "not (as we may ethnocentrically as-

36. Kraft, *Christianity in Culture*, 135.

sume) because our hearers *could not* be saved (for lack of knowledge) but because they, like those in our home country, *will not* ordinarily respond in faith to God on the basis of knowledge and stimulus they now have."[37] What is needed is the kind of translations, communications, and theologies that will stimulate such revelatory responses as occurred in Bible times.

Dynamic-Equivalence Outcomes

Finally, we might well ask, "What do the products of Kraft's process look like?" In terms of field results that is not an easy question to answer because Kraft's approach has met with a mixed response in the Third World as well as on the home front. But in Kraft's own projections the question is not difficult to answer at all. Let us look at some of the practical outcomes as he envisages them.

1. *Dynamic-equivalence translations and transculturations.* Bible translations such as Phillips, Today's English Version, the New English Bible, and the Living Bible are praised by Kraft. But he would go beyond them in the direction of transculturation. Translation tends to be tied to historical events, but in transculturation of the message "the aim is to *represent the meanings of those historical events as if they were clothed in contemporary events.*"[38] *Letters to Street Christians* and Clarence Jordan's *Cotton Patch Version* are selected by Kraft as illustrations of good cultural translations or transculturations. For specific illustrations of what Kraft has in mind, see figure 3.

2. *Dynamic-equivalence ethnotheologies.* All theologies are made by people and therefore reflect the cultural settings and personal perspective of those who engage in the theologizing process. Western theology represents the answers to questions asked by contemporary Westerners and their forebears. Not only that, it represents ways of thinking about those questions and ways of framing those answers that are appropriate to Western thought patterns. But it does not speak to the concerns of, nor in accordance with the ways of thinking of, Third World cultures.

Taking a cue from Daniel von Allman, Kraft turns to the New Testament and views it as containing the theological product of a process in which the gospel of the Aramaic preaching tradition was ultimately contextualized in the Hellenistic formulations of Pauline theology. But Pauline theology does not speak to many of the issues being raised today in either Western or Third World cultures. What is important, then, is not that the theological systems of the West be passed on to the

37. Ibid., 257.
38. Ibid., 280.

Figure 3
Levels of Abstraction

1. Basic Ideals: Highly abstract.	2. General principles: Ideals translated into transcultural concepts. Less abstract.	3. Specific Cultural Forms/Symbol level: Principles translated and concretized for a culture.
◀ – – – – – – – – – More General ◀ ––––▶ More Specific – – – – – – – – – ▶		
A. *Love your neighbor as you love yourself (Matt. 22:39).*	1. Do not steal (Exod. 20:17).	a. Do not take your neighbor's donkey (Hebrew).
		b. Do not take your employer's money (USA).
	2. Do not covet. (Exod. 20:17).	a. Do not desire your neighbor's house (Hebrew).
		b. Same for USA.
	3. Do not show partiality (1 Tim. 5:21; James 3:17).	a. Treat Gentiles, blacks, and women as human beings.
		b. Rebuke whoever needs it (1 Tim. 5:20).
B. *Love the Lord your God with all your heart. . . (Matt. 22:37).*	1. Worship no God but me (Exod. 20:3).	a. Do not bow down to worship an idol (Exod. 20:5) (Hebrew).
		b. Do not pledge primary allegiance to material wealth (USA).
	2. Seek by all means to save people (1 Cor. 9:22).	a. Live as a Jew to win Jews (1 Cor. 9:20).
		b. Live as a Gentile to win Gentiles (1 Cor. 9:20).
		c. Live as an African to win Africans.
C. *Everything must be done in a proper and orderly way (1 Cor. 14:40).*	1. Leaders should be beyond reproach (1 Tim. 3:2; Titus 1:6).	a. They must be self-controlled, etc. (1 Tim. 3:2).
	2. Christian women should not appear out of line.	a. They should cover their heads when praying (Greek culture) (1 Cor. 11:10).
		b. They should not wear their clothes too tight (USA).
	3. Christians should live according to the rules of their culture as long as they do not conflict with Christian principles.	a. Women should learn in silence (Greek culture).
		b. Woman may speak in mixed groups (USA).
		c. Pay the government what belongs to it (Matt. 22:21).
		d. Obey governmental authorities (Rom. 13:1).
		e. Wives, submit to your husbands (Greek and some segments of USA culture) (Eph. 5:22; Col. 3:18).

Charles H. Kraft, "Interpreting in Cultural Context," *Journal of the Evangelical Theological Society* 21, 4 (December 1978): 356–66. Used by permission.

Third World. Nor is it essential that the theological systems of the past be passed on to another generation. What is required of Western and Third World theologians is that they emulate the theological process of the Bible and produce theologies that will display the foci, understandings, and expressions appropriate to the cultures from which they emanate. Examples of this kind of theologizing are discoverable very early in the history of the church. In fact, according to Kraft, it is likely that many of the so-called heresies of the early centuries should be recognized as valid contextualization attempts rather than as theological aberrations.

3. *Dynamic-equivalence conversions.* Kraft believes that contemporary communicators tend to succeed in getting people to accept the forms of Christianity without experiencing a true Christian conversion much as the early Judaizers attempted to get Gentiles to adopt Jewish culture forms. Dynamic-equivalence conversion, on the other hand, is more concerned with meanings than with forms, and more concerned with the direction in which people are moving than in the precise position in which they find themselves. In relation to God's ideal, people start at different points and move at different rates. God accepts this. Hence, the message may well come with more impact if it draws attention to people's failure to live up to their own cultural ideal, with which they are familiar, than with failure to measure up to God's ideal, with which they may not be familiar. By moving them in the direction of true conversion in accordance with their cultural understandings, timing, and methods of decision making, we avoid the kind of false conversion which contents itself with conformity to certain forms instead of evidencing a change in worldview.

4. *Dynamic-equivalence churches.* When it comes to the church and its leadership, what is required today is an appropriateness of function rather than of form. Our contemporary world will be vitally affected by Christian churches only if churches reproduce the impact of the early churches, not their form.

Kraft turns to the pastoral Epistles to indicate what he has in mind. When in Titus 1 and 1 Timothy 3 Paul provided lists of qualifications for church leaders, he was actually listing the characteristics of ideal leadership in Greco-Roman cultures. For Kraft these are "cultural ethical lists" that may have to be modified in four ways if churches in their various cultures are to influence their own societies (see fig. 4). First, qualifications may have to be modified. Second, old qualifications may have to be omitted. Third, new qualifications may have to be added. Fourth, the order of the listing (representing priorities) may have to be changed. Accordingly, in American culture we may need to change the stipulation "having one wife (forever)" to "faithful to spouse" to reflect

Figure 4
Leadership Lists for Greco-Roman, American, and Higi Cultures

Greco-Roman	American	Higi

1. Irreproachable:
   One wife (forever)
   Serious
   Self-controlled
   Courteous
   Not quarrelsome
	1. Irreproachable:
	   Faithful to spouse
	   Self-controlled
	   Serious
	   Courteous
		1. Royal social class

2. Hospitable	2. Doctrinally sound	2. Hospitable
3. A good teacher	3. Vigorous	3. Mature

4. Not a money lover	4. A good preacher	4. Irreproachable:
		   Generous
		   Patient
		   Self-controlled
		   Serious
		   Courteous

5. Manage household well	5. Personable	5. Manage polygamous Household well
6. Mature in faith	6. Mature in faith	6. A good teacher
7. Good reputation outside	7. Manage household well	

Charles H. Kraft, *Christianity in Culture* (Maryknoll, N.Y.: Orbis; Exeter: Paternoster 1979), 352. Used by permission.

contemporary American values which make more allowance for divorce and remarriage. Such an amendment would still value faithfulness and would recognize the right of women to a leadership role. Similarly, since in Higi culture (Nigeria) there is a common proverb which says, "You cannot trust a man with only one wife," it may be necessary to at least temporarily change "managing a (monogamous) household well" to "managing a polygamous household well."

5. *Transformation of culture.* If Kraft cannot be accused of lack of creativity neither can he be accused of smallness of vision. In his view the larger objective of the complex and demanding process we have attempted to summarize is nothing less than the transformation of culture. In subsequent chapters we will point out the strengths, weaknesses, and even the errors of his approach. But the worthiness of his motives and his objectives will not be impugned. Kraft is convinced that only by following the pattern he has so carefully outlined will we be enabled to transform culture with God.

Increasingly, Anglo-American scholars in most of the disciplines related to theological education are being drawn into the discussion of contextualization. The widening conversations, however, serve to amplify differences that surfaced very early in the consideration of contextualization meanings and methods. The decidedly different approaches of two self-professed evangelicals, Bruce J. Nicholls and Charles H. Kraft, serve notice that even those with important theological affinities may not agree on the subject. It is not easy to see how "relational-centers dogmatic theology" and "dynamic-equivalence transculturation" open-endedness can stem from the same theological rootage. It would seem to be a part of our task to determine whether they actually do or not.

6

Asia
M. M. Thomas and Kosuke Koyama

A New Independence

Religion is part and parcel of Asian life and history. Asia is the home of all of the great religions—Hinduism, Buddhism, Islam, Judaism, and Christianity—as well as Confucianism, Taoism, Shintoism, and lesser religions. As for Asian Christianity, the churches in Asia are older than churches in most other parts of the world. The Syrian churches in India go back at least as far as the third century and perhaps to the first century. The first non-Western missions were carried out in Asia; Nestorians in the seventh century were followed by Franciscans in the fourteenth, Jesuits in the seventeenth, and Lutherans in the eighteenth. Nevertheless, observers speak of the Teutonic captivity of Asian theology to Western theological formulations,[1] of the fact that Christianity is a "potted plant" and not a "transplanted plant" in Asia,[2] and of the

1. Alan Geyer, "Toward a Convivial Theology," *Christian Century* 86 (23 April 1969): 542.
2. Daniel T. Niles, as noted in Douglas J. Elwood, ed., *Asian Christian Theology: Emerging Themes* (Philadelphia: Westminster, 1980), rev. ed. of *What Asian Christians Are Thinking* (Quezon City: New Day, 1976), 27.

"ghetto mentality" that until very recently has prevented Asians from responding sensitively to the concerns of their own cultures.[3]

As a consequence of these and other factors, Asian Christians are faced with some unique problems in contextualizing the Christian message for their peoples. We are faced with similar problems in analyzing their contextualization attempts.

In the first place, Asia comprises one of the broadest areas of the world and is home of a wide diversity of peoples and cultures. For our purposes Asia can be divided into three principal regions: the South, the Southeast, and the Northeast. But to characterize adequately the uniquenesses and the theological formulations coming from each of these regions would take us far beyond the bounds of this work.

In the second place, the fact that Asian Christians "live in a world of great religious traditions, modernization impacts, ideologies of left and right, international conflicts, hunger, poverty, militarism, and racism"[4] means that contextualizers must respond to a bewildering variety of questions and challenges. Though common themes and threads are discoverable, generalizations are particularly risky.

In the third place, while the division between liberal and conservative Protestantism apparent in the modernist-fundamentalist debates of the late nineteenth and early twentieth centuries tends to be a more recent feature of African and Latin American church life, it has a longer history in Asia and has made greater inroads within the laity. On the surface this may seem to be of limited significance because contextualizations of both liberal and conservative theologies are discoverable everywhere. But at a deeper level we should know that when it comes to Asian Christianity, radical contextualizations are not so much bidding for attention and acceptance as they are reflecting liberal theological commitments that are already in place. Western observers do not always take this into account.

Apart from some early attempts to indigenize theology in the 1930s, Asian theologians generally have devoted themselves to mastering Western theological formulations. Over the last twenty-five years or so, however, more attention has been given to Asian contextualizations of theology, first on the part of liberals and then on the part of conservative evangelicals. A 1966 Faith and Order Conference in Hong Kong sponsored by the East Asia Christian Conference (since 1973 the Christian Conference of Asia) set the tone by addressing the theme, "Confessing the Faith in Asia Today." Subsequent conferences and

---

3. Gerald H. Anderson, ed., *Asian Voices in Christian Theology* (Maryknoll, N.Y.: Orbis, 1976), 5.

4. Kosuke Koyama, Foreword, in Elwood, *Asian Theology,* 14.

consultations involving ecumenically-minded Protestants, Anglicans, Roman Catholics, and independent Catholics have dealt with the formulation of an Asian theology.

Evangelicals of the Asia Theological Association (related to the World Evangelical Fellowship) have also sponsored a series of consultations on the subject. Perhaps one of the most significant of the series was held in Seoul, Korea, in 1982. That particular consultation enjoyed a wide participation and included some representatives from other parts of the world. It resulted in the Seoul Declaration and a variety of essays which are to be found in *The Bible and Theology in Asia Contexts.*[5]

Reports of various other consultations and insights into Asian theological thinking are available in *The Human and the Holy,*[6] *The Voice of the Church in Asia,*[7] *Asian Voices in Christian Theology, Asian Christian Theology—Emerging Themes, What Asian Theologians Are Thinking,* and *Living Theology in Asia Today.*[8]

After years of examining such Asian theologies as the pain of God theology (Japan), waterbuffalo theology (Thailand), third eye theology (for the Chinese), yin yang theology (Chinese and Korean), theology of change (Taiwan), Minjung theology (Korea), as well as Indian and Sri Lankan theology, the executive secretary of the Asian Theological Association, Bong Rin Ro, groups these theologies into four categories:[9]

1. *Syncretistic theologies* as in Raymond Panikkar's *Unknown Christ of Hinduism* (1964)
2. *Accommodation theologies* of the type found in Kosuke Koyama's *Waterbuffalo Theology* (1970) and Batumalai Sadayandi's *Prophetic Christology for Neighbourology* (1987)
3. *Situation theologies* as can be found in Kazoh Kitamori's *Pain of God Theology* (1965), Kim Yong Bock's *Minjung Theology: People as the Subjects of History* (1981), and various other liberation theologies
4. *Biblically oriented Asian theologies* of which Ro does not give

5. Bong Rin Ro and Ruth Eshenauer, eds., *The Bible and Theology in Asian Contexts: An Evangelical Perspective on Asian Theology* (Taichung, Taiwan: Asia Theological Association, 1984).

6. Emerito P. Nacpil and Douglas J. Elwood, eds., *The Human and the Holy: Asian Perspectives on Christian Theology* (Maryknoll, N.Y.: Orbis, 1980).

7. Bong Rin Ro, ed., *The Voice of the Church in Asia* (Taichung, Taiwan: Asia Theological Association, 1975).

8. John C. England, ed., *Living Theology in Asia Today* (Maryknoll, N.Y.: Orbis, 1982).

9. Bong Rin Ro, "Theological Trends in Asia: Asian Theology," *Asian Theological News* 13 (October/December 1987): 2–3, 15–17.

specific examples but would undoubtedly include those found in his coedited volume, *The Bible and Theology in Asian Contexts* (1984), and Vinay Samuel and Chris Sugden, who edited *Sharing Jesus in the Two-Thirds World* (1984)

We will summarize some of the proposals of two prominent Asian contextualizers: the theology of Madathilparampil M. (M. M.) Thomas, a layman from Southeast Asia (India), and that proposed by Kosuke Koyama, a missionary and theologian from Northeast Asia (Japan). This choice is confirmed by the primary reference Gerald Anderson makes to Thomas and Koyama in his introduction to Asian theology.[10]

M. M. Thomas: "Christ-Centered Syncretism"

Arnold Toynbee believed that if Christianity is to be the religion of the future it must become less exclusivistic, more open to change and to accepting various ways of expressing the results of the religious quest. Stated another way, Christianity must become more inclusivistic, more like Hinduism in its ability to incorporate a wide variety of views without losing its own identity. If widely accepted, the theology of M. M. Thomas would eventuate in just that kind of Christianity.

A layman of the Mar Thoma Church of South India, Thomas is director emeritus of the Christian Institute for the Study of Religion and Society, Bangalore, and editor of its journal, *Religion and Society.* He is past chairman of the Central Committee of the World Council of Churches. This analysis of his theology is based in the main upon two monographs, "India: Toward an Indigenous Christian Theology"[11] (which provides the essential thought of his book, *The Acknowledged Christ of the Indian Renaissance*),[12] and "Theological Insights for a Secular Anthropology,"[13] the epilogue of *Secular Ideologies of India and the Secular Meaning of Christ.*[14] Use is also made of *Man and the Universe of Faiths.*[15]

10. Anderson, *Asian Voices,* 4–5.
11. Madathilparampil M. Thomas, "India: Toward an Indigenous Christian Theology," in Anderson, *Asian Voices,* 11–35.
12. Madathilparampil M. Thomas, *The Acknowledged Christ of the Indian Renaissance* (Bangalore, India: Christian Institute for the Study of Religion and Society, 1970).
13. Madathilparampil M. Thomas, "Theological Insights for a Secular Anthropology," in Elwood, *Asian Theology,* 289–98.
14. Madathilparampil M. Thomas, *Secular Theologies of India and the Secular Meaning of Christ* (Madras: Christian Literature Society, 1976).
15. Madathilparampil M. Thomas, *Man and the Universe of Faiths* (Madras: Christian Literature Society, 1975).

Thomas's *indigenous theology* is perhaps best understood within the somewhat turbulent stream of World Council discussions regarding the Christian attitude toward non-Christian faiths which date back to the Jerusalem conference in 1928. To understand the attitude and the issues involved one must perceive the openness to other religions expressed at Jerusalem and by William Hocking and the members of the Laymen's Inquiry in the early 1930s; the exclusivistic position taken by Hendrik Kraemer at the World Missionary Conference in Tambaram, India, in 1938; the inauguration of interreligious dialogues by the WCC; and, of course, various efforts to contextualize theology during the 1970s and 1980s. Over the years of his involvement Thomas has responded to the ebb and flow, the central current and the side eddies, of ecumenical discussion. Though some observers find indications of a more evangelical posture in his most recent writings, generally he has taken a position that has broad ecumenical support.

Like Koyama's, but with a closer affinity to liberation theologians, Thomas's view of history is central to his way of doing theology. For Thomas God is not reaching into human history from the outside to effect his purposes. Rather he is working out his purpose from within history. Inevitably, therefore, all theology involves an understanding of both a general and a particular history. A Christian theology for India—or, perhaps better, an Indian Christian theology—must recognize God's past and present workings in the Hindu renaissance and in the incursion of secularism in India and work for the realization of his future purpose.

The Acknowledgment of Christ in the Indian Renaissance

Kraemer felt that Indian religions revolve around a central and unchanging monistic core. Thomas disagrees with Kraemer. He says that the Hindu renaissance in modern times "represents an effort to put meaning-content into the term 'personal' as applied to God, man and society, and to affirm God's purposive work in world life as directed toward an end."[16] Largely as a result of the impact of Westernization and Christianity, Thomas believes, India is in tension. Monism no longer provides the unified center for Indian life and thought.

The church has not been entirely unresponsive to this state of affairs. Increasingly the church in India has opened up to the idea of an *Indian* church, "witnessing to Christ within the context of the Indian realities of life, and in this sense, indigenous."[17] (Thomas has continued to use the older term *indigenous* long after the new term *contex-*

16. Ibid., 77.
17. Thomas, "India: Toward an Indigenous Christian Theology," 17.

tualization became current.) Five tributaries have led to this new openness.[18]

1. *Theological education.* In 1968—the year of the appointment of the advisory group to the TEF which recommended the third (reform) mandate—the National Consultation on Theological Education was held in India. The report coming out of that meeting noted that Western models of ministry were slowly giving way to models better adapted to the Indian environment. It called for a new and more radical adaptation which would share in India's search for new meaning and a new humanity by seeking to lead people out of poverty, by an open encounter with other religions which would discern the values resident in them, and by learning to minister to those who must make decisions in the face of unprecedented change in political, economic, intellectual, religious, and cultural life.

2. *Discussion on church union.* Gradually progress has been made in the struggle for a unity among Indian churches which expresses both the life and thought of the church universal and the spiritual values of the Indian heritage. Thomas draws encouragement from the fact that this sentiment has now found expression in the constitution of the Church of South India.

3. *Christian apologetics.* The crucial issues of an indigenous Indian theology have been formulated and clarified in dialogue with proponents of a renascent Hinduism over a long period of time. In fact, very soon after the coming of William Carey, Rammohan Roy fought against the monism and polytheism of traditional Hinduism and interpreted Christ as a great moral teacher and religious messenger. To Roy, Christ was the "pre-existent firstborn of creatures." Forgiveness is available through repentance without Christ's atonement. (One of the famous Serampore trio, Joshua Marshman, took issue with Roy.)

Over the years the contributions to dialogue and a rethinking of both Hindu and Christian teachings by such men as Ramakrishna, Vivekananda, J. R. Chandran, Aiyadurai J. Appasamy, Surjit Singh, and Mahatma Gandhi have pointed in the direction of an indigenous theology. Ramakrishna "experienced" identity with Kali, Rama, Brahman, Mohammed, and Christ and espoused the equality of religions. Building on this, Vivekananda taught that experience with a personal God may be a step toward identity of the soul with Brahman and that Jesus himself progressed through stages to the point where he could say, "I and my Father are one." Chandran viewed this as the abandonment of religious discrimination but insisted that Christianity must grapple with the truth behind ideas of the Impersonal Ultimate and the ultimacy of the

18. Ibid.

mystical experience. Appasamy advocated that Christians speak to Hinduism "from the inside." Singh used Radhakrishnan's ideas to develop a new Christology. Gandhi was attracted to Jesus, but believed in him not as a historical person but as the personification of nonviolence.

4. *Thinking on Christianity and other religions.* Most early missionaries in India thought Hinduism was a product of the devil, but theological liberalism came to affirm its treasures and worth. Some liberals believed that it is possible to be a Christian within Hinduism apart from baptism and joining a Christian church. Others believed that those who came to recognize Christianity as the fulfilment of Hinduism should become part of the Christian communities. The Hocking report and Kraemer's response contributed to a tension in this area which has not been entirely resolved by more recent efforts at interreligious dialogue, but Thomas believes that the tension will be overcome.

5. *A theology of nationalism.* Thomas speaks of the contributions of educational missionaries such as Alexander Duff, John Wilson, and William Miller who saw the substitution of Western culture for Indian culture as a preparation for the gospel. Christian Nationalists such as Charles F. Andrews, S. K. Rudra, S. K. Datta, and K. T. Paul in one way or another reinforced the notion that the gospel of Christ could contribute greatly to the breakdown of caste and the building up of a new, unified Indian nation.

One would be hard-pressed to understand Thomas's indigenous theology apart from these tributaries. Concerning them he writes, "The five streams . . . have contributed to the development of the idea of an Indian church witnessing to Christ within the context of the Indian realities of life, and in this sense, indigenous. It must be immediately pointed out that the contemporary Indian reality *is not the traditional one, but the traditional one renewed under the impact of the West and of the awakening*" (emphasis added).[19]

The Secular Meaning of Christ

Thomas believes that Christ is present, not alone in the renaissance of a religious India influenced by Christianity and Westernization, but also in secular ideologies which have some Christian roots. With his view of history and an enlarged definition of theology as "the intellectual articulation of man's faith in God or in a structure of meaning and sacredness which is seen as his ultimate destiny,"[20] Thomas can restate in theological terms the ideologies of all of the political systems of India

19. Ibid., 27–28.
20. Thomas, "Theological Insights," 289.

from liberal nationalism and democratic socialism to Marxism-Leninism. Conversely, he is able to redefine theological doctrines in secular terms. As in the case of the religious renaissance, this process has two primary and positive results, according to Thomas. First, these ideologies are understood as sacred though secular—as having a *Christ meaning*. Second, it discloses their errors and myopias. Let us see how this works out in particular instances.

1. *A realistic ideology of social humanism.* Some elements of Christian theology (in this case, anthropological) are relevant to social humanism and therefore should be restated in secular terms:
   a. Man as created in the image of God. In secular terms this affirms that man is a spiritual being and is called to fulfill himself by mastery over nature and by engaging in dialogue and communion with others in society.
   b. Man as a fallen creature. In secular language this can be interpreted as the tendency to self-alienation in man's spirit resulting from the self-love and self-centeredness which seek to wield power over others.
   c. The crucified and risen Christ. Christ is the true man. He is the source of the renewal of human nature (humanization) and, through this, the renewal of all things. Secularly this involves a recognition that the ultimate pattern of life, a life of self-giving love as the criterion of true humanity and social community, is the pattern of Jesus' humanity.
   d. The kingdom of God as the absolute future of man and society. Christian hope for the future is based on the power of the Spirit that raised Christ from the dead and which is at work renewing all societies and all of creation. Secularly put, there is a transcendent reality, a providence, or a presence which determines man's future and is available for the humanization of man, nature, and society even when conditions are seemingly hopeless.

2. *A critique of secular humanism.* According to Thomas this kind of syncretized theologizing opens the eyes of the church to what God is doing outside her walls and opens the mouths of Christians to dialogue with secular humanists. It also enables a critique of secular humanism in, though not necessarily on, its own terms. Why not on its own terms? Theology rules out all closed forms of secular humanism which not only oppose the gospel but are devoid of a comprehensive understanding of man and therefore become dehumanizing. Positively, however, a secular humanism which espouses humanization, liberation,

creativity, love, and purpose in history is "integral to the faith and hope of the Christian gospel."[21]

The Hidden Christ Revealed

Traditionally missions in India found Christ in the Bible, preached this Christ to the people without respect to Indian understandings, and worked to raise up a Christian church that had but little relevance to Indian life and thought. But there is now an openness to the Christ who in all of history is working out his new-creation and new-humanity purposes. This hidden Christ is being revealed as a result.

Sunand Sumithra and Bruce J. Nicholls summarize Thomas's approach in four steps:[22]

1. His starting point is *man's quest*. He analyzes what man is searching for and discovers that the primary search is for human dignity, freedom, creativity, and meaning in history.
2. He asks what *Christ offers* to these quests. He responds that Christ is offering exactly those things for which man is searching. Christ is the new man, the new humanity. Humanization is the most relevant point of entry for dialogue between Christianity and the other religions.
3. Then what is the *mission of the church?* It is to participate with Christ in the liberation movements of our time, so that man may receive what he is searching for. The confession of participation is the essence of the mission of the church.
4. Finally, what is the *goal of humanity?* It is the humanity of mankind leading ultimately to a just world society. This utopian world society is at best the preparation for the coming kingdom of God, for the kingdom of men is necessary raw material for the kingdom of God.

Sumithra and Nicholls go on to say that Thomas's theology is situational, "born out of the meeting of the living church and its world" and always moving in the direction of synthesis.[23] In the Indian case the results of this meeting of church and world become evident in, among other things, a "Christ-Centered Hindu Church" that will transform Hindu patterns in accord with the missionary goal.

---

21. Ibid., 291.
22. Sunand Sumithra and Bruce J. Nicholls, "Critique of Theology in Indian Cultures," in Ro and Eshenauer, *The Bible and Theology*, 196–97.
23. Ibid., 197.

Nicholls has since said that Thomas has moved toward "a more evangelical appreciation of the relationship between text and content."[24] One hopes that this is so.

Though many will be tempted to feel pessimism when they survey contemporary events in the religious and secular worlds, Thomas has a profound faith in the process he describes.

> The historical process is affirmed through its transformation which is as radical as the one which happened quietly in the inhominization of God in Jesus in the history of the world, or as what happened with greater trauma in the resurrection through death of the historical humanity of Jesus. Such an eschatological hope alone can give natural necessity, human determinism, and transcendent providence each its due place in the interpretation of the historical process as a whole and the human reality in any historical situation. . . . The meaning of every historical action directed to love and justice in history and every fragmentary realization of truth, goodness, and beauty in life is protected, redeemed, and fulfilled in the end. How, we do not know. But our guarantee is the risen Jesus Christ.[25]

A profound faith this is; but is it also apostolic? That is the important question.

Kosuke Koyama: Waterbuffalo Theology

One of the most imaginative and widely-read Asian theologians is Kosuke Koyama of Japan. Koyama has served as a missionary to Thailand where he taught in the Thailand Theological Seminary; as executive secretary of the Association of Theological Schools in Southeast Asia; as dean of the Southeast Asia Graduate School of Theology; and as editor of the *South East Asia Journal of Theology*. Subsequently he became a member of the faculty of Union Theological Seminary in New York. Koyama has had a part in contextualization discussions from their beginning. He subscribes to the basic approach advocated early on by the third mandate committee of the Theological Education Fund. He "points out that in contextualizing the Christian faith we do not begin with 'adjustments to a transplantation'—like the transplanting of a grown tree from Amsterdam to Djakarta, or from New York to Manila—but with 'locating the *living seed* of faith in what was re-

24. "Hermeneutics, Theology, and Culture with Special Reference to Hindu Culture," ibid., 254.

25. Thomas, "Theological Insights," 297–98.

ceived,' and then guarding, watering, and nurturing it as it roots itself in the native soil."[26]

That being his approach, Koyama is intriguing to Westerners. But he is also somewhat exasperating, especially to those who look for a systematic and logical development of his theology and methodology. In keeping with its Asian roots, Koyama's contextualized theology tends to be heuristic, less concerned with rigorous logic than with exploring cultural issues. There is something refreshing about this, for Koyama does not claim to have all the answers—not even answers to all the questions he himself raises. But there is also something disconcerting about it because for him Third World theology begins with raising issues.[27] If this is the starting point, who is to say when theology has asked the important questions, or even that it has asked the right questions?

This brief analysis of Koyama's waterbuffalo theology is based upon two of Koyama's works: the book for which he is best known, *Waterbuffalo Theology*, and a monograph entitled "Thailand: Points of Theological Friction."[28] The latter represents a significant sampling of Koyama's theologizing for his own mission field of Thailand. As long as our purpose is to provide a brief summary rather than a critique, it is probably best to proceed as Koyama himself does, with prods to rather than prescriptions for, contextualized thinking and involvement.

Waterbuffalo Theologizing

Often overlooked, Asian history must be reinterpreted and reclaimed. Koyama attempts to do this for various Asian countries, but central to waterbuffalo theology as a theology is the history of Thailand.

1. *Rooting theology in Thai history.* Most Westerners are introduced to Thailand within the confines of a large, busy airport with its converging jets and jostling taxis and limousines. From there, however, it is impossible to go anywhere—even to Bangkok with its ancient temples and modern hotels—without traveling between a patchwork of rice paddies tended by Thai farmers and lumbering waterbuffalos. The real Thailand can be understood and penetrated by Christian faith only as it is seen to be a combination of hotels and temples, motor cars and waterbuffalos.

---

26. Douglas J. Elwood, "Asian Theology in the Making," in *Asian Christian Theology*, 27.

27. Kosuke Koyama, *Waterbuffalo Theology* (Maryknoll, N.Y.: Orbis, 1974), 3.

28. Kosuke Koyama, "Thailand: Points of Theological Friction," in Anderson, *Asian Voices*, 65–86.

For Koyama the history which has led to this situation sets the stage for an encounter between a Thai interpretation of history and Israel's theology of history, an encounter that prepares Thailand for the ultimate encounter with Christ.

The fact is that there is not just one Thailand today. There are two in the one society. "Thailand One" is a Thailand of traditional values shaped by various forces, especially the values of Theravada Buddhism imported from India and Ceylon. It is characterized by *apatheia-anthropology* and *apatheia-history*—a dispassionate view growing out of the kind of honest observation of the decay and demise of humanity which occasioned Gautama Buddha's withdrawal to the life of a recluse. A strict empiricism presents us with birth, growth, aging, sickness, and death in seemingly endless cycles. And the laws of nature, after all, are more trustworthy than such arbitrary categories as the historical and the personal.

"Thailand Two" is a product of Western colonialism with its guns and ointments. The colonial powers brought a wounding, but they also brought modernization and Christianity. Their anthropology and history involved *patheia*, a passion that can ultimately be traced back to the special love and concern of a personal God who by his love and involvement made Israel's history unique among the nations of this world. A theologically and teleologically determined *patheia-anthropology* and *patheia-history* in the forms of Christianity, modernization, and secularization characterize Thailand Two. Here there is an existential interest in history, and personhood has special meaning.

As Koyama sees it, Thailand One and Thailand Two currently confront one another. There are various ways of describing this confrontation, but one way is to think of it in terms of the "theological friction caused at the intersection of Thailand and Israel."[29] Thailand One makes its contribution by magnifying points of tension and by providing a framework for the discussion of modernization. Inadvertently the modernization of Thailand Two also makes a theological contribution because it involves the transformation of the social systems, including religious and psychological, by which man organizes society. Amid the shaking foundations of Thai culture theologians may condemn both the Buddhist notions of man's predicament and the basic notion of modernization and secularization, which is that man makes his own history. But God's pathos is at work in Thailand as it was in Israel, and both traditionalism and modernization are making their contributions to his working. The tension points are creative in that they prepare Thai spirituality for a realization of the new creation in Jesus Christ.

29. Ibid., 75.

All of this is purposed by the Lord of history who is preparing good soil in Thailand. As Koyama puts it,

> The monsoon rain cannot make God wet! God is the Lord of monsoon rain. He sends his monsoon for his purpose. The biblical view of history is not circular. It is linear. But life in Thailand is strongly influenced by the circular movement of nature. This circular nature is not of demons. It is, as we understand, from God. We see the glory of God both in history and in nature. Circular nature shows God's glory as much as linear history. In this proper location, circular nature finds it purpose. When two images, circular and linear, are put together, why can we not have the image of an ascending spiral view of one unified history-nature?[30]

Thus everyone lives not only in universal history, but also in a particular situation in history. Each history has that which is true, honorable, and just, for which we should be thankful and which must be incorporated into what Koyama calls "particular orbit" theology.

2. *Rooting theology in Thai cultural thinking*. Koyama believes that the historical, cultural, and religious situation should lead us in our interpretation of theology. His own work includes several culturally imaginative ideas:

a. Aristotelian pepper and Buddhist salt. In the kitchen we use pepper and salt to season our food to our taste without asking questions about it. Something similar happens in the church. The Western church flavors its theological food with the Aristotelian pepper of rationalism and causal relationships. The Thai church picks up on this and discusses the Aristotelian-inspired cosmological argument for the existence of God but sprinkles it with the Buddhist salt of the doctrine of "dependent originations." Then it adds the salt of the lifestyle of detachment. Both Aristotelian pepper and Buddhist salt lead to a blurred Christ and a dimmed gospel. But the solution is not to be found in rejecting the pepper and salt. It is to be found in using them to make Christ tasty, so that in Thailand we do not speak simply of salvation through the blood of Christ or of salvation through the *dharma* (the Buddhist message, Buddhist truth). Instead we say that the content of the *dharma* is the sacrificial death of Christ.

b. "Neighborology." The Thai are not interested in Christology, but they are concerned about neighborology. The message of Christ, then, must be put in neighborological language—in the discipline

---

30. Koyama, *Waterbuffalo Theology*, 41.

involved in knowing Thai neighbors immediately and straightfor-
wardly.

c. Asian issues and Christian theology. If theologians in Asia want
to root Christian theology in their respective cultures they must
deal with ten issues: (1) an interdependent world, (2) the Bible, (3)
proclamation, accommodation, and syncretism, (4) men of other
faiths and ideologies, (5) the West, (6) China, (7) the haves and
have-nots, (8) the animistic world, (9) spirituality, and (10) doctrinal clarity.

3. *Rooting theology in Thai Buddhist life.* Waterbuffalo theology
focuses on Buddhists rather than Buddhism. It looks at persons who are
made in the image of God rather than at manmade institutions. It looks
through "incarnate eyes" rather than through "doctrinally-trained
eyes." And thus it "sees" differently.

It sees, for example, the cool Thai and the hot God. Buddhist concepts such as *dukkha* (unsatisfactoriness, suffering), *anicca* (transitori-
ness), and *anatta* (self-destruction) result in a cool Thai who eats not to
satisfy his palate but his hunger; who is homeless, at least in the sense
of emptying one's self; who is without history in the sense that he is
not greedy for a place in it. But God is hot. He is engaged in history. He
is concerned with the restoration of the "I." He does not reject the cool
man, but he wants to warm him. Therefore, the personhood of God
himself must be made meaningful to the Thai audience.

To take another example, waterbuffalo theology sees how the Book
of James fits the Thai people. James is cool in content but hot on
practice. Things are transitory and changing, but faith in the change-
less God is expressed, not in detachment, but in involvement in the
world of marginal people.

4. *Rooting theology in a Christian lifestyle.* The center of theology is
the crucified Christ and the mission of believers in the world. It is at
the cross that Jesus Christ draws all men to himself. It is by costly
participation in saving history that Christians serve God and the world.
Personal ambitions and institutional goals often obstruct this. Both the
praise of men and the criticism of men prevent the glorification of God.
Identification with Christ expresses itself in involvement in a suffering
world. The Christian is attached to the Lord's table and is free from the
"saving messages" of other tables such as secularism, technocracy,
communism, and the world's great religions.

Doing Waterbuffalo Theology—The Faith of a Gentile Mother

Concerning the doing of theology Koyama writes,

Theology is a reflection. Reflection on what? *History in the Light of the Word of God.* The word here must be understood in the solemn theological message of John 14:26. . . . It is understanding God's understanding of history and man in the illumination of John 14:26. In this way man finds his spirituality enlightened and he discovers his spiritual identity. To engage in the historical context does not mean then that the context, whatever it is, is there as something unchangeable and beyond our control. . . . Context is something which must be constantly challenged and forced to change. "At the name of Jesus every knee should bow, in heaven and on earth and under the earth" (Phil. 2:10).[31]

To see how this approach works in a specific instance we turn to Koyama's discussion of the "beginning of faith."[32] The biblical case in point is the amazing faith of the Gentile woman who came to Jesus out of concern for her demon-possessed daughter (Matt. 15:21–28). Martin Luther found in this Gentile woman a faith that was strong enough to refuse to be put off even by the seeming refusal of Jesus. She exhibited a strong faith in the midst of, and in spite of, severe *Anfechtung* (which Koyama translates as "assault"). Koyama says that he was so impressed by Luther's interpretation that he determined to share it with his small Thai congregation. He was sure that the Thai would be impressed by this "assault interpretation." But instead they were confused and concluded that the Christian faith must be neurotic.

Dismayed, Koyama returned to the biblical account. This time he attempted to look at the story through eyes enlightened by Thai historical, cultural, and religious backgrounds. He concentrated on the beginnings of the woman's amazing faith and discovered two important elements in it: faith in the Son of David and the disclosure of her problem. It was the latter that propelled her to the former. Human, natural love (*erōs*) met and merged with divine self-giving love (*agapē*) and produced strong faith. Koyama concluded that "the beginning of faith must contain some universally valid and relevant factor which can erase religious, cultural and political demarcations."[33] And he gives credit to the Thai for that insight: "My interest in this *beginning* of faith did not come from myself but was forced on me by my Thai neighbours."[34]

Luther's assault interpretation must have had profound meaning in the contexts of Wittenberg and Reformation times. But it is the beginning of faith, growing from a universal such as a mother's love for her

31. Ibid., 106–7.
32. Ibid., 73–75.
33. Ibid., 75.
34. Ibid.

daughter, that has meaning in Buddhist Bangkok. This is the meeting point of the two Thailands. For Koyama, in this instance and in this sense, waterbuffalo theology takes precedence over Reformation theology. Should it? That is the question that must yet be answered.

If there is anywhere outside of the Western world where it might be misleading to speak of a regional theology as though it exhibits homogeneity that place would be Asia. The expanse and cultural and religious diversity of Asia are overwhelming. The history of the church and missions is long and variegated. Yet contextualized theologies in Asia often exhibit a characteristic mixture of Asian religious concerns and Western influences. Hailing from the different parts of Asia that nevertheless share some basic religious outlooks—India and Japan—M. M. Thomas and Kosuke Koyama display a deep understanding of both Eastern and Western traditions in their respective contextualizations. Their formulations therefore challenge those who would cross the boundary between the ever-meeting and never-meeting East and West with the gospel of Christ.

7

Latin America
Gustavo Gutiérrez and José Míguez-Bonino

Theologies of Liberation

To many observers liberation theology appears to be a direct out-growth of Christianity's response to the sociopolitical givens of Latin American society. That society, which until recently had not changed significantly since the days of the *conquistadors*, can be viewed through the relationships among four major groups or classes. The oligarchy is made up of a few wealthy families who own the vast majority of the land and thus control its use. In El Salvador, for example, fourteen families representing about 2 percent of the total population are said to own 60 percent of the land. The oligarchy's hold on that property is generally supported and in some cases made possible by the military. Ever since the days of the Spanish invasions military might has been used to acquire, forcibly redistribute, and maintain natural resources which constitute the wealth and define the social standing of the upper class. Unfortunately the church has consistently sided with or been associated with the existing order. There have, of course, been isolated voices of protest. In 1541, for example, Bartolomé de Las Casas protested to the King of Spain about the evils associated with the conquest of Mexico. Unable to sway either the crown or the church, Las Casas's archetypal theology of liberation was tabled for more than four centuries. The church joined the alliance of the rich and the military. The last component in this social structure is represented by the poor peasants, the *campesinos* who make up about 85 percent of the general population. With few legal rights to protect them from oppression these mostly landless serfs have become dependent on the oligarchy, afraid of the military, and alienated from the church.

During the 1960s several developments converged to set into motion a politicoreligious reorientation which began to address the inequities of the old order. Two streams of this reorientation are of particular importance to our inquiry. The first stream was initiated by a number of theologians who were influenced by such Europeans as Jürgen Moltmann and Johann Baptist Metz to follow the precedent set by Las Casas. They began to rethink the process of theology, the role of Christianity, and the implications of the gospel in the light of the sociopolitical realities of Latin America. These attempts to contextualize the gospel added to the unrest and self-questioning which engulfed the Roman Catholic church in the wake of Vatican II.

The second stream dates to 1968 when the church endorsed a major policy shift and embarked on a course which ultimately led to a break with the old alliance and included what many churchmen referred to as a "preferential option for the poor." In spite of the ongoing debate and internal tension this decision provided official sanction and support for the liberation theologians. As a result the movement has gained momentum and is today associated with an ever-increasing array of models and a growing number of proponents who span a broad spectrum of theological and political positions. They include Rubem Alves, Hugo Assmann, Leonardo Boff, Dom Helder Cámara, Emilio Castro, Samuel Escobar, Paulo Feire, José Porfirio Miranda, Rene Padilla, and Juan Luís Segundo.

The two theologians chosen for brief summary here belong to the seminal vanguard of the movement. Gustavo Gutiérrez, a Peruvian priest, was the first Roman Catholic writer to gain a wide reading and thereby popularize the movement with *A Theology of Liberation,* first published in 1973. José Míguez-Bonino, an Argentinian, has provided the major Protestant contribution with *Doing Theology in a Revolutionary Situation,* published in 1975. These two thinkers provide a systematic and coherent statement of the fundamental tenets of liberation theology.

Gustavo Gutiérrez: Theology as Critical Reflection on Praxis

Traditionally theology has been a meditative activity "geared toward spiritual growth"[1] and an intellectual activity "born of the meeting of faith and reason."[2] Although both spirituality and rational knowledge are necessary parts of theology, both have to be "salvaged . . . from the division and deformation they have suffered throughout history."[3] That is, theology has to be rediscovered as a critical reflection on praxis.

Praxis

Gutiérrez defines praxis as the "existential and active aspects of the Christian life," which include (1) charity, the gift of one's self to the Other (Christ) and ultimately to others; (2) spirituality, in the form of *actione contemplativus* which culminates in a recognition of the value of the profane and Christian activity in the world; (3) the anthropological aspects of revelation which focus attention away from the supernatural realities and toward man and his world; (4) the life of the church as *locus theologicus*—participating by service in the social upheavals of its day; (5) the signs of the times, which involve not only intellectual analysis but also a call to pastoral activity and service; (6) eschatology or understanding the church's role in history. "If human history is above all else an opening to the future, then it is a task, a political occupation, through which man orients and opens himself to the gift which gives history its transcendent meaning: the full and definitive encounter with the Lord and with other men."[4]

Thus Christians are called to "verify" (from the Latin *verus*, "true," and *facere*, "to do") their faith by doing the truth. This activity, referred to as orthopraxis, emphasizes the essential importance of concrete behavior, deeds, and action.

To this list could be added the influence of Marxist thought which, focusing on praxis, is geared to the transformation of the world. According to Gutiérrez theology finds itself in direct and fruitful confrontation with Marxism.

Theology then is critical reflection on practice which grows out of Christian faith. It is a second step, and as such it follows pastoral activity. Reflecting on the presence and the action of Christians in the

---

1. Gustavo Gutiérrez, *A Theology of Liberation*, trans. and ed. Caridad Inda and John Eagleson (New York: Orbis, 1973), 4. This work remains Gutiérrez's definitive statement on liberation theology and is used for this summary.
2. Ibid., 5.
3. Ibid., 6.
4. Ibid., 10.

world means looking beyond the visible limitations of the church. It requires believers to be open to human history in order to fulfil several critical functions over against ecclesial praxis and society. The church engages in the prophetic activity of interpreting history by revealing and proclaiming its ultimate meaning. This implies nothing short of a new way of doing theology.

> Theology as critical reflection on historical praxis is a liberating theology, a theology of the liberating transformation of the history of mankind and also therefore that part of mankind—gathered into ecclesia—which openly confesses Christ. . . . It is a theology which is open—in the protest against trampled human dignity, in the struggle against the plunder of the vast majority of people, in the liberating love, and in the building of a new, just, and fraternal society—to the gift of the Kingdom of God.[5]

Implications

What then are the implications of this radically new orientation for the various aspects of theological thought and practice? The central problem with which liberation theology has to wrestle is the relationship between salvation and the historical process of the liberation of man.[6] Although the interface between faith and human existence is often unclear, the politicization of thought has brought men to a new level of maturity and social consciousness in Latin America. Human reason has become political reason.[7] That change compels the believer to ask what it means to be a Christian in the Latin American setting. To put it another way, what do the biblical concepts of liberation, salvation, and conversion mean in that revolutionary environment?

1. *Liberation assumes several levels of meaning.*[8] Liberation expresses the aspirations of oppressed peoples and social classes, emphasizing conflicts within the economic, social, and political processes which put the oppressed at odds with wealthy nations and oppressive classes. Liberation can also be applied to an understanding of history, as people assume conscious responsibility for their own destiny. Liberation allows an approach to Scripture which elevates the presence and actions of humanity in history. Christ is the liberator who frees people from sin to live in communion with him and with others. Sin is defined

5. Ibid., 15.
6. Ibid., 45.
7. Ibid., 47.
8. Ibid., 36. Liberation is contrasted with development. Although development synthesizes the aspirations of the poor it can only find its true meaning and possibilities within the radical framework of liberation.

as the ultimate root of all disruption of friendship and of all injustice and oppression.[9]

2. *Salvation*. Gutiérrez asserts that our understanding of salvation will depend on our ability to move from the traditional quantitative orientation, which emphasized the salvation of the pagans, to a qualitative orientation which affects every aspect of human life.[10] Salvation is a personal and intrahistorical reality. It involves the daily events of human life so that there are not two histories but rather one Christo-finalized history, every dimension of which is embraced by Christ's redemptive act. The history of salvation is therefore the very heart of human history. Several biblical themes help put the relationship between history and salvation into proper perspective:

a. Creation, the first salvific act. Biblical accounts such as Isaiah 43:1 show that God saves in history. Yahweh is Creator and Redeemer.[11]

b. Political liberation, the self-creation of man. The liberation from Egypt is linked to the creative act. Isaiah 51:9–10 speaks simultaneously of creation and liberation (Isa. 42:5–7). The exodus is a political action.[12]

c. Christ is the fulfilment of this process. He brings a new creation and frees people to continue the work of creation, for "to work, to transform this world, is to become a man and to build the human community; it is also to save. Likewise, to struggle against misery and exploitation and to build a just society is already to be part of the saving action which is moving towards its complete fulfillment."[13]

d. Eschatological promise, the hope of ultimate fulfilment of history. This creation of a new man and society is the basis of that hope.[14]

Gutiérrez builds on Ernst Bloch, Metz, and Moltmann, but he rejects their ambiguity and develops two further thoughts. First, he emphasizes the political nature of Christ's ministry. Although he was not in the Jewish zealot movement, Christ constantly confronted those in authority and the political power structures of his day, and he was crucified by those very political powers. By attacking the root of social

9. Ibid., 36–37.
10. Ibid., 150–51.
11. Ibid., 154–55.
12. Ibid., 155–57.
13. Ibid., 159.
14. Ibid., 145–78.

injustice Jesus tied present liberation to the universal, permanent revolution of salvation history. The political is grafted into the eternal, and Christ's acts take on political significance precisely because of their salvific nature.[15]

Second, Gutiérrez points out that faith and political action are related efforts to create a new type of person in a different society. Faith reveals the deep meaning of the history which we fashion with our own hands. Thus, to the degree that they are oriented toward the construction of a new and better society, our acts are salvific.

In light of the nature of history and the call to liberation, it is necessary to radically revise what the church has been and what it now is.[16] As it accepts universal salvation the church's purpose is no longer to save in the sense of guaranteeing heaven. The work of salvation really occurs in history. Thus the church is to be an active part in the recreation of society. It partakes in the sacrament of history.[17]

3. *Conversion.* As with liberation and salvation, Gutiérrez redefines conversion in terms of his understanding of liberation. The intense spiritual experience of liberation leads not only to a radical transformation of our relationship to God, but also to specific and concrete ways to respond to the needs of the oppressed, exploited, poor, and despised. Accordingly, our conversion to the Lord implies a conversion to our neighbor. "To be converted is to commit oneself to the process of the liberation of the poor and oppressed, to commit oneself lucidly, realistically, and concretely. It means to commit oneself not only generously, but also with an analysis of the situation and a strategy of action."[18]

For Gutiérrez the contextualization of theology involves reflection on the experience and meaning of faith which is based upon a commitment to overcome injustice and create a new societal order. Faith can be verified only by the actualization of that commitment in active participation in the struggle for the liberation of the exploited.

José Míguez-Bonino: Doing Theology in a Revolutionary Situation

José Míguez-Bonino is one of only a few Latin American Protestants who have begun to reflect theologically on the concept of liberation. According to him, Protestant theologians "used to be satisfied with translations, reproductions, or adaptations of European or North Ameri-

15. Ibid., 225–39.
16. Ibid., 251.
17. Ibid., 255–306.
18. Ibid., 205.

can religious books. Lately, however, a certain creativity seems to have been kindled in some Protestant quarters."[19] In a sense Míguez-Bonino himself typifies the new breed of Christians so aptly described in his significant work, *Doing Theology in a Revolutionary Situation*. They, like their non-Christian counterparts, have been forced to respond to a "new reality" in Latin America. The social and economic reality of the Latin continent defies, by its very nature, neutral or indifferent responses. "It refuses to be merely assimilated in traditional categories or placed side by side with other religious 'products' available in the market."[20] The new, revolutionary environment requires a new way of doing theology which grows out of a clearly definable set of presuppositions and is based on a fresh hermeneutic.

Presuppositions

Míguez-Bonino writes (or, he would say, does theology) "from the point of view of a person who confesses Jesus Christ as his Lord and Savior."[21] For him this means that everything else is to be viewed in relation to that basic orientation. The cardinal tenets of Christianity, such as the reality and power of the triune God, the witness of Scripture, and the story of God's salvation, are admittedly matters of faith and can only be justified eschatologically. However, they are not hypotheses which need proving but are rather the foundation for life, action, understanding, and hope. Thus, there can be no thought of abandoning to secularists the task of establishing just structures. The community of believers is called to participate in a consciously Christian manner. Yet they cannot expect their secular colleagues to fully understand what can become clear only when faith becomes sight, and all men shall see him. Thus the struggle for liberation is itself not inherently Christian and will not be accomplished by a new idealism of Christian theology. A desacralization of politics is required, in which there is no room for theocratic dreams of any sort, either from the right or the left.[22]

Given the history of the Latin American experience, Míguez-Bonino is convinced that "revolutionary action aimed at changing the basic economic, political, social and cultural structures, and conditions of life is imperative today in the world."[23] Simple development or re-

---

19. José Míguez-Bonino, *Doing Theology in a Revolutionary Situation* (Philadelphia: Fortress, 1975), 73.

20. Ibid., xxiv.

21. José Míguez-Bonino, *Christians and Marxists: The Mutual Challenge to Revolution* (Grand Rapids: Eerdmans, 1976), 7.

22. Ibid.

23. Ibid., 8.

arranging will not be sufficient. What is needed is basic and revolutionary change. This is not necessarily to be equated with violence, but in
order to be accomplished, these changes must be implemented, and so
be turned into history.[24]

Indispensible for this revolutionary change are "the socioanalytical
tools, the historical horizon of interpretation, the insight into the dynamics of the social process and the revolutionary ethos and programme [of Marxism]."[25] The assumption here is that Marxism is
taken not as dogma but rather as method. Míguez-Bonino observes that
there seems to be a consensus that Latin America is moving toward
some form of socialism and that Marxist analysis is "realization of
human possibilities in historical life."[26] But the new order will not
simply copy existing systems. Similarly, the Marxist analysis, which at
present appears to provide the most adequate insights, will itself have
to be reevaluated and will have to develop its own categories and methods. From this it can be seen that he is willing to seek common ground
with the Marxists, to accept their criticism and use their methods.
This, however, should not be understood as an uncritical adoption of
the whole system. Those elements of Marxism which do not square
with the gospel will have to be eliminated.

> I have never felt attracted to Marxism as a system, neither have I felt
> inclined to enroll in any anti-Marxist crusade. . . . I have more and more
> come to think in terms of a long humanist-socialist tradition, with early
> Christian and Hellenic roots which have developed in the modern world,
> in which Marx has played an insistent—even decisive—part, but which
> he has neither created nor fulfilled.[27]

Hermeneutic Circulation

Míguez-Bonino's understanding of the proper interpretation of the
Word begins with a reevaluation of the relationship between truth and
practice. According to him the classical conception assumes an absolute Christian truth which is somehow enshrined in Scripture or in
pronouncements of the church. It is then applied to a particular historical situation. Precisely this concept is rejected by the liberation theologians. For them truth is not simply something which is applied or even
related to an application, but rather truth is part of the historical context. There is no truth outside or beyond the concrete historical events

24. Ibid.
25. Míguez-Bonino, *Doing Theology*, 35.
26. Ibid., 97.
27. José Míguez-Bonino, "For Life and Against Death: A Theology That Takes Sides,"
in *Theologians in Transition*, ed. James Wall (New York: Crossroad, 1981), 175–76.

in which people are agents. "There is . . . no knowledge except in action itself, in the process of transforming the world through participation in history."[28]

It is at this interface between truth and praxis that two instruments created by Sigmund Freud and Karl Marx take on significance. The first, criticism, forces one to examine every proposed interpretation in relation to the praxis out of which it comes. The theologies coming from the rich cannot be accepted without asking, for example, why they have chosen to ignore obvious political motifs in the life of Christ. Does this reflect simply oversight or an ideology which relegates religion to the realm of individual privacy? The second tool is verification of Christianity as it operates historically. Traditionally this has been approached apologetically, that is, in showing that Christianity made sense within the framework of certain philosophical systems. However, ideas and words should never be divorced from their historical significance, the total experience of a given time and people. We are not dealing merely with ideas and feelings but with acts. Thus, today Christianity must be verified in terms of its relationship to issues such as integration, apartheid, and self-determination, all of which signal its obedience. Determining the correlation between Scripture, understood in the light of its own historicity and our own historical reading of it, is crucial for understanding Christian obedience today.

Such a determination involves us in an interpretive process, which Míguez-Bonino refers to as "hermeneutical circulation."[29] This method is limited by two important facts. First, the proper reading of the Word is not a matter of philosophical argumentation or theological acumen, but rather the synthetic discernment of the Spirit. Obedience grows out of this prophetic discernment promised the community of believers and received through faith. Second, no formal correspondence between either the form or the precedents of the law as recorded in Scripture and a particular historical setting can be expected. For that reason it is important to mediate our understanding by "reading the direction" of the biblical text with regard to liberation, righteousness, and peace, and their complementary "elucidation in history." Further refinement can be achieved by "the determination of the historical conditions and possibilities of our present situation, as discovered through rational analysis."[30] It is this correlation between historical and conceptual mediations which provides a usable framework for Christian obedience.

28. Míguez-Bonino, *Doing Theology*, 88. This, Gutiérrez believes, is in keeping with John's use of *logos*.

29. Ibid., 102.

30. Ibid., 103.

Theology of Liberation

According to Míguez-Bonino Latin American theology in the context of the struggle for liberation has developed after reflection about reality had already evoked a response from Christians. However, once they began to explain, understand, and communicate their convictions, a new theology was born. At the heart of this theology is its verifiability. Within it God can be named only with reference to the concrete actions of historical existence, in relation to which words define their meanings through obedience. Theology is not viewed as an attempt to give a correct understanding of God's attributes or actions but rather an articulation of the action of faith and realized obedience. It provides the framework for the Christians' response to the economic and social injustices of the Latin American environment.

For both Gustavo Gutiérrez and José Míguez-Bonino Christian faith can be verified only by *doing* the truth. Since there is no possibility of establishing a norm for understanding outside of praxis itself, orthopraxis rather than orthodoxy becomes the criterion of sound theology. As Míguez-Bonino puts it, this understanding of the theological task leads to a Copernican revolution in theology. So, whether we are dealing with a theology of liberation or critical reflection on praxis, it becomes clear that we are dealing with nothing short of a new way of doing theology.[31]

31. Ibid., 82.

8

Africa
John S. Mbiti and Byang H. Kato

Traditional Religion and the African Church

Whether Africa will be a Christian continent by the year 2000, as was widely predicted by mission analysts a few years ago, depends on what groups are included in the category *Christian* and a variety of other factors. Nevertheless, among the six continents the church of Africa is one of the fastest growing in the world. At the same time, that church is characterized by great diversity in Christian expression and church leadership. Given the large size of Africa and the vitality and diversity of its church, some distinctions should be made from the outset.

First, in speaking of the church and theology in Africa our focus is on sub-Saharan Africa. The nations of North Africa (and, to a lesser extent, the nation of South Africa) represent special cases that would require separate treatment.

Second, African theology should not be confused with black theology, a theology of decolonization, or Ethiopic theology. Black theology, which originated in the United States but is also strong in South Africa, adheres to a black Messiah and stakes its spiritual claims to validity on the basis of skin color—blackness. One of the major themes of Ethiopic theology is "Africa for the Africans": it aims to rid

Africa of whites and even whiteness. The theology of decolonization represents a synthesis of these two with special emphasis on a sociopolitical response to the cry of the oppressed in Africa, but also in other parts of the world. African theology may share in various of these emphases, but it must be distinguished from them. Sergio Torres, for example, says that one basic criterion for an authentic African theology is the "concern for structural change, for a new economic order."[1] Whether that is a basic criterion could be debated, though as described by liberal theologians it would seem to be the case. It may well be that other distinctives more clearly distinguish African theology from those already identified, however.

Third, African theology has a variety of sources: the Bible, especially the Old Testament; the Christian tradition; African history; the history of missions and the church in Africa; traditional religion and the symbols of African art, sculpture, drama, dance, and ritual. John Pobee essentially agrees with this (though he prefers to speak of African theologies in the plural) and says that he advocates a phenomenological approach to African religions *and* a literary-critical approach to the Bible which will enable African theologians to draw from Africa's "collection of myths, proverbs, invocations, prayers, incantations, rituals, songs, dreams, and so on."[2]

Tite Tienou says African theology is beset by major problems because so much weight is given to African sources. For example, it is sometimes pointed out that ecclesiology is not well developed in Africa because many African theologians are persuaded that a more important need of African Christianity is selfhood and identity after long foreign domination. But when people such as Bengt Sundkler, Harry Sawyerr, and Edward W. Fashole-Luke propose a contextualized ecclesiology based on African kinship, Tienou contends that they go too far. They include both dead ancestors and the as-yet-unborn in the "Great Family" of the church in a way that does violence to both biblical ecclesiology and the Christian tradition.[3] Tienou would agree with Byang H. Kato when the latter concludes that many African theologians "exalt African culture, philosophy and religion beyond proportion."[4]

Fourth, African theology is being worked out at two distinct levels,

1. Sergio Torres, "Opening Address," in *African Theology en Route*, ed. Kofi Appiah-Kubi and Sergio Torres (Maryknoll, N.Y.: Orbis, 1979), 6.

2. John S. Pobee, *Toward an African Theology* (Nashville: Abingdon, 1978), 21.

3. Tite Tienou, "The Church in African Theology: Description and Analysis of Hermeneutical Presuppositions," in *Biblical Interpretation and the Church: Text and Context*, ed. D. A. Carson (Exeter: Paternoster, 1984), 151–65.

4. Byang H. Kato, *Theological Pitfalls in Africa* (Kisumu, Kenya: Evangel, 1975), 53–54.

at the academic level in the schools, and at the practical level in the churches, particularly the independent churches. Adrian Hastings believes this distinction is of the utmost importance.[5] He says the African theology being worked out in the religious departments of the universities by scholars such as Sawyerr of Sierra Leone, E. Bolaji Idowu of Nigeria, John S. Mbiti of Kenya, J. K. Agbeti of Ghana, and others is being done on a western model. Their proposals run the twin risks of overlooking the diversity of African religiosity on the one hand and of viewing all African religion as continuous with Christianity and marginalizing doctrines not reflected in traditional African religion on the other. He also believes that there is an important sense in which the more authentic contextualization is being worked out in what are called independent churches such as the Kimbanguist church in Zaire and the Aladura in Nigeria. The prophets and other leaders of these churches adopt African forms of music and worship, yet recognize local distinctives and stress the discontinuity between Christianity and traditional African religion. Thus in these movements fetishes are often burned, ancestral spirits are replaced by angels, healing of the body is stressed along with salvation of the soul, and the uniqueness of Christ as the one Savior is maintained. This, however, is not to be construed as Hastings's imprimatur on all such contextualizations.

We conclude that as a category, African theology does not yield itself to either commendation or criticism any more than does European, Asian, or any other geographically identified theology. Rather each theological proposal must be judged on its own merit. This will become apparent as we look at the theology of one of the most prolific authors yet produced by the church in Africa, John S. Mbiti, and then look at the counterproposals of perhaps the first evangelical scholar to be recognized on a continent-wide basis, Byang H. Kato.

John S. Mbiti: A Theology of Ontology and Time

Without question, one of the most influential African theologians is one of the recipients of a Theological Education Fund grant, John S. Mbiti. Brought up in a Christian home in his native Kenya, Mbiti was educated in Kenya, the United States, and Europe. He has served as head of the Department of Religions and Philosophy at Uganda's Makerere University and as director of the Ecumenical Institute at Bossey, Switzerland. Judged from the standpoint of an early and lasting impact on contextualization thinking, his most significant works are *African Religions and Philosophy*, *Concepts of God in Africa*, and *New Testament*

5. Adrian Hastings, *African Christianity* (New York: Seabury, 1976), 49–59.

Eschatology in an African Background.[6] *Concepts of God* is an impressive work in which Mbiti collects anthropological data relating to African deities from close to three hundred tribes and attempts a theological interpretataion of these data. *New Testament Eschatology* is his doctoral dissertation. In more recent years Mbiti has continued to write primarily poems, monographs, and shorter works. But the key to understanding Mbiti's contextualized theology for Africa had already been provided in his earlier major work, *African Religions and Philosophy.*

Mbiti believes that in spite of the growth of the church in Africa and the fact that almost one-third of his own Akamba tribe are Christians, the missionary effort in Africa has largely been a failure. Missionaries have been unable to contextualize the gospel with an understanding of and appreciation for African thought and religion. As a result the gospel has not yet been made relevant to Africans, conversions have not been real, and African Christianity is superficial. The same is true of African Islam, though to a somewhat lesser degree.

In a sense Christians must begin all over again. Their starting point must be to develop a theology for the African church that accommodates African culture better than the Western theology communicated by missionaries of the past. Mbiti does not leave us in the dark as to the direction he would see such a theology take. In *African Religions and Philosophy* he writes, "My approach in this book is to treat religion as an ontological phenomenon, with the concept of time as the key to reaching some understanding of African religions and philosophy."[7]

The Ontological Basis of African Theology

Mbiti is disenchanted with many of the anthropological attempts to understand Africa. He finds such classifications as "animism," "primitive religions," "magic," "dynamism," "totemism," "fetishism," and "naturism" to be inadequate if not entirely misleading. Similarly, the attempts of people such as Placide Tempels and Janheinz Jahn to emphasize force as a key explanatory concept are suspect because they overstate the case. He finds John V. Taylor to be too sympathetic to and uncritical of African religions. He is less critical of such anthropologists as Edward G. Parrinder and Hubert Deschamps who gather information from various tribes and attempt to treat African religion systematically, or Godfrey Lienhardt and E. E. Evans-Pritchard who study in-depth reli-

---

6. John S. Mbiti, *African Religions and Philosophy* (New York: Praeger, 1969; Garden City, N.Y.: Doubleday, 1970); *Concepts of God in Africa* (New York: Praeger, 1970); *New Testament Eschatology in an African Background* (London: Oxford University Press, 1971).

7. Mbiti, *African Religions*, 14.

gion within individual tribes. It is apparent that Mbiti has learned from the anthropologists, including some whose approach he criticizes. It is also apparent that he has learned from Western theologians, particularly those who view the various religions as complementary efforts in the pursuit of an understanding of God.

1. *An anthropological analysis.* African ontology is anthropocentric. It can readily be divided into five categories:
   a. God, the Originator and Sustainer of humanity
   b. Spirits, concerned with human destiny
   c. Humanity
   d. Animals and plants, part of the human environment
   e. Phenomena and objects without biological life, also part of the environment

For a reappraisal of the African situation there must be an understanding of the African concept of God in this scheme. Mbiti concludes from his research on the concept of God in various African tribes that Africans already knew and worshiped the one supreme God long before the coming of the missionary. As examples of the kind of interpretation that lends itself to this conclusion we note Mbiti's references to divine attributes that are discoverable in the ways in which various tribes refer to their deities. The Shona refer to him as "the one who can turn things upside down." Mbiti interprets this as an indication that the Shona are aware of God's immutability—God can change things, but he himself is unchangeable.[8] The Karanga speak of God as "the great pool, contemporary of everything." According to Mbiti, the idea of the great pool is suggested by the Zambesi and its tributaries which annually flood the area in which the Karanga live. Interpreted theologically the idea demonstrates an awareness of the omnipresence of God.[9] For the Ila the association between the sun and God is so intimate that when the temperature is unusually high they say, "God is much too hot, let it be over-clouded." According to Mbiti this speaks of an appreciation for God's presence and providence.[10] Mbiti treats data relating to various aspects of the African religious experience, whether shamanism, worship, sacrifice, or spirit involvement, looking for similar types of content.

2. *A theological response.* For Mbiti the strength of African traditional religions lies in the integration of faith into the whole of human existence. If we think that these religions must be *supplanted* by Chris-

---

8. Mbiti, *Concepts of God*, 13.
9. Ibid., 5.
10. Ibid., 57.

tianity, we are faced with a tremendous problem. But if we recognize that in the main they represent valid African understandings of the divine and that Christians need only *supplement* these understandings, this is indeed a strength. After all, true religion should have to do with the whole of life, with the whole of existence, with all "beingness." Therefore, to ask a religious question should be to ask, not about detached theory, but about what actually is.

Contextualization of the concept of God in Africa must be based on a reinterpretation of African ontology. Mbiti's assumption is that pre-Christian Africa knew God in a valid, albeit imperfect, way. In light of this, the anthropological data can be reinterpreted theologically so as to build upon the truth already present in the African religious experience. Reinterpreted in this way, God concepts speak of his true nature. Sacrifice, whether to God alone or to the spirits, is a valid form of worship. The medicine men are benefactors of African society. Ancestor worship is not worship as such but is reflective of the kind of profound respect for the departed which is enjoined by Scripture.

The Time Orientation of African Theology

Mbiti deals with the African orientation to time in much the same way. In his view no single aspect of Western Christianity renders it so foreign to Africa as the Western view of time inherent in it. The African understanding of time is so different from the Western view and in many respects so much closer to the biblical view, that a viable African theology must be oriented to it.

1. *An anthropological analysis of time.* Mbiti analyzes African time from a variety of perspectives, each of which provides clues both to the foreignness of Christianity and the direction that must be taken in constructing a viable African theology.

    a. Potential time and actual time. Time is simply a composition of events which have occurred, are occurring, or soon will occur. That which has not occurred, or has no likelihood of occuring immediately is in the category of *no-time.* That which is certain to occur or is part of the cyclical rhythm of nature is in the category *potential time.* Time, therefore, is two-dimensional. It is composed of past time and present time but has virtually no future time. The Western idea of linear time with an indefinite past, a present, and an infinite future is almost completely foreign to African thinking. For the African, actual time moves backward rather than forward. While Westerners face forward and plan for the future, Africans face backward and set their minds on what has already taken place.

    b. Time reckoning and chronology. African time is connected to

Figure 5
Analysis of the African Concept of Time as
Illustrated by a Consideration of Verb Tenses
among the Kikamba and Gikuyu of Kenya

	Tense	Kikamba	Gikuyu	English	Approximate Time
Sasa	1. Far Future or Remote Future	Ningauka	Ningoka	I will come	About 2 to 6 months from now
	2. Immediate or Near Future	Ninguka	Ninguka	I will come	Within the next short while
	3. Indefinite Future or Indefinite Near Future	Ngooka (ngauka)	Ningoka	I will come	Within a foreseeable while, after such and such an event
	4. Present or Present Progressive	Ninukite	Nindiroka	I am coming	In the process of action, now
	5. Immediate Past or Immediate Perfect	Ninauka (ninooka)	Nindoka	I came (I have just come)	In the last hour or so
Zamani	6. Today's Past	Ninukie	Ninjukire	I came	From the time of rising up to about two hours ago
	7. Recent Past or Yesterday's Past	Nininaukie (nininookie)	Nindirokire	I came	Yesterday
	8. Far Past or Remote Past	Ninookie (ninaukie)	Nindokire	I came	Any day before yesterday
	9. Unspecified Tene (Zamani)	Tene ninookie (Nookie tene)	Nindookire tene	I came	No specific time in the 'past'

John S. Mbiti, *African Religions and Philosophy* (London: Heinemann, 1970), 22. Used by permission.

concrete and specific events, not just mathematics. Numerical calendars rarely exist, and when they do they reach back only a few decades. Rather, Africans have phenomenon calendars. An expectant mother counts the lunar months of her pregnancy. A traveler calculates the number of days required to get from one place to another. In fact, the day is often divided in relation to events. Among the Ankoro of Uganda, for example, the day is divided in terms of milking time, resting time, draw-water time, drinking time, grazing time, return-home time, and so forth. It follows that for the African, time is not a commodity to be spent, bought, or sold. It is something to be made or created.

c. The concepts of past, present, and future. Building upon tenses in the languages of the Kikamba and Gikuyu and using the Swahili words *sasa* and *zamani* rather than the English words *past* and *future*, Mbiti attempts to show that *sasa* time includes everything from the recent past to as far into the future as the African thinks, or about six months. *Zamani* includes everything from the immediate past (it overlaps somewhat with *sasa*) to the far or remote past (see fig. 5).

There are many important aspects of *sasa* and *zamani* time reckoning. One important aspect is that in *sasa* the emphasis is on an elongated now composed of the very recent, the present, and the immediate future. It is important because people are participating in it. This contrasts with a superficial, Westernized Christianity that is interested only in the hereafter.

Another important aspect is that *sasa* feeds or disappears into *zamani*. Events move backward. *Zamani* is where people go after death when they join their ancestors. *Zamani* is the graveyard or storehouse of time where everything is absorbed into a reality that is neither after nor before. It is the period of the myth which explains the origins of the tribe and much else. Accordingly, Africans "back" into the future with their gaze fixed upon the past.

d. The concept of history and prehistory. In traditional Africa there is no concept of history moving forward to a future climax. There is no belief in progress, no planning for the distant future, no messianic hope, no final destruction of the world, no world to come. African eyes are focused on *zamani* and a prehistory which is telescoped into a compact tradition with no dates to remember—only events.

e. Human life in relation to time. Human life moves with the rhythm of nature. At the individual level it includes birth, puberty, initiation, marriage, procreation, old age, death, entry to the community of the departed, and entry to the company of spirits. At the community or national level it includes the cycle of seasons and activities like sowing, cultivating, harvesting, and hunting. Abnormal events such as the birth of twins or an eclipse are usually taken to be bad omens.

f. Death and immortality. An individual is not a complete person until marriage or even procreation. All the while he is moving from *sasa* to *zamani*. Death is part of the process. The deceased is remembered by relatives and friends who talk of his character, words, and exploits. If he should reappear, he is remembered by name. As long as one is remembered in this way life somehow continues; he is "living-dead" and in a state of personal immortality. Afterward, the individual becomes completely dead and sinks into *zamani*. Individual immortality is exchanged for collective immortality. This is the state of spirits. Now if he should appear no one remembers his name and his appearance will likely cause fear. There is no personal communication in this state, but there may be communication through mediums. The departed may become guardians of the clan or intermediaries between God and man.

This helps us to understand the importance of marriage and

procreation in Africa. If a person has no relatives to remember him physical death means that he vanishes out of human existence. Procreation is the gateway to personal immortality. The remembrance of the name is essential to this. And the provision of food and drink for the departed is a symbol of communion and fellowship. The oldest member of the family has the longest *sasa* and memory of the departed and therefore supervises these acts of remembrance. Not to do so is tantamount to excommunicating the departed family member. It is in the light of this that Mbiti insists that these acts do not constitute ancestor worship but only respect.

g. Space and time. Africans often use the same word for space and time. As with time, it is content that defines space. What is geographically near is important. What is far away is not. Africans are tied to their land. It is the concrete expression of their *sasa* and *zamani*. They walk on the graves of their ancestors for fear of being separated from them. To leave their home place may be very difficult psychologically.

Mbiti's data and conclusions have been roundly criticized by Africans and Westerners alike. He admits that Western influence has extended the future dimension of time in Africa, making planning possible. But he insists that the transition is not smooth, and in the secular and political spheres it has caused instability. In the church it has resulted in strong expectations of the millennium and in the shunning of present responsibility. According to Mbiti a right understanding of the African concept of time and an incorporation of this understanding into a contextualized African theology would have great potential for the African church.

2. *The eschatological response.* As a part of the African Inland Church, Mbiti was taught a futurist eschatology: that many events connected with the last days such as the second coming of Christ, the millennial kingdom, the judgment at the great white throne, and the creation of new heavens and a new earth are still to take place in the future. As a result of his theological studies in the West and a reexamination of the African concept of time, he espouses a realized eschatology. He believes the Bible passages that refer to these teachings must be interpreted symbolically and christologically to refer to what has already occurred, or is now occurring, in Christ. In Mbiti's view, the futurist understanding grows out of the Western linear view of time. A realized eschatology is in accord with both Scripture ("That which is has already been, and that which will be has already been, for God

seeks what has passed by." [Eccles. 3:15 NASB]) and the African *sasa-zamani* philosophy of time.

Instead of attempting to place events into a distant future foreign to African thinking, African theology should interpret Scripture to provide Africans with the significance of Christ for their past and present. In this connection Mbiti deals with eight eschatological symbols and words which require reinterpretation, though he himself is not entirely clear as to their meaning.[11]

a. Gehenna is the negation of incorporation into Christ, is at least partly realized in the present, and is a useful psychological tool for evangelistic purposes.
b. Fire does not have moral, religious, and hereafter associations as such, though it is connected to the last judgment. It should be related somehow to the present and the departed.
c. Treasures and rewards speak of fellowship with God.
d. The new Jerusalem is another symbol of the fellowship of God with his people. For the African it has many of the connotations of "home."
c. The future country to which Christians as pilgrims go has to do with abiding in Christ as our permanent home.
f. Eating and drinking and the marriage supper of the Lamb are to be understood sacramentally and christologically, as in communion or the Eucharist.
g. The escaping of tears and pain has to do with sorrows of the present experience.
h. Heaven is not a place as such. Mbiti writes, "The New Testament is explicit that Jesus never promised us a heavenly utopia, but only His own self and His own companionship both in time and space and beyond."[12]

If Mbiti is not entirely clear in his interpretation of Scripture at these and other critical points, he is nevertheless clear in his designs. We do not know exactly how he would respond to a call for more explicit explanations and more pointed applications in these cases, but we are sure he believes that he is marking out new trails, that the doing of African theology is in its early stages and is still in process, and that pioneers cannot always describe with complete precision that land which they strive to possess.

Mbiti has been charged with many errors—from universalism to

11. Mbiti, *New Testament Eschatology*, 64–90.
12. Ibid., 89.

misreading and generalizing his data to grossly inconsistent logic. An evaluation of contextualization approaches such as his will come later. We would stress that, despite his weaknesses and perhaps even heresies, Mbiti has had, and continues to have, a profound impact. Proofs of this could be given, but it may be sufficient simply to point to the attention that conservative evangelicals have been forced to give to his work.

Byang H. Kato: Safeguarding Biblical Christianity in Africa

To those familiar with the church in Africa it may seem incongruous that we choose to deal with Byang H. Kato's approach to contextualization in this context. He died before he had reached his prime, and others have developed more elaborate contextualizations during the last decade. However, Kato was among the earliest evangelical African theologians to respond to African theology as it was being worked out by TEF proponents, so it is difficult to overlook him. Like the writings of Bruce J. Nicholls his work takes on two tasks. Since the meaning and methods of contextualization were first proposed by more liberal theologians, conservative evangelicals felt early on that they had to respond to contextualizations which they believed did injustice if not violence to the biblical gospel. They also saw the necessity to propose meanings and methods which they deemed to be biblically warranted.

Kato's biography was recently published by the Africa Christian Press.[13] He was general secretary of the Association of Evangelicals of Africa and Madagascar (AEAM). He was one of the speakers at the Lausanne Congress of 1974, and his presentation on that occasion forms a part of the basis for this analysis.[14] Several of Kato's works were published in Africa and have had a limited circulation outside that continent.[15] His major work and the primary focus of this introduction to his thought, *Theological Pitfalls in Africa*,[16] is based on his doctoral dissertation at Dallas Theological Seminary. The foreword was provided by Billy Graham, and Charles C. Ryrie of Dallas wrote the introduction. At the time of its publication, Harold Fuller, deputy

13. Sophie de la Haye, *Byang Kato: Ambassador for Christ* (Achimota, Ghana: Africa Christian, 1986).

14. Byang H. Kato, "The Gospel, Cultural Context, and Religious Syncretism," in *Let the Earth Hear His Voice*, ed. J. D. Douglas (Minneapolis: World Wide, 1975).

15. I refer to *African Cultural Revolution and the Christian Faith*, published by Challenge Publications in Nigeria, and *The Spirits* and *Biblical Christianity in Africa*, both published by Africa Christian Press.

16. Kato, *Theological Pitfalls in Africa*.

director of the Sudan Interior Mission, called it "the most significant publication ever produced for and by evangelicals in Africa."[17]

In the book Kato sets the background by describing African traditional religion and by delineating the various types of theological systems which have special reference to Africans. Then he evaluates major aspects of African theology and the ecumenical movement which has given rise to it. Finally, he speaks of the challenge facing biblical Christianity in contemporary Africa and makes basic proposals for an evangelical contextualized theology for that continent and its peoples.

Four Challenges Facing Biblical Christianity in Africa

The perceptive Kato sees four fundamental challenges facing Christianity in Africa. These are intimately related yet distinct from one another.

1. *Rising universalism.* Such factors as universalism in the homelands of missionaries going to Africa, the search for solidarity in the human race, reformation of African traditional religions, scholarships from liberal sources for rising African theologians, and the gregarious nature of the African have conspired to produce an incipient universalism in Africa.

2. *African traditional religions.* A great deal of confusion surrounds African religions because of the profusion of terms used to describe them. Animism, idolatry, paganism, heathenism, fetishism, witchcraft, *juju,* primitive—all of these words and others are used. Kato prefers to speak of African traditional religions. What must not be lost sight of is the "paradoxical yes-and-no principle," according to which we recognize that in these religions man both seeks to find God and seeks to escape from him. If in the past many have emphasized the no and have simply read off these religions as devilish and idolatrous, currently many are emphasizing the yes and are seeking to elevate them to the same status as that of biblical Christianity. This latter approach results in relativism and syncretism, both of which are inimical to true faith.

3. *African theology.* For Kato the designation *African theology* is vague and ambiguous, but he understands it as the product of liberal theologizing. It presupposes that God has revealed himself in African traditional religions and therefore gives expression to that kind of revelation. Understood in this way, African theology constitutes an important aspect of the contemporary challenge to biblical Christianity.

4. *Ecumenism in Africa.* April 23, 1963, was an important date for

17. Quoted in de la Haye, *Byang Kato,* 105.

African Christianity according to Kato. On that date "the long-time dream of ecumenical enthusiasts" culminated in the formation of the All Africa Conference of Churches (AACC). He calls attention to the air of optimism that characterized the event and quotes one description of it: "The solemn silence was then swept away as the assembly hall reverberated with the loud and clear beats of African drums signalling the birth of AACC. This was the voice of Christian Africa, not drums calling to the past darkness of pagan rituals, but drums dedicated to God, the transformation of an age-old instrument into an instrument of the church proclaiming unity, and common witness."[18]

Despite the euphoria of the occasion, the wording of the description, and the references to the Scriptures and Christ as the *only* Savior in the doctrinal bases of the World Council of Churches (WCC) and the AACC, Kato sounds an alarm. In his view the ecumenical movement is largely in the hands of liberals who reject a fully authoritative, inspired, and inerrant Bible and who espouse a theology open to universalism and other aberrations. A massive infusion of WCC funds into Africa and the influence of teachers such as Paul Tillich and James Cone on scholarship recipients can only mean an incursion of the poisonous elements of liberal ecumenism into Africa.[19]

Kato's Assessment of the Work of Two African Theologians

Far from contributing to the solution of problems facing the church in Africa, Kato is convinced that certain theological works have actually exacerbated the situation. Of the various proposals that come in for criticism in *Theological Pitfalls*, those of Mbiti and Idowu attract the most attention. Kato weighs them in the balance and finds them wanting.

1. *The proposals of John S. Mbiti.* Kato gives most of his attention to the theology of Mbiti because he believes Mbiti is one of the most influential of African theologians, and his proposals are misleading and damaging even though offered in good faith. Generally speaking, he faults Mbiti for being self-contradictory, for dealing with African religion as though it were one organized system, for engaging in inadequate though extensive research, and for espousing unbiblical teachings. But he also deals with such particulars as Mbiti's views on African concepts of God and African philosophy of time as it relates to eschatology and other matters.

---

18. *Drumbeats from Kampala* (London: Lutterworth, 1963), 10, as quoted in Kato, *Theological Pitfalls*, 138.
19. Kato, *Theological Pitfalls*, 140.

According to Kato three problems accrue to Mbiti's analysis of African concepts of God. First, his sources are inadequate. It is impossible to cover nearly three hundred tribes in less than a year as Mbiti did and still gather accurate and adequate data. For example, Mbiti speaks of the Kagoro as having a divinity of cattle, but Kato replies that he has an intimate acquaintance with the Kagoro tribe, and they do not raise cattle at all, let alone have a divinity of cattle. Second, Mbiti makes hardly any reference to the evil attributed to God in African traditional religions. Third, Mbiti interprets his data so as to substantiate his premises. Thus he rationalizes ancestral worship to remake it into ancestral respect. Similarly, idolatry is interpreted as the worship of the one God.

Concerning the African philosophy of time and African eschatology, Kato cites leading African scholars who dispute Mbiti's analysis of African time. In contrast to Mbiti, he concludes that Africans definitely do have a concept of a distant future. Other ideas, such as Mbiti's notion that the African philosophy of time is cyclic, are open to question. As for eschatology in Africa, Kato finds Mbiti's ideas on such subjects as resurrection and judgment at odds with both African reality and biblical teaching. In his estimation Mbiti's realized eschatology stems from his bias in favor of universalism.

2. *E. Bolaji Idowu's implicit monotheism.* Kato also deals with a Nigerian theologian who has served as president of the Methodist Church in that country as well as head of the Department of Religious Studies at the University of Ibadan, E. Bolaji Idowu. Idowu espouses a philosophy of peaceful coexistence with the various religious systems of Africa—a philosophy which he identifies as *implicit monotheism*, but which has also been called *diffused monotheism*. Idowu believes that the gods in African religions are ministers of the one God. Consequently representatives of all religions should seek for peaceful coexistence rather than taking a proselytizing approach. Christian influence should be exerted, if at all, in presence rather than proclamation.

Kato faults Idowu for not taking the Scriptures seriously, as when he makes Micah condone all worship as worship of Jehovah. He cites Idowu's commentary on Micah 4:3–5:

Here, in defining "total peace" as the end of religion, Micah adds startlingly the acceptance and understanding of each people in the religious context in which they lived. This would be as already asserted, because Yahweh was in control everywhere; and maybe that he [Micah] would like to have added that, therefore, every impulse to worship at all, and the resulting practice of essential worship, was of "the everlasting God, the Creator of the ends of the earth."[20]

In these few words Idowu has distorted the peace of which Micah speaks by making it into the acceptance of "each people" in their own religious context. He also puts words in the prophet's mouth when he says that "maybe . . . he would like to have added" that all worship is Yahweh's.

Kato accuses Idowu of an epistemological relativism and universalism ("all religions are heading in the same direction"), of giving fresh and unwarranted meaning to idol worship ("underneath their acts of worship is the deep consciousness that Olodumare is above all"), and of confusing general with special revelation ("God has spoken from the very beginning to every heart of all the peoples of the earth").

If we are to understand Kato's polemics, we must understand that he does not simply adopt an accusatory posture in his critiques of Mbiti, Idowu, and others. He gives them credit for their scholarship and good intentions. But he believes he must take them to task on the bases of scriptural authority, sound hermeneutical principles, traditional orthodox theology, and logical reasoning—all of which constitute the foundation for a defensible Christian theology.

A Program for Safeguarding Biblical Christianity in Africa

Kato sees history as having come full circle. The church in Africa is now confronted with many of the same problems the church faced in the first century—competing religions, complex cultures, the conjoining of politics with religion, and humanitarian concerns. He urges sensitivity to the need to preserve cultural distinctives, to the call for patriotism, to the remembrance of ancestors, and to the plight of those who have never heard the gospel. Above all, if Christians are to obey God and bless Africa they must safeguard biblical Christianity as Africa's only hope.

At this point Kato proposes a ten-point foundation for a contextualized approach to Africa.[21] He did not live long enough to build the superstructure on this foundation, a task for which he was eminently qualified, but those who follow him would be remiss if they did not give attention to the foundation. The following summary of Kato's proposal combines his precise words (in quotation marks) and our summarizations.

1. "Adhere to the basic presuppositions of historic Christianity."
   These include: God has revealed himself in creation and con-

20. E. Bolaji Idowu, *Orita: Ibadan Journal of Religious Studies* 4:89, as quoted in *Theological Pitfalls*, 96–97.
21. Kato, *Theological Pitfalls*, 181–84.

science; non-Christian religions demonstrate both that man has a concept of God and that he rebels against God; there is redemption in Christ but only to those who believe; God's image has not been obliterated in man but, nevertheless, God is creating a new man; and the Bible is the final and infallible rule of faith and practice. In Kato's view these propositions are indispensable to African Christianity.

2. "Express Christianity in a truly African context, allowing it to judge the African culture and never allow the culture to take precedence over Christianity." The way to do this is not by creating an African theology but by "expressing theological concepts in terms of the African situation" and by "scratching where it itches"—by tackling characteristically African problems related to polygamy, family structure, the spirit world, and liturgy, presenting biblical answers to these problems.

3. Train men in the Scriptures and its original languages so that they have the ability to exegete the Word of God correctly.

4. Give careful study to the non-Christian religions remembering, however, that for us, as for the New Testament writers and evangelists, this study is secondary.

5. Engage in aggressive evangelism and so avoid a repetition of the error of third-century African Christian leaders who became so involved in doctrinal strife that they neglected evangelism.

6. "Consolidate organizational structures based on doctrinal agreements." It is the nature of Africans to require fellowship, but this need not be organic union and should not be unity at any cost.

7. "Carefully and accurately delineate and concisely express terms of theology as a necessary safeguard against syncretism and universalism."

8. "Carefully present apologetics towards unbiblical systems that are creeping into the church. This calls for more leadership training."

9. Show concern for social action but not at the expense of a message of personal salvation. True conversions to Christ result in Christians who revolutionize society for the good.

10. Know that Africa needs her Polycarps, Athanasiuses, and Martin Luthers who are ready to contend for the faith whatever the cost.

We can only conjecture as to exactly how Kato would have fleshed out this skeleton of contextualization. But it is the foundation that largely determines the type and shape of the building, and it is the skeleton that determines the type and shape of the body. It would not be at all surprising if, while showing appreciation for the insights of African colleagues such as Mbiti and Idowu, Kato nevertheless would have proceeded along the lines indicated in his ten-point program.

African theology is easily confused with black theology or Ethiopic theology or a theology of decolonization. In fact, African theology itself is sometimes identified with the search for a new economic order and the struggle for structural change. But beyond the quests of these theologies, the African church is producing contextualized theologies that also aim to be authentically African in traditional religiosity and understandings while authentically Christian in biblical authority and teaching. The contributions of Mbiti and Kato illustrate that it is not easy to resolve this tension.

9

The Middle East
Kenneth E. Bailey and Tim Matheny

The Bible in Its Own Cultural Setting

Contextualization in the Middle East presents a unique, double-sided challenge. We are dealing with the fountainhead of the biblical culture data we seek to interpret and contextualize. For that reason any attempt to apply biblical teaching to this context ultimately involves a form of reverse contextualization since the contextualizer must apply the gospel to the very cultural setting from which it was received. Since the current situation differs little from the biblical milieu, it affords the exegete an opportunity to rediscover the cultural context of biblical texts. Kenneth E. Bailey's *Poet and Peasant*[1] is one such attempt to use Middle Eastern literary forms as a framework for interpreting Jesus' parables.

Yet the Near East is also the cultural center of Islam. Cultural proximity has not made contextualizing the gospel for Muslims easier. Quite to the contrary, the overlap of biblical materials has made this a notoriously difficult task. Recent attempts have centered on the unique nature

1. Kenneth E. Bailey, *Poet and Peasant: A Literary-Cultural Approach to the Parables in Luke* (Grand Rapids: Eerdmans, 1976) and *Through Peasant Eyes: A Literary-Cultural Approach to the Parables in Luke* (Grand Rapids: Eerdmans, 1983).

113

of Muslim culture and common ground. One example is Phil Parshall's *New Paths in Muslim Evangelism*.[2] It represents a ground-breaking attempt to apply the principles of contextualization to the Muslim environment. The approach is based, among other things, on the premise that certain Muslim rituals and patterns of worship associated with the mosque should be incorporated into a radically new type of church designed to meet the needs of a Muslim convert. Another example of this basic orientation is provided in Tim Matheny's *Reaching the Arabs*.[3] Although not as widely known as Parshall's, Matheny's model is equally innovative and instructive. Since it is based on an analysis of only one type of Muslim—the transient Arab—it is somewhat narrower in scope and has, for that reason, been chosen for consideration in this chapter.

Kenneth E. Bailey: Poet and Peasant

After reviewing several approaches to interpreting the parables of Jesus, Bailey suggests that

> Eastern Literature must be examined using its own literary art forms. Then when the question is asked, "What are the primary literary art forms in Eastern literature?" the almost exclusive answer is, "Stories and poems." Thus, if we would investigate the parables aesthetically we must examine them to see if Eastern poetical forms occur in the text, and if the stories have a distinct literary form.[4]

This leads to Bailey's conviction that "the historical must be re-examined in the light of additional evidence from the cultural milieu of the parables."[5] That is, to understand the theology of the parables one must recapture the culture that informs the text. This is what he calls the cultural problem.

Oriental Exegesis

In order to solve the cultural problem Bailey proposes a process which he calls Oriental exegesis. It involves (1) discussing the cultural aspects of the parable with Middle Easterners, (2) examining pertinent ancient literature, and (3) consulting the Oriental version of the gospel.

2. Phil Parshall, *New Paths in Muslim Evangelism* (Grand Rapids: Baker, 1980).
3. Tim Matheny, *Reaching the Arabs: A Felt Need Approach* (Pasadena, Calif.: William Carey Library, 1981).
4. Bailey, *Poet and Peasant*, 25–26.
5. Ibid., 26.

Initial findings indicate that "each parable has a 'cluster' of theological motifs that together press the listener to make a single response."[6]

1. *Ancient literature.* Ancient Middle Eastern literature has been examined for clues regarding the culture that informs the text. What is the exegete looking for?

2. *Contemporary Middle Eastern culture.* Archaic lifestyles of Middle Eastern peasants have been preserved by their isolation and by the fact that they regard changelessness as an important societal value. To preserve meaning is to preserve the status quo. The same thing applies to intellectual life, as in the poems and stories preserved from the past.[7] There are three approaches to data acquisition: the view from the saddle—"riding through"; the view from the study window—"the outsider looking in"; and the view from the single village and from the *mastaba,* the mud-brick or stone bench outside the peasant's house on which he sits and talks with his friends by the hour.[8] Information gained by such study introduces a fresh set of questions which, when asked of the Bible, uncover a new layer of perception. These questions concern attitude, relationship, response, and value judgment. For example, what is the attitude of the sleeping neighbor who is called upon for help in the night?[9]

3. *Oriental versions.* Since all translation is inevitably interpretation, the decisions made by Arabic and Syriac translators will reflect an understanding of the culture that informs the text. This examination will include major Arabic and Syriac versions, as well as medieval and modern translations by Eastern scholars. How can we be sure that the Middle Eastern peasant has not changed his culture and attitudes across the intervening centuries? We cannot be sure. Thus, if an older and in any way more authentic alternative is available, it will be given preference. The ultimate question is, "Whose culture shall we allow to inform the text for us?"[10] Searching for the answer to this question, Bailey develops a new methodology which facilitates a more precise interpretation of the culturally bound elements of the New Testament parables. He also discovered a series of literary types which have led to a "more accurate division of traditional materials into pericopes and a new understanding of the original meaning of the material itself."[11]

6. Ibid., 27.
7. Ibid., 31.
8. Ibid., 34.
9. Ibid., 35.
10. Ibid., 37.
11. Ibid., 207.

Figure 6
Elements of a Parable

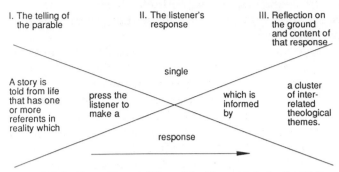

Kenneth E. Bailey, *Poet and Peasant: A Literary-Cultural Approach to the Parables of Luke* (Grand Rapids: Eerdmans, 1983), 41. Used by permission.

On the basis of this new methodology Bailey comes to the conclusion that a parable has three basic elements (see fig. 6):

1. *Multiple referents,* that is, one or more points of contact within the real world of the listener (symbols). The concept of multiple real-life referents is crucial in determining the theological center of the parable. The interpreter must shake "himself loose from the stance that sees the parable as a secret cryptogram, with a code that must be broken."[12] Once this is done, a parable can be seen to contain several symbols which may point to several referents without losing its unity.

2. *A single response.* The listener is pressed to make a response to the parable. Depending on its nature, that response could be either "a decision to act in a particular way or to accept a new understanding of the nature of God's way with men in the world."[13]

3. *A cluster of theological themes.* In this combination of explicitly stated or presupposed theological motifs which press the listener toward the desired response, the unity of the parable can be found.

In the parable of the sower (Matt. 13:3–8; Mark 4:1–12; Luke 8:4–10) the listener is called to hear and bear fruit. This is based on a cluster of motifs and referents which include (a) the kingdom of God is like a growing seed, (b) the sower sows liberally (grace), (c) fruit-bearing is an essential mark of the kingdom, and (d) there is hope for a harvest in spite of difficulties. This cluster of motifs forms the ground and con-

12. Ibid., 39–40.
13. Ibid., 40.

**Figure 7
The Structure of Galatians 3:5–14**

A Spirit, faith, righteousness
  B Gentiles, blessing of Abraham
    C Curse
      D Law
        E Righteousness by faith
      D' Law
    C' Curse (Christ)
  B' Gentiles, blessing of Abraham (Christ)
A' Spirit, faith, promise

From Kenneth E. Bailey, *Poet and Peasant: A
Literary-Cultural Approach to the Parables in Luke*
(Grand Rapids: Eerdmans, 1976), 55. Used by
permission.

tent of a single response. Thus, "a parable is not an illustration but is a mode of theological speech used to evoke a response."[14]

Types of Literary Structure

On the basis of his research Bailey recognized a number of patterns of semantic relationships.[15] They can be summarized:

1. Sections of prose that use an inversion principle for an outline, such as *a b c d c' b' a'*. According to Bailey, Galatians 3:5–14 exemplifies this pattern (see fig. 7).
2. Poetic sections which use a variety of parallelistic devices including standard parallel (*a a' b b'*), step parallel (*a b a' b'*), and inversion (Luke 11:29–32).
3. Sections that have tight parallelism encased in one or more sets of matching prose (Acts 5:1–6).
4. The parabolic ballad, a narrative form distinct from the others and typical of Luke's parables (Luke 10:30–35).

Recognizing the literary structure of a given text is important for several reasons. The structure may help the interpreter find the climactic center, it shows how that center is related to the outside, it identifies the turning point, and it provides a key to match words, phrases, or sentences and so aids understanding.

Exegesis of Luke 15:4–7

Bailey provides a detailed analysis of several parables to demonstrate the validity and usefulness of this contextualized approach to exegesis.

14. Ibid., 43.
15. Ibid., 45–75.

Figure 8
The Structure of the Parable
of the Lost Sheep

```
1 which man of you
2 one
3 ninety-nine
    A the lost
      B find
        C joy
            D restoration
        C' joy
      B' find
    A' the lost
1' I say to you
2' one
3' ninety-nine
```

From Kenneth E. Bailey, *Poet and Peasant: A
Literary-Cultural Approach to the Parables in Luke*
(Grand Rapids: Eerdmans, 1976), 144–45. Used
by permission.

Selected portions of his study of the parable of the lost sheep (Luke 15:4–7) may serve to illustrate his method.[16]

The structure of this parable involves three stanzas in which the first and the third are semantically related while the second uses a different poetic device. "It has strong auditory, as well as semantic correspondences. Both inverted and step parallelism are used. The climax, which is joy in restoration, is highlighted by the parallelistic structure and by the word-rhyme between 'one' and 'joy' " (see fig. 8).

An analysis of the cultural aspects of this parable reveals several significant insights:

1. Jesus shocked the sensitivities of his listeners by referring to them as shepherds, an occupation none of them would have likely taken up.
2. Anyone rich enough to have owned one hundred sheep would probably have hired a shepherd. However, this person is likely to have been part of the owner's extended family, which may help explain the community which rejoices at the restoration.
3. The shepherd is blamed for having lost the sheep, which were probably counted and left in the wilderness.

Four theological themes form the center of this parable:

16. Ibid., 144–56.

1. The joy expressed by the shepherd and shared with the community at finding the lost sheep is an invitation for the listener to share in the joy over the conversion of the sinner.
2. The joy is related to the burden of restoration. In this case Jesus is defending his own acceptance of sinners. Like the shepherd Jesus himself would have to pay a heavy price for shouldering the burden of a sinful world; nevertheless he accepts the task with joy.
3. It is gracious love which seeks the sinner.
4. The parable raises questions with regard to the subject and nature of repentance. In contrast to the idea that the "completely righteous" had no need of repentance, Jesus teaches that all men must repent. The structure of the parable underscores with irony the fact that no one can be that sure by forcing the listener to relate stanzas 1 and 3. In stanza 1 the ninety-nine are still in the wilderness, and it is not clear where they are in stanza 3. As for the nature of repentance, Jesus clearly rejects the early Jewish notion that repentance would be instrumental in bringing about the kingdom. "The sheep does nothing to prompt the shepherd to begin his search except to become lost. In the parable, there is reported joy over 'one sinner who repents.' Here 'being found' is equated with 'repentance.' "[17]

According to Bailey, then, a knowledge of both the culture that informs the text of the biblical parables and the literary structures used are crucial to an accurate understanding of them. By using this approach to exegesis we are brought closer to a clearer perception of the person of Christ and a more precise understanding of him as a theologian.

Tim Matheny: Reaching the Arabs by a Felt Need Approach

Basic Assumptions

Tim Matheny calls his model for evangelism among Arabs *a felt need approach*. The model grows out of two informed assumptions.

Some groups of Muslims are more receptive to the gospel than are others. On the basis of previous investigation, Matheny suggests that transitional Arabs are the most receptive. These are individuals who are in the process of modernization, that is, they are moving from a traditional way of life to a more complex, technological, and rapid-paced style of living. Most were born in rural settings and have subsequently relocated to urban centers. Most have attended high school and

17. Ibid., 155.

college and are materially secure. This group has been shown to consistently respond positively to the communication of innovations.

The results of social scientific research as it applies to innovation can be used to more effectively communicate the gospel and assure the acceptance of its ideas.

On the basis of these assumptions Matheny initiates his study by analyzing cultural and religious themes and social structures. These "regulate the behavior of the Transitional Arab . . . and become very important in constructing a relevant Christian message."[18]

Cultural Analysis

Rather than undertake an exhaustive treatment of cultural themes Matheny attempts to "isolate those themes that would be of crucial importance to the communicator of religious innovations."[19] One must understand the basic components of the Arab value system in order to relate to it supracultural Christian values. The following illustration represents how Matheny deals with values:

1. *Honor.* Honor is one of the most important cultural themes, since in Arab society it provides the framework which governs the individual's "protection of and behavior toward his kinsman."[20] The concept is directly related to family solidarity and ultimately group survival. All good achievements, whether realized by personal effort or by laborious efforts of other members of the kin group to which a man belongs, build up or contribute to his *sharaf* (highness, honor). "Thus a man's honor is largely determined by his own personal behavior and by the behavior of his kinsmen."[21]

This pan-Arabian theme is expressed in many areas of social life. It establishes and maintains proper relationships between the sexes, setting up a mechanism to guard against dishonorable sensual behavior and punishing misbehavior. Since sexual crimes are an affront to a man's honor, they must be avenged to avoid permanent dishonor. The concept of honor determines the relative desirability of certain types of work. Most Arabs, for example, despise any kind of manual labor, including agricultural work, in which many of them are by necessity involved. Honor dictates a high degree of respect for the elderly. Thus the tolerance, politeness, and deference required led most Arabs to favor the son who lied to his father in Jesus' parable (Matt. 21:28–30), since his answer reflected the proper respect.

18. Matheny, *Reaching the Arabs*, 9.
19. Ibid., 14.
20. Ibid.
21. Ibid., 15.

2. *Hospitality.* Another important cultural theme in Arab society is hospitality, which governs the way in which the individual protects and behaves toward a guest. This concept, like most other Arab values, is intended to strengthen group solidarity. In a sense it grows out of the harsh environment in which the bedouins have traditionally lived. A number of researchers have concluded that this has led to a great deal of hostility, which at any moment could break out into open violence. As a result, social interaction takes place within a strictly controlled framework in which everything from the greeting and seating arrangement to the course of the conversation unfolds according to a prescribed pattern. Upon meeting, for example, the individuals will engage in an extended greeting which includes prescribed inquiries and stereotypical responses. Supposedly, this provides a means of "sizing each other up" without arousing sensitive tempers. No matter how short a visit may be, the guest is never allowed to leave before he is offered food or drink. A guest may even be forced to stay until a meal is prepared. These intricate behavioral patterns have almost ritualistic significance and are carried out in the most lavish manner possible, regardless of one's financial standing. From that it can be seen that hospitality is closely related to the concept of honor. Lavish hospitality shows the host's wealth and increases his personal prestige. Refusing to accept hospitality offends the honor of the potential hosts "by indicating that one thinks they might not be good hosts or might do one harm."[22]

3. *The welfare of the group.* As has already been pointed out, the welfare of the group often takes precedence over that of the individual. In many cases that group is one's own family unit. This determines the way in which the individual relates his own needs and desires to those of his family members. Family loyalty is a dominant theme. The family's place in society also determines the individual's position. "His chances of success, his expectations of education and attainments of wealth are largely determined by the family into which he is born."[23] This may help explain why the family must be viewed as the major unit of identity and the object of intense feelings of loyalty. In fact some have gone as far as to suggest that the individual participates with the larger groups of society—economically, politically, socially, and religiously—through family membership rather than as an individual. Few, if any, important decisions are made without conferring with the family, to which the individual usually submits. That being the case, "the cohesiveness of the Arab extended family, which has been the primary barrier to individ-

22. Ibid., 17.
23. Ibid., 19.

ual religious conversions in the Middle East, can become the primary vehicle of culture change and innovations."[24]

4. *The function of religion.* Not only is observing the presence of a well-defined religious belief system important for understanding Arabs, but it is also important to see that religion's function. In the West the function of religion has shrunk considerably and covers only one area of life, but in the Arab world it is the fundamental motivating force from which all else radiates. Religious convictions influence practically every act during each moment of life.[25]

Thus Islam has to be viewed as a societal structure and an integrative worldview and not merely as a religion. It represents the one factor which integrates almost every aspect of social life. As a result religion has tremendous psychological sustaining power. Since Christianity is also characterized by this claim to exclusive allegiance, there seems to be considerable similarity between the two belief systems. However, there are significant differences in the area of each religion's normative and psychological function. The crucial difference between Islam and Christianity is more functional than doctrinal.[26]

As this applies to social structure, it should be pointed out that religion functions as an important factor in social differentiation. According to Matheny, understanding this depends upon grasping the significance of a twofold distinction between a religion and a sect. A religion is a system of beliefs and symbolic acts concerned with the supernatural and therefore relatively theoretical and unrelated to everyday life. A sect is a group of people that has not only a religious identity, but also its own internal social structure and its own external political relationships with other sects and groups.[27] In keeping with the unity between religion and society, sectarian behavior includes a wide range of religious as well as nonreligious concerns. Adherence to a particular sect will determine if and how an individual may participate in political affairs, whom he may and may not marry, and even where he will live.

Matheny draws a distinction between *great* and *little* traditions which, when combined with the religion/sect distinction, helps account for the complexity of religious life in the Arab world (see fig. 9). These distinctions offer four categories which provide an understanding of the role religion plays in the lives of Arabs: (a) The religious great

---

24. Ibid., 42.
25. Ibid., 21.
26. Ibid., 22.
27. John Gulick, *The Middle East: An Anthropological Perspective* (Pacific Palisades, Calif.: Goodyear, 1976), 164, quoted in Matheny, *Reaching the Arabs*, 44.

Figure 9
Great and Little Traditions

	Great Tradition	Little Tradition
Religion	The "Five Pillars"	Reverence for saints
		Dhikr
		Evil eye
	jinn	
	life-crisis rituals	
Sect	Ulama and specialized functionaries	Marabouts Brotherhoods

John Gulick, *The Middle East: An Anthropological Perspective* (Pacific Palisades, Calif.: Goodyear, 1976), 172. Adapted by Tim Matheny, *Reaching the Arabs: A Felt Need Approach* (Pasadena, Calif.: William Carey Library, 1981), 47. Used by permission.

tradition includes the formal aspects of Islam, such as the five pillars, the Koran, and the Hadith and governs three rites of passage—marriage, birth, and death. (b) The religious little tradition includes animistic and superstitious behavior. (c) The sectarian little tradition includes major Sufi orders and brotherhoods, which at times have sprung up around charismatic leader-saints. This "saint complex" facilitates emotional discharge and provides support mechanisms for the individual. (d) The sectarian great tradition is embodied in the leadership of the various sects. Islam, even if it cannot be considered superior to Christianity, does meet a number of practical needs across the entire spectrum of social, political, and religious life. It is essential to recognize these need-fulfilling functions "if the evangelist is to effectively introduce the religious innovation of the Christian message in such a way. . . that the Arab people will accept it as a viable alternative."[28]

Strategy

Before setting out his contextualization suggestions Matheny sets four goals for evangelism within the Islamic value system:

1. *Disassociating the gospel from Western forms of culture.* This provides an opportunity for the gospel to "pass through the Arab mind."[29]
2. *Preparing evangelists to recognize their role as agents of change.* This requires (a) a knowledge of Islam, (b) a knowledge of Arabic, and (c) the ability to make concessions in customs. Even more important than specific skills is the ability to identify with the Muslim, which is not so much a matter of costume and eating

28. Ibid., 49.
29. Ibid., 104.

habits, but rather developing "a mind that can understand, hands which join in with others in a common task, and a heart which responds to other's joys and sorrows."[30]

3. *Facilitating valid decisions for Christ.* Conversion is based upon a direct encounter between God and the non-Western people according to their own patterns of decision making. The evangelist will have to overcome sociological restrictions by working within the family network rather than tearing individuals out of it.

4. *Providing an environment in which one can work for persistence of obedience.* The basic concern here is to establish an indigenous church for Arab converts. After rejecting the three-self formula as an inadequate concept of indigeneity Matheny once again draws upon the theory of innovation and information diffusion. In the work of Luther P. Gerlach and Virginia H. Hine, he finds five key factors which explain successfully innovative movements. Matheny believes all five were used in the first-century church.

   a. A segmented, usually polycephalous, cellular organization
   b. Face-to-face recruitment using preexisting social relationships
   c. Personal commitment generated by an act or experience
   d. An ideology which forms the basis for conceptual unification of a segmented network of groups
   e. Real or perceived opposition from society[31]

Applying these factors to the Arab world, Matheny spells out the need for indigenous leadership and, above all, worship.

Picking up on the suggestions made during the Lausanne Congress on Evangelization, Matheny proposes an indigenous form of worship which essentially modifies Muslim practices. Daily prayers could be retained. Fasting in keeping with biblical instruction could be accepted. Scripture memorization and recitation could take the place of readings from the Koran. Removing one's shoes and bowing for prayer could also contribute to a noncompromising identification with the convert's background. Formal prayer being an important element of worship in Islam involves not only the lips, but the whole body. Could not a Muslim convert be encouraged to maintain a similar form of prayer as a Christian?[32]

30. Eugene A. Nida, *Customs and Culture: Anthropology for Christian Missions* (New York: Harper, 1954), 257, quoted in Matheny, *Reaching the Arabs*, 116.

31. Luther P. Gerlach and Virginia H. Hine, *People* (New York: Bobbs-Merrill, 1970), xvii, quoted in Matheny, *Reaching the Arabs*, 125.

32. Matheny, *Reaching the Arabs*, 126.

Matheny adds a modification of the time of worship. In keeping with the Arab concept of time,

> a gathering could take place on Sunday morning or evening for the purpose of worship, observing the Lord's Supper, and teaching. A specific time to begin would not be necessary. . . . As each member arrived at the place of worship he would immediately begin a period of private mediation, scripture reading, or prayer. As the group became larger, various forms of corporate worship could begin with spontaneous singing, prayer, scripture reading, and exhortations interspersed by quiet periods of meditations. . . . When all had arrived, the Lord's Supper could then be observed. This could be followed by a period of teaching and exhortation. A thirty-minute sermon would not be necessary every week.[33]

Having thus suggested ways in which the formal practice of the Christian faith could be applied to the Arab setting, Matheny raises a question related to the limits of contextualization: "How far can one go in adapting (or accommodating) before one has gone too far?"[34] In answer he proposes a threefold distinction which enables the missionary to categorize the various elements of Arab culture and religion.

  a. *Biblically supported items which should be retained:* honor to parents, hospitality, strict regulation of sexual behavior, giving to the poor, fasting, loyalty, ban on drunkenness.
  b. *Neutral items which can be maintained:* types of clothing, sitting on the floor, ways of greeting, ways of making decisions, removing shoes in places of worship, circumcision, bowing prostrate when praying, ways of getting married, religious gatherings on Friday.
  c. *Items which must be rejected as contrary to biblical principles:* polygamy, animistic superstitions, belief in Muhammed as Prophet, maintaining honor at any price, fatalistic practices.

Matheny suggests that for the gospel to be relevant to transitional Arabs it must be related to their felt needs. "A state of dissatisfaction or frustration . . . occurs when one's desires outweigh one's actualities. It is produced by a tension in the psychological field which seeks readjustment. The achievement of the goal towards which it is directed relieves the stress and results in satisfaction."[35] Our understanding of

---

33. Ibid., 127.
34. Ibid., 131. Matheny adopts Byang H. Kato's definition of contextualization. See Byang H. Kato, "The Gospel, Cultural Context and Religious Syncretism," in J. D. Douglas, *Let the Earth Hear His Voice* (Minneapolis: World Wide, 1975), 1217.
35. Matheny, *Reaching the Arabs*, 140.

these needs grows out of the analysis of Arab culture. It will be important to address the message to the need to preserve honor, to show hospitality, and to live in community.[36] Felt needs, however, represent only one aspect of an individual's actual state. Ultimate needs, those seen from God's perspective, also have to be taken into account. Thus the evangelist will have to patiently teach his listeners and "bring them to see the needs that they have as God sees them."[37]

The models introduced in this chapter typify the two major components of all cross-cultural communication and contextualization: (a) bridging the gap between the communicator and the culture which informed the biblical texts and (b) introducing that text's informed understanding into another cultural matrix. Bailey has unveiled the richness of an exegesis based on firsthand exposure to contemporary bearers of the cultural tradition in which the parables were first formulated. Matheny has made us privy to his search for culturally appropriate means of communicating the gospel to a highly resistant people. Where else but in the Middle East do the "three cultures" (see p. 200) involved in contextualization lie in such proximity?

36. Ibid., 146–52.
37. Ibid., 153.

Frameworks for Analysis

Introduction to Part 3

The examples presented in part 2 demonstrate that the various attempts at contextualization span a wide spectrum both theologically and methodologically. The reader has probably formed some preliminary opinions and rightly concluded that not all contextualization schemata are valid, that is, not every effort to transculturate revealed truth remains faithful to the original gospel. Evangelical believers respond almost instinctively to the perceived inadequacies in the respective models. In some cases this involves the assumed or real threat of a theologically liberal orientation. In other cases, our reservations may be triggered by a supposedly unorthodox methodology, an unacceptable political agenda, or the danger of syncretism. In any case we feel the need to evaluate.

But by what standard should these models be evaluated? Surely we need something more objective than our own culture-bound theological instincts. In part 3 a set of five analytical tools will be introduced. Each provides a perspective which, if rigorously applied, will further our search for the normative "bottom line" of contextualization.

10

A Philosophical Perspective
Genres of Revelational Epistemology

The "Revelation" Behind the Contextualization

Whatever its definition, contextualization involves knowledge of both a message and an audience. To be more explicit, it involves understanding a message revealed by God in Holy Scripture and respondents who have an inadequate or distorted understanding of God's revelation. The contextualizer must take into account the nature of biblical revelation and also the nature of the scriptures of the various religious traditions. Eric J. Sharpe says that "since virtually all scripture is understood in revelatory terms . . . there must be some prior understanding of Hindu, Jewish, Christian, Muslim and other doctrines of God and doctrines of revelation."[1] Contextualizations (translation, explanation, and application) then should be faithful to the nature (and message) of biblical revelation, and yet correct the inadequacies and distortions connected with revelational understandings of other religious traditions.

In this chapter we will not focus so much on the biblical message itself as on the nature of biblical revelation. Also, we will not focus on

---

1. Eric J. Sharpe, *Fifty Key Words: Comparative Religion* (Richmond: John Knox, 1971), 64–65.

the distorted messages of other religious traditions so much as on the kind of revelation other traditions claim to possess. To be valid and authentic Christian contextualization must conform to the kind of revelation God—Father, Son, and Holy Spirit—and the Bible writers claim for the written Word. And to be effective Christian contextualization must correct any misunderstandings attached to the revelatory claims and products of other religions.

Generally speaking we can think of four very different kinds or genres of special, usually written, revelation: myths, the writings of the enlightened, divine writing, and inspired writings. Proponents of the various faiths invariably lay claim to one or another of these types of revelation in relation to their scriptures. More than that, when they undertake to communicate their faith to people of other traditions and cultures sheer logic demands that they "contextualize" their faith in a manner consistent with the kind of revelation they claim to possess. Insofar as their contextualization is consistent with that understanding it can lay claim to validity and will probably be compelling. Insofar as it is not consistent it lays itself open to criticism from within and without. For example, Buddhists who insist that this or that sutra is the "very word" of a certain deity make a claim that runs afoul of the historic Buddhist understanding of the nature of any and all scriptures. Shintoists who insist on Japanese supremacy on the basis of the historicity of the Yamato myth may persuade some, but they invite derision in the company of informed believers and unbelievers alike because informed Shintoists have not held that the significance of the Yamato tale rests upon its historicity. Of course, Christian contextualizations that betray Buddhist or Shintoist epistemic bases rather than the historic Christian basis or that are ambiguous as to the nature of the divine authority of Scripture should expect criticism for those reasons. It is to the explication and illustration of this important point that we dedicate this chapter. Contextualization must be consonant with the genre of the revelation it claims to possess and seeks to communicate to others.

Myth and Its Contextualization

Myth as a Genre of Special Revelation

We may think of myths as phantasmagoric narratives thought to convey basic information about god(s), the world, and men which bind a people together in a common origin, loyalty, and destiny. In modern as in ancient times, the origin and significance of mythical language have been viewed in different ways. Moderns generally divide into rationalists and intuitionalists as regards their views of myths. Rationalists—Benedict Spinoza, Thomas Hobbs, Carl Jung, Bennet Tyler, Andrew Lang, Robert R. Marett, James George Frazer, and others—have understood myths as erroneous interpretations of natural phenomena. Intuitionalists—Christian Heyne, Johann Herder, Ernst Cassirer and Friedrich Schelling—understand mythical language as growing out of inner states, a function of intuition. Herder also suggested that myths are created more by the genius of nations (*Volksgeist*) than by the genius of individuals, and this sociological interpretation was adopted by Francois Voltaire, Auguste Comte, and Emile Durkheim.

Whether myth is understood as the aberrant product of intellect or the creative product of intuition, myths do command the loyalty of individuals and societies. Moreover, to the people who hold to them, they usually represent something more than the product of mere intelligence or intuition. They represent the truth as revealed by god(s) or by revered ancestors who occupy a status that is almost divine. They may be handed down orally from generation to generation and never reduced to writing. Or they may be inscripturated at one point or over a period of time. Whatever their origin they come with the force of divine revelation.

A classic case of such a myth is that of the ancient Yamato people of Japan which became the basis of Shinto and ultimately of imperial Japan. To avoid being cut off from their roots by the incursion of foreign ideas and faiths (particularly the Buddhist faith) the ancient Japanese committed the Yamato myth to writing in the *Kojiki* and *Nihongi* (primarily) by the middle of the eighth century. For over a millennium and in spite of the vicissitudes and vagaries of Japanese history, this myth has provided the foundation for Japanese nationalism.

The *Kojiki* and *Nihongi* purport to be historical and to trace the origins of Japan and its people back to the gods. All reputable scholars recognize that these books present pseudohistory, and no conscientious person would seriously attempt to defend either the existence or character of the myth's numerous capricious and cavorting deities. Certainly these books do not constitute a basis for study or meditation for the overwhelming majority of the Japanese people. Nevertheless, the Shinto myth which they contain has conferred a divine authority on a sociopolitical system that still commands the total allegiance of millions of Japanese.

The Contextualization of the Shinto Myth

Within the genre of mythological scripture one is at a loss to find parameters which contextualization attempts could not legitimately cross. After all, though the myth may include some historical data, it characteristically will reach far beyond history into fantasy. While the myth may contain something of truth, characteristically it will mix truth and falsehood without providing criteria for distinguishing between them. Whatever claims may be made for a myth by the people who hold to it, the myth itself neither demands nor lends itself to the kind of critical analysis that leads unbiased minds to accept its genuineness and authenticity.

The only impingements that bear upon the contextualization of a myth, therefore, are brought to the myth by the preunderstanding, ethic, and imagination of the contextualizers themselves. The myth provides the raw materials for contextualization—the symbols, the *leitmotiv*, the *dramatis personae*—and, of course, these are somewhat limited in quantity and kind. But the only other limitations are those imposed by the contextualizers—what they can do with the given materials and what they will do with them. They will be praised or blamed largely on bases extrinsic to the myth itself.

As an illustration of non-Christian contextualization within this genre look again at the Japanese case. Many untutored Japanese have thought of their icons as *deities* while others have thought of them as *symbols* of the deities. Some have taken the myth of the *Kojiki* and *Nihongi* literally while others have taken it symbolically. The important thing is that at critical stages in the history of Japan the myth has been made to fit the particular mentality of the people and purposes of their leaders by well-constructed and effective presentations. We may confidently call this "Shinto contextualization."

The case with which most of us are best acquainted is the monumentally successful effort by the militaristic government of Japan in the 1930s and early 1940s to convince the Japanese people of the validity of this myth and its implications, namely, that their divinely ordained destiny was to share the beneficent rule of the *Tenno Heika* (Heavenly Emperor) with the rest of the world. There were two major aspects of that endeavor, persuasion and, if that failed, coercion. The fact that hundreds of thousands of Japanese willingly gave their lives, and millions of others stood ready to give their lives, attests to the effectiveness of the persuasion.

How did the militarists convince highly literate and intelligent Japanese of the validity of a fantastic myth such as that which unfolds in the *Kojiki* and *Nihongi?* Certainly they did not try to marshal evidence for the historicity of the text. Such an undertaking, if it betrayed any kind of objectivity at all, would have been met with opprobrium and opposition. Nor did they undertake a new translation designed to convey the meaning of the original texts with more accuracy and contemporaneity. Of course not. The ambiguity and inaccessibility of the language of the texts was an advantage to the contextualizers! No, let the texts be as products of their time and place. What then was the approach? As Daniel C. Holtom makes clear, the ancient texts simply provided the symbols out of which a very contemporary faith could be fashioned:

> [I]n order to understand modern Japan and her significant trends, we must deal first and foremost with a highly successful, rigorously centralized, religiously founded educational program whereby the national mentality is fixed in terms of forms that are governmentally expedient and necessary to military control. But these forms are not arbitrarily manufactured out of makeshift materials in the social and political life. They have come down out of an ancient past, they are erected on literary foundations that have the sanctity of holy scripture, and they survive as almost instinctive elements in the folkways. In all this we come to recognize that the center of that ethical certitude that stands so firmly in the midst of the storm of Far Eastern politics is lodged in the conviction of the possession as a race of unique divine attributes, of a peerless national structure, and of a sacred commission to save the world.[2]

Such "Shinto contextualization" *par excellence* was the case in the Japan of the 1930s and 1940s, and some would argue that it may yet be the case again in the future.

The Writings of the Enlightened and Their Contextualization

The Writings of the Enlightened as a Genre of Special Revelation

In original Buddhism, Lao-tze's Taoism, and Hinduism in its most widely-held understanding, we encounter a very different understanding. Hinduism, for example, is an inclusivistic religion that encompasses a wide variety of deities, sacred books, and religious expressions. If there are any basic epistemological commitments that run through this extensive divergency, they are (1) that knowledge of ultimate reality comes through the experience of *moksha* (enlightenment), and (2) that the highest written authority is that of the Vedic literature.

Hinduism admits to primary and secondary types of knowledge. Primary knowledge accrues to the enlightenment experience alone. All other knowledge, including the theological and the scientific, is secondary knowledge. The Hindu scriptures are also divided into two types: *shruti* ("that which is heard" or *revelation*), and *smriti* ("that which is remembered" or *tradition*). Strictly speaking, the Vedas alone come

---

2. Daniel C. Holtom, *Modern Japan and Shinto Nationalism* (Chicago: University of Chicago Press, 1943), 25.

into the *shruti* category, though brahmanical (priestly) and upanishadic (philosophical) appendages are usually included as a matter of course. *Smriti* literature is a voluminous and ever-expanding corpus.

Although the Vedas have always held a unique place in Hindu literature, there has been some disagreement as to how they are divinely authenticated. A minority believe that the Vedas were communicated directly by the great lord of the universe who, for this purpose, is considered to be personal. The majority recognize the need for some special authority, but they do not offer a historical frame of reference for the Vedas nor do they put forward objective proofs for the validity of the Vedic corpus.

Philosophically inclined Hindus have recognized the weakness of these positions and have realized that the authority of the Vedas requires some explanation. They sometimes think of eternal ideas of reality as resounding in the highest spheres of the universe. Highly spiritual, disciplined *rishis* (sages) of old were translated into these higher spheres where they could "hear" or directly intuit these truths. They then conveyed them to posterity in the words of the Vedas. *Shruti* knowledge depends on direct perception of the kind experienced by those unidentified *rishis* of long ago. With a greater or lesser degree of sophistication, this is the view that probably is held by the majority of Hindus.

For must Hindus primary knowledge is attainable only in the enlightenment experience. The experience itself being ineffable, any propositional report, no matter how genuine and authentic, comprises and conveys only secondary knowledge. The Vedas are accorded a special authority in this scheme of things because they report the experiences of the earliest *rishis* and therefore are the most normative. Nevertheless, even they can do no more than aid readers and hearers in the quest for experiential knowledge of the reality behind the phenomenal world.

The Contextualization of the Message of the Vedas (Upanishads)

Since the reports of enlightened persons are involved in the Vedic scripture, textual criticism is more important than with mythic literature, but not as important as in the two genres yet to be considered. If a given text purports to contain the teachings of the inspired seers who "experienced truth initially," it is to be expected that the reader will want to know whether it is the seer who spoke or wrote, and whether this is what he said or wrote.

However, one does not proceed very far in the study of scriptures of this type before he discovers that, though adherents do address themselves to authorship and textual questions, these questions are not essential. The overriding purpose of such writings is not so much to provide objective, authoritative knowledge as to assist the adept in attaining personal authoritative enlightenment experiences. In a very real sense, the validity of the text, therefore, depends more upon its utility, effect, and impact than upon its genuineness. Indeed, to place too much confidence in the words of the enlightened betrays one's ignorance of the true source of knowledge.

Contextualizers of writings of this sort, therefore, may and do exercise a considerable freedom in both translation and interpretation of the text. Form is not crucial. The purpose and the proof of the contextualized pudding are to be found in the eating of it. Indeed, the revelatory corpus is neither final nor closed. Having experienced enlightenment, the contextualizer may translate and interpret the text in the light of the impact the text had on his own experience and may have on his hearers or readers.

Swami Prabhavananda and Frederick Manchester offer an introduction to and translation of certain Upanishads for Westerners. In the introduction they point out the importance of the Vedas: "All orthodox Hindus recognize in them the origin of their faith and its highest written authority."[3] Then they explain that there are four Vedas, each of which is divided into two parts: work and knowledge. Work is mainly made up of hymns, instructions regarding rites and ceremonies, and rules of conduct. Knowledge is concerned with God and religious truth.[4]

> We have said that the orthodox Hindu regards the Vedas as his highest written authority. Any subsequent scripture, if he is to regard it as valid, must be in agreement with them: it may expand upon them; it may develop them, and still be recognized, but it must not contradict them. They are to him, as nearly as any document can be, the expression of divine truth. At the same time it would be a mistake to suppose that his allegiance to their authority is slavish or blind. If he considers them the word of God, it is because he believes their truth to be verifiable, immediately, at any moment, in his own personal experience. If he found on due examination that it was not so verifiable, he would reject it. And in this position the scriptures, he will tell you, uphold him. The real study, say the Upanishads, is not study of themselves but study of that "by which we realize the changeless." In other words, the real study in religion is firsthand experience of God.[5]

3. Swami Prabhavananda and Frederick Manchester, *The Upanishads: Breath of the Eternal* (New York: New American Library, 1957), ix.

4. Ibid.

5. Ibid., xi–xii.

Prabhavananda and Manchester approach this task of translation in a manner entirely consistent with this epistemic preunderstanding. They "allow themselves the freedom" as "seems desirable" to convey the "sense and spirit" of the original in English. Though the original Sanskrit is verse, they render it in prose except in some special instances where they use a "form which is not verse perhaps, save by courtesy, but which has seemed to us to produce a heightened effect not readily attained to prose."[6] This approach, we maintain, is not only permissible but commendable within this genre. The form is relatively unimportant. The sense and spirit are very important because the effect and impact in the experience of the reader are all-important.

Divine Writing and Its Contextualization

Divine Writing as a Genre of Special Revelation

Orthodox Muslims recognize two types of inspiration—*ilham* or lower-level inspiration and *wahy* or higher-level inspiration.[7] It is widely believed that the *ilham* may be experienced by holy men as well as prophets. It is a gift of Allah which accords knowledge to men, but it is subjective and cannot be trusted fully.

Wahy, on the other hand, confers knowledge that is objective and fully trustworthy. It comes directly from Allah through true prophets. The inspired messages of prophets antedating Muhammad in this category were corrupted. Therefore, the Koran alone qualifies today as being the product of *wahy* inspiration and as possessing infallible authority. W. Montgomery Watt says that the absolutely essential features of Muhammad's *wahy* experience are "the words in his conscious mind; the absence of his own thinking; and the belief that the words were from God."[8]

Orthodox Muslims consider the Koran to be a partial reproduction of an eternal original called the "Well-Preserved Tablet" or "Mother of the Book" which is in heaven. The reverence that Muslims entertain for the prophet Muhammad is not simply attributable to Muhammad's personality, character, or gifts, though they value all of these. The unprecedented importance of Muhammad rests in faith that Allah delivered his message to Muhammad by an angelic messenger (usually

6. Ibid.

7. H. A. R. Gibb and Johannes H. Kramers, *Shorter Encyclopedia of Islam* (Ithaca, N.Y.: Cornell University Press, 1965), 163, 622–24.

8. W. Montgomery Watt, *Islamic Revelation in the Modern World* (Edinburgh: University Press, 1969), 69–70.

said to have been Gabriel) over a period after his prophetic call.[9] Allah had spoken through a number of prophets, but in revealing his word to Muhammad he gave his final word. Note that it was Allah's word; Muhammad was a passive receptor or recorder. His mind, his heart, his feelings—none of these entered into the recording of the words of the Koran. It is the eternal, uncreated word of Allah which has existed through all time as an expression of his will. Furthermore, in view of the distortions which had overtaken his previous revelations Allah undertook to insure this final revelation against distortion for all time to come.

This understanding lies at the heart of the Muslim attitude toward the Koranic scripture. First, the Koran is the undisputed supreme authority in Muslim law and theology, faith, and practice. Second, it is on the heart, mind, and tongue of millions of Muslims who have memorized it, at least in part. Third, the Koran has traditionally been held to be untranslatable—the Arabic words being the words of heaven and therefore divine in their sound and rhythm.

The Contextualization of the Koran

Islamic contextualizers are confronted with a unique set of problems. What does one do—what *can* one do—with a book that is "made in heaven" and admits of no human element whatsoever? A book written, so to speak, in the "language of God"? Consistency here demands that the book be delivered, interpreted, preached, taught, and memorized—but not translated. The traditional position of Islam is that the Koran translated into another language is not really the Koran. In a sense all inquirers into the faith must themselves become contextualizers. They must learn the Arabic language and culture. As Islam has come to rely less on power and more on persuasion to propagate the faith, practicality has demanded translations. Nevertheless, translators sympathetic to Islam reflect a loyalty to the Arabic text that is unmistakably characteristic of the genre.

A. J. Arberry, who has provided us with one of the most widely used of these translations, writes as though he possessed an inner compulsion to bring the Koran and its message to his English-speaking contemporaries. He concedes that the Koran is untranslatable. Granting "the rhetoric and rhythm of the Arabic," he says, "any version is bound to be a poor copy of the glittering splendour of the original."[10] The chief reason he gives for attempting a translation is that no "serious attempt has previously been made to imitate, however imperfectly, those rhe-

9. Samuel Zwemer, *The Heirs of the Prophets* (Chicago: Moody, 1946), 17–25.
10. A. J. Arberry, *The Koran Interpreted* (New York: Macmillan, 1955), 24.

torical and rhythmical patterns which are the glory and sublimity of the Koran."[11] Though a self-confessed "infidel" at the time of translation, Arberry exudes a disciple's passion and a missionary zeal when he explains what he has set out to accomplish:

> There is a repertory of familiar themes running through the whole Koran; each Sura elaborates or adumbrates one or more—often many—of these. Using the language of music, each Sura is a rhapsody composed of whole or fragmentary *leitmotivs*; the analogy is reinforced by the subtly varied rhythmical flow of the discourse. If this diagnosis of the literary structure of the Koran may be accepted as true—and it accords with what we know of the poetical instinct, indeed the whole aesthetic impulse, of the Arabs—it follows that those "wearisome repetitions," which have proved such stumbling-blocks in the way of our Western appreciation will vanish in the light of a clearer understanding of the nature of the Muslim scriptures. A new vista opens up; following this hitherto unsuspected and unexplored path, the eager interpreter hurries forward upon an exciting journey of discovery, and is impatient to report his findings to a largely indifferent and incredulous public.[12]

All of this accords well with what we know about the people, religion, and language of Arabia in Muhammad's day. In pre-Islamic Arabia, the *kahin* (priest) regularly gave oracles in rhythmic prose that were similar in form and content to the Koran, especially to its earlier suras. The form of Muhammad's pronouncements, therefore, was of special significance to his earliest hearers and has remained so to the faithful of the present day.[13]

Wilfred Cantwell Smith's assessment is that Arberry's work is "certainly [the] most beautiful English version, and among those by non-Muslim translators the one that comes closest to conveying the impression made on Muslims by the original."[14] It is significant that Arberry has accomplished this by giving close attention to the literary form of the Koran, and that he is content to call his work an "interpretation" rather than a translation.

---

11. Ibid., 25.
12. Ibid., 28.
13. Zwemer, *The Heirs of the Prophets*, 19–25.
14. Arberry, *The Koran Interpreted*, cover.

Inspired Writings and Their Contextualization

Inspired Writings as a Genre of Special Revelation

Christians characteristically speak of the Old and New Testament Scriptures as constituting the "inspired Word of God." This grows out of the King James rendering of *theopneustos* in 2 Timothy 3:16. As B. B. Warfield noted a number of years ago, the word really means "breathed out by God."[15] In context the reference is specifically to the written word of the Old Testament, but by extension it is applied to the New Testament as well.

As Warfield was careful to point out (with special reference to the New Testament authors), inspiration in this sense does not refer to the psychological or even the spiritual state of the human writers as such; rather it refers to the activity of God whereby he "breathed out" his Word through the Bible authors. In this process God did not discount the personality, background, experience, or research of the authors. Nevertheless, all of these human elements were divinely employed in such a way that the product is more than the word of the author. The author's words are, in a more profound sense, the Word of God. This claim is everywhere made in Scripture and is made most incontrovertibly and arrestingly by our Lord himself. What Scripture says, God says. When men hear the words of Scripture they hear the Word of God. Of course, a further work of the Holy Spirit is necessary for them to perceive and receive it as the Word of God. The Westminster Shorter Catechism (31) refers to this as effectual calling. Nevertheless, the Bible does not become the Word of God when hearers are called; it became the Word of God when its authors were inspired to write it.

We insist that this is the traditional and orthodox understanding of biblical revelation. A recent attempt to identify it as an invention of post-Reformation European theologians and nineteenth-century Princetonians[16] has been demonstrated to be untenable.[17]

The Contextualization of the Bible and Its Message

From both logical and practical viewpoints it would seem obvious that the genre or nature of the canonical Scriptures as inspired writings

15. B. B. Warfield, *The Inspiration and Authority of the Bible* (London: Marshall, Morgan, and Scott, 1951), 245.

16. See Jack B. Rogers and Donald K. McKim, *The Authority and Interpretation of the Bible: An Historical Approach* (San Francisco: Harper and Row, 1979).

17. John D. Woodbridge, "Biblical Authority: Towards an Evaluation of the Rogers and McKim Proposal," *Trinity Journal* 1 (Fall 1980): 165–236. Woodbridge specifically answers the charge of Rogers and McKim and demonstrates that a more careful reading of the sources they themselves cite undermines their position.

takes precedence over its message. In the final analysis the answers to such questions as "What is the nature of the authority of the Bible?" "Does the Bible (in its original autographs) contain errors?" and "Is the Bible truth-oriented or task-oriented?" are logically prior to questions having to do with the biblical message. Our answers to these questions will go a long way toward determining how we translate, interpret, and contextualize the Bible.

To illustrate the contextualization of genres of special revelation in non-Christian traditions we chose examples that were logically consistent with these genres. But if we return to the examples of Christian contextualization overviewed in part 2 of this book, it becomes apparent that not all of them are consonant with the view of the Bible as inspired writings which has been the understanding of historic Christianity. Some contextualizers we have considered make their position on Bible revelation clear; others do not. Some contextualizations clearly fit into one or another genre of revelation; others fall somewhere in between them. Furthermore, an orthodox view of the Bible does not always yield an orthodox contextualization, nor does a suborthodox view of the Bible always yield suborthodox contextualizations. Many other factors are involved. We believe, however, that contextualizations (and translations and interpretations) that grow out of a view of Scripture in accord with the revelational epistemology of Shintoism, Hinduism, Islam, or some faith other than historic Christianity may well be suborthodox. In any case, they will have sacrificed biblical authority by defining that authority in terms more suitable to the Kojiki, the Upanishads, the Koran, or some other understanding of revelation. This is always dangerous and can be disastrous.

It is incumbent upon us to give due consideration to the way in which those who translate and interpret the biblical text and those who communicate its message view its nature and authority. When they are explicit in stating their view this is not difficult. When they are not the task becomes more difficult and tenuous but no less important. Let us see how this is so.

Relating Contextualizations to Revelational Epistemology and the Authority of the Bible

Let us examine some proposals relating to contextualization in this light. In doing so, we will make primary reference to some of the scholars whose proposals were outlined in part 2 and to Rudolf Bultmann and Edward F. Hills among the many whom we were forced to overlook there.

The Bible as Myth

Contextualizations growing out of a belief that the Bible is basically mythological usually display a profound respect for biblical symbols, motifs, stories, and parables while downplaying biblical history (qua history) and authority. Extrabiblical history and culture assume unusual importance in this view. Gustavo Gutiérrez, for example, explicitly espouses an epistemology which takes as its starting point participation in the contemporary struggle for justice. The reader will discover more than four hundred references to the Bible in his *Liberation Theology* but minimal attention to the biblical text and content. Again, though M. M. Thomas might be expected to treat the Bible as "writings of the enlightened" in accord with a Hindu view of the Vedas, he actually seems to have imbibed so much of Western theology that he comes closer to the-Bible-as-myth epistemology. That posture enables him to "read" the history of India with extreme seriousness and propose, not a biblical Christ, but a syncretized Christ.

Whether Gutiérrez and Thomas would actually say that the Bible is myth is not clear. That theologians such as Bultmann and Paul Tillich do is clear in their writings. For Bultmann the theologian's task is to make the Bible believable and meaningful to modern man, and modern man cannot be expected to respond as people did in prescientific times. Bultmann calls for demythologization which, he says, "is to reject not scripture . . . but the worldview of a past epoch."[18] He goes on to say that demythologization eliminates "a false stumbling-block and brings into focus the real stumbling-block, the word of the cross." In effect, Bultmann was a precontextualization contextualizer in the sense that he adapted the Christian message to moderns before the word *contextualization* was even coined. But in doing so he parted company with orthodoxy.

If the Bible is myth, or a combination of myth and cultural history with insufficient criteria to distinguish the two, almost any contextualization is allowable. This is so because, as almost any historian worth the name will admit, there are many ways to read history. That Christian contextualizations of this variety may prove to be as appealing and deceptive as the Shinto contextualizations of Japanese chauvinists a generation ago should give pause to all of us.

The Bible as Writings of the Enlightened

Inasmuch as Kosuke Koyama approaches the theological task as one of interpreting history in the light of the Word of God, it seems he is

18. Rudolf Bultmann, *Jesus Christ and Mythology* (London: SCM, 1960), 35–36, quoted in Anthony Thiselton, *The Two Horizons: New Testament Hermeneutics and Philosophical Description* (Grand Rapids: Eerdmans, 1980), 258–59.

epistemologically close to Gutiérrez and Thomas. The difference is that Koyama seems to take the phrase *in the light of the Word of God* much more seriously. He wrestles with the text. At the same time he searches for religious and cultural materials at hand that will make the text come alive, allowing it to speak to persons in their existential situation. The results are either happy or unhappy, depending upon where one sits.

Charles H. Kraft makes his view of the Bible explicit. Kraft is a firm believer in the apostolic faith. He believes that the Bible has "supracultural truths floating around in it." He is convinced that the prophets and apostles had genuine encounters with God. He agrees that the Bible is without error as concerns its intended teachings. But there is much more to the Bible than a message. There is also a method. The Bible is a casebook. What happened to the prophets, apostles, and others in Bible times must happen today. The Bible is only potentially revelation. Revelation is not objective and closed; it is subjective and continuing. Understood and used correctly, the Bible can provide the stimuli necessary for revelation to occur today. The anthropologist is bicultural and so is better equipped than the grammarian or historian to aid us in ethnolinguistic interpretation and application of the Bible.

Now if this sounds similar to the Hindu approach to the Vedas (including the Upanishads), that is understandable. The two epistemologies are so similar that it is scary. The frightening element is not so much where Kraft's approach takes his conclusions (though his conclusions give us considerable pause). More frightening is where his view of Scripture may lead others. Also, on a cognitive plane at least, Kraft leaves the proponent of Christianity all but defenseless in the encounter with adherents of Hinduism, Buddhism, Taoism, and similar traditions.

The Bible as Divine Writing

Readers may wonder who among Christian scholars would look upon the Bible as Muslims look upon the Koran. No one that we considered in part 2 is even close to this position. However, conservative evangelicals are often accused of holding a position akin to that of Islam. Their more liberal protagonists sometimes take delight in building a conservative straw man who holds to "mechanical dictation" and thinks of the Bible writers as automatons who held the brush while God somehow moved the hand.

One answer to this false depiction is that it accords well with the Muslim's view of the Koran but hardly describes the orthodox view of the Bible. At the same time we should recognize that there are ultraconservative Christians such as Wilbur N. Pickering and Edward F. Hills whose views come perilously close to the view of Islam.[19] Hills, for example, accepts Warfield's understanding of inspiration, but goes on to propound an "inferred doctrine" of providential preservation. According to this doctrine, God chose the Greek church to preserve a pure text (the Byzantine text) which became the basis of the Textus Receptus and then the King James Version of the Bible. Therefore to supplement the King James Version is acceptable but to substitute for it is "to fly in the face of God's providence."[20] It is superior to all other versions in that it is the historic Bible of English-speaking Protestants. "Its majestic rhythms easily lend themselves to memorization"—a use to which modern translations do not lend themselves.[21] Some expressions may be modernized and certain renderings bettered, but changes should be minimal and introduced only with great care, "in order that the matchless beauty of this great piece of classic English prose may in no wise be impaired. Thus slightly revised, the King James Version will doubtless continue for another three hundred and fifty years (if the Lord tarry so long) to preserve for faithful readers the true New Testament text undamaged by the ravages of naturalistic New Testament criticism."[22]

For all of Hill's good and understandable intentions, it is apparent that this position goes well beyond the requirements of Scripture and historic Christianity that it makes the historic view extremely vulnerable to criticism from within and without the Christian tradition, that it renders most, if not all, contextualizations suspect, and that for missionary translators it poses problems similar to those that have plagued Muslims for centuries.

The Bible as Inspired Writings

Among contextualizers we have considered those who most explicitly espouse the historic understanding of the Bible are Bruce J. Nicholls and Byang H. Kato. Were Tim Matheny to spell out his understanding his position would seem to be within this rubric. Perhaps he is somewhat vague because of the Muslim understanding of Jews and Christians as also being "people of the Book." It is important to note that in spite of Matheny's dependence upon the contributions of social science (e.g., innovation theory and felt needs), he presses beyond these

19. See Wilber N. Pickering, *The Identity of the New Testament Text* (Nashville: Thomas Nelson, 1977); Edward F. Hills, *The King James Version Defended* (Des Moines: Christian Research, 1956).

20. Hills, *The King James Version Defended*, 142.

21. Ibid.

22. Ibid., 142–43.

to emphasize ultimate needs, conversion, and Bible instruction. Nor does he treat Christian forms such as baptism and the Lord's Supper in a cavalier fashion. But perhaps the clearest indication of his commitment to Scripture is his insistence that Christian contextualizations for Muslims retain what can be biblically supported and reject what is contrary to biblical principles.

A fundamental question with respect to human knowledge is how we know what we claim to know. This is no less true with knowledge about God and divine truth than it is with knowledge about the world in which we live—and certainly no less important!

The major religions of the world lay claim to scriptures which adherents believe contain truth about God (or gods) and the world. When categorized by the kind of revealed truth these various scriptures are thought to contain, at least four major genres of scripture are discoverable. These "revelational types" mightily affect the kind of translation, interpretation, and communication that can be undertaken because of the logical connection between the type and the way the text is perceived and treated.

Lying beneath every contextualization attempt that purports to be Christian, then, is a revelational epistemology that either explicitly or implicitly allows for it. If the Christian contextualizer consciously or unconsciously shifts ground and builds on a view of Scripture and theological knowledge that accords better with one or another of the non-Christian views, he not only sacrifices the uniqueness of the Bible but also finds himself standing on the shaken epistemological foundations of other faiths.

11

A Theological Perspective
The Contextualization Continuum

Theological Perspectives and Contextualization Outcomes

The concept of contextualization was neither conceived nor developed *ex nihilo*. Its initiators were expert theologians and experienced churchmen. They brought existing theological perspectives to their discussions and formed contextualization meanings and methods out of them. The same could be said for other contextualization endeavors. All of these endeavors have grown out of existing theological bents and matrices which have in large measure determined the results. It is essential, therefore, that in analyzing the contextualization attempts of others or in attempting our own we are sensitive to the theological soil which nurtures and sustains them. After all, we are members of the body of Christ, a body which includes great minds and hearts that have wrestled with theological issues down through the centuries. To disregard that which they have bequeathed to us is to dishonor the Head of the church whose special gifts they were and are. Of course, there also have been false teachers whose aberrations have been rejected as unchristian and heretical. An awareness of the intimate relationship that exists between orthodox and suborthodox theological models and current contextualization meanings and methods will go a long way toward dispelling the confusion that so often attends contextualization discussions and endeavors.

When we proceed in this way we again are brought face to face with the critical nature of biblical authority. The foundations of major theological orientations are identifiable by the ways in which their proponents view the Bible and handle the biblical materials. We are justified in locating them on a continuum which, in effect, indicates the relative weight they ascribe to supracultural and to cultural and human factors in the production, preservation, and interpretation of the biblical text. But if this is the root of theological differences we should not lose sight of the fact that different roots yield different fruit. Representing opposite ends of the continuum, orthodoxy and liberalism give rise to divergent Christologies, soteriologies, and eschatologies. Not only that; the varied roots bear varied meanings and methods of contextualization and, therefore, divergent *contextualized* Christologies, soteriologies, and eschatologies. In this chapter we explore some of these divergences.

Matrices of Contextualization

Four profoundly different and universally recognized theological orientations—orthodoxy, liberalism, neo-orthodoxy, and neoliberalism—tend to yield very different contextualizations. Let us look at these in some detail.

Orthodoxy

To many if not most Christians, their own view is orthodox while any competing one is heterodox. But a strong case can be made for saying that there is one basic theological orientation that can correctly be thought of as both biblical and orthodox. It is biblical because, as Carl F. H. Henry says, "the O.T. prophets consistently speak of their words as the words of God. . . . The N.T. apostles, moreover, speak of divine revelation in the form of definite ideas and words. . . . The Bible nowhere protests against the identification of Scripture with revelation, but rather supports and approves this identification."[1] It is orthodox because, as Henry goes on to say, the historic Christian view is that the Bible itself is a form of revelation specially provided for man in sin as an authentic disclosure of the nature and will of God."[2]

As a result of this commitment, orthodoxy has embraced Christian doctrines (e.g., the virgin birth, the bodily resurrection of Christ) that

---

1. Carl F. H. Henry, "Revelation, Special," in *Baker's Dictionary of Theology*, ed. Everett F. Harrison (Grand Rapids: Baker, 1960), 458–59.
2. Ibid., 459.

are biblical but which cannot be explained on naturalistic or rationalistic grounds. More than that, orthodoxy has held to doctrines such as the lostness of man, the blood atonement, and conscious punishment of unbelievers that run contrary to human sentiment. Adherence to doctrines such as these is often attributed to obscurantism or callousness, but it should not be. They are enjoined by Scripture and discoverable in the historic creeds of the Christian church.

Liberalism

Bernard Ramm writes that religious liberalism (classical, traditional liberalism) had a "fourfold rootage":

> First, philosophically it was grounded in some form of German philosophical idealism (e.g., Schleiermacher in Romanticism; Ritschl in neo-Kantianism; Biedermann in Hegelianism). Secondly, it placed unreserved trust in the new critical studies of the Scriptures which contained implicitly or explicitly a denial of the historic doctrines of revelation and inspiration. Thirdly, it believed that the developing science of the times antiquated much of the Scriptures. Fourthly, it was rooted in the new learning and believed in a harmony of Christianity with the new learning. In this sense it is modernistic (preference for the new over the traditional) and liberal (the right of free criticism of all theological claims).[3]

Religious liberalism is usually thought to have begun with Friedrich Schleiermacher's *Über die Religion: Reden an die Gebildeten unter ihren Verächtern* (1799) and to have ended with Karl Barth's *Römerbrief* (1919). In some forms it is still very much with us, however. As Ramm goes on to explain, the method of religious liberalism is to accept a current philosophy as a conceptual framework out of which a doctrine of religious experience is developed. It then proceeds to interpret this philosophy and experience in Christian terms, and alter Christianity to suit this philosophy and doctrine of religious experience.

Ramm offers a corollary of this orientation, "in that the radical division of saved-or-lost was denied, and all men held to possess the same religious potentiality, all men formed the so-called brotherhood of man whose corollary was the Fatherhood of God."[4] Liberalism, therefore, tends to accept all sincere strivings after, and expressions of, truth as having validity. None has final validity, however. Therefore Christian doctrine is constantly being reshaped according to contemporary human understandings and cultural preferences.

3. Bernard Ramm, "Liberalism," in *Baker's Dictionary of Theology*, ed. Harrison, 322.

4. Ibid.

Neo-orthodoxy

Neo-orthodoxy became prominent in the United States after 1930 and owes a signal debt to Søren Kierkegaard and Karl Barth. It is orthodox in the sense that it returned to some of the primary themes of the Reformation such as the depravity of man and the need for grace and pardon. It is new because, in contrast to liberalism, it does not assume the continuity between the divine and the human and does not regard the Bible simply as great literature. It is also new because, in contrast to orthodoxy, it concludes that though the Bible is unique, it is also human and therefore contains the Word of God in imperfect form. For this reason, neo-orthodoxy employs the methods of higher criticism in biblical interpretation and doctrinal formulation, usually without apology.[5]

Neoliberalism

The views of men such as Walter Marshall Horton and G. Bromley Oxnam fall somewhere between neo-orthodoxy and classical liberalism. Horton holds "that the new liberalism will give a central place to biblical revelation. It will not try to confine the understanding of God to a closed rational system but will, however, continue to maintain a place for reason as a most necessary check to any fanatical dogmatic religious revelation."[6]

Oxnam's view illustrates this formulation. He acknowledges that God has revealed himself through the centuries but emphasizes that human limitations played a decisive role in that process:

> The revelation was conditioned by their [human beings'] ability to understand, and their reports of the limitations that current events, current thought, and current practice evoke. Take the cosmology accepted by the Old Testament writers, for instance; or the belief in demons; or Paul's attitude toward women. To hold that Paul's advice on women is truth revealed by God and binding upon all is as sorry as to hold that God commanded the Jews to commit atrocities on their enemies in war. Nonetheless, truth is revealed.[7]

Horton and Oxnam tend to take biblical revelation more seriously and to assess culture more critically than did the proponents of classical liberalism. But it is somehow left up to perceptive Christians to enter the struggling world and read the Bible in such a way as to hear

5. "Neo-orthodoxy," in *Corpus Dictionary of Western Churches*, ed. T. C. O'Brien (Washington, D.C.: Corpus, 1970), 531–32; Paul K. Jewett, "Neo-orthodoxy," *Baker's Dictionary of Theology*, ed. Harrison, 375–79.

6. Cited in Robert P. Lightner, *Neo-liberalism* (Chicago: Regular Baptist, 1959), 43.

7. G. Bromley Oxnam, *A Testament of Faith* (Boston: Little, Brown, 1958).

Figure 10
The Contextualization Continuum (a)

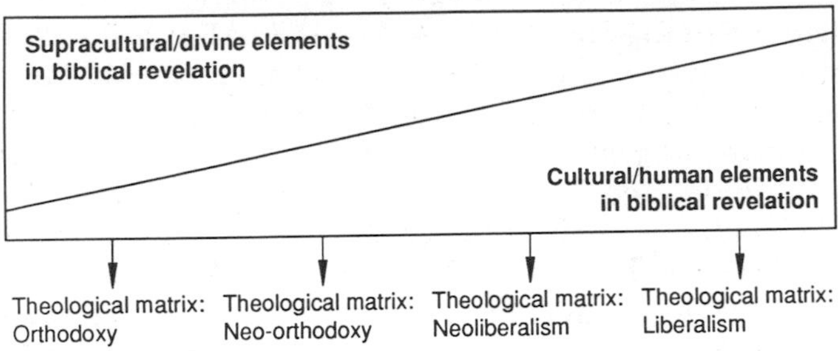

and see that which other men may not hear and see, the *contemporary* word and work of God. The underpinnings of such an approach are existentialist or rationalist or perhaps a hybrid of the two.

Three conclusions are obvious when these theological orientations become bases of theology and theologizing. First, both supracultural/divine elements and cultural/human elements are somehow involved in all four orientations. Second, the proportionate weights given to these elements vary greatly. Third, though both divine and human elements are always recognized, the closer one gets to classical orthodoxy the greater the weight given to the biblical revelation, and the closer one gets to classical liberalism the greater the weight given to human reason and culture (see fig. 10).

Meanings of Contextualization

The importance of context to meaning has been emphasized by communicologists for a long time. The phrases *he stole first, we wuz robbed,* and *murder the guy in blue* mean something altogether different in a baseball park than they do in a local bank.

The relation of the theological matrices of contextualization to the meanings ascribed to contextualization is equally important. Reflect on some of the definitions of contextualization that have been surveyed in previous chapters. Why are they so different? One reason is that they are rooted in disparate theological orientations. The more liberal theologies allow for greater concessions to the contemporary context. The more conservative and orthodox theologies are more restrictive in this regard. Some contextualizations, therefore, result in the formation of a "new gospel." Others enhance the communication of the "old gospel." This needs to be demonstrated.

Apostolic Contextualization

One understanding of contextualization is reflected in the definitions offered by Bruce J. Nicholls and George W. Peters (among others). One of Nicholls's definitions for contextualization is "the translation of the unchanging content of the Gospel of the Kingdom into verbal form meaningful to the peoples in their separate cultures and within their particular existential situation."[8] Peters's definition is similar but more restrictive: "Contextualization properly applied means to discover the *legitimate implications* of the Gospel in a given situation. It goes deeper than application. Application I can make or need not without doing injustice to the text. Implication is *demanded* by a proper exegesis of the text."[9]

It is apparent that these scholars and many others of similar conviction emphasize the supracultural nature of the biblical gospel. They recognize that the biblical revelation is not acultural. It was given to and through prophets and apostles from Joel to John—men who received and reported the divine message in linguistic and cultural frames of reference. But they believe that the sovereign God ordered the cultural circumstances, the prophetic and apostolic authors, and the linguistic forms in such a way that in both the revelation and the inscripturation *his message* was transmitted. The biblical message, therefore, is unique. The impingements of circumscribed cultures, imperfect authors, and human languages are transcended in such a way as to provide a perfect gospel. Having endorsed the word of the prophets and having ensured the word of the apostles, our Lord gave the Great Commission to "make disciples of all nations . . . teaching them to obey everything I have commanded you" (Matt. 28:16–20).

For the sake of brevity and convenience we will say that Nicholls and Peters are representative of a class of theorists who espouse apostolic contextualization. Their emphasis is on taking the apostolic faith "once for all entrusted to the saints" (Jude 3) and contextualizing (translating, interpreting, adapting, applying) that faith (body of truth) to the people of a respondent culture in such a way as to preserve as much of its original meaning and relevance as possible.

---

8. Bruce J. Nicholls, "Theological Education and Evangelization," in *Let the Earth Hear His Voice*, ed. J. D. Douglas (Minneapolis: World Wide, 1975), 647.

9. George W. Peters, "Issues Confronting Evangelical Missions," *Evangelical Missions Tomorrow*, ed. Wade T. Coggins and Edwin L. Frizen, Jr. (Pasadena, Calif.: William Carey Library, 1977), 169.

Prophetic Contextualization

The definitions proposed by the members of the TEF committee are different. Recall Shoki Coe's definition:

> In using the word *contextualization*, we try to convey all that is implied in the familiar term *indigenization*, yet seek to press beyond for a more dynamic concept which is open to change and which is also future-oriented.
>
> Contextuality . . . is that critical assessment of what makes the context really significant in the light of the *Missio Dei*. It is the missiological discernment of the signs of the times, seeing where God is at work and calling us to participate in it. . . . Authentic contextuality leads to contextualization. . . . This dialectic between contextuality and contextualization indicates a new way of theologizing. It involves not only words, but actions.[10]

This definition is clear and forthright. The primary emphasis here is on the "prophetic" insight of the contextualizer and the cultural, political, and other circumstances in which he finds himself. Contextualization entails entering a cultural context, discerning what God is doing and saying in that context, and speaking and working for needed change. In short, it is prophetic contextualization. The mission of the Old Testament prophets and the prophetic mission of Christ become models for perceptive men and women of mission today.

There are neoliberal and neo-orthodox versions of this approach. The neoliberal tends to put less emphasis on Scripture and more emphasis on the insights gained by participation in the struggles of the marketplace, as does Gustavo Gutiérrez. The neo-orthodox tends to put more emphasis on the insights gained from reflection on Scripture and history. Kosuke Koyama is representative when he says. "Theology is reflection. It is an intelligent reflection inspired by the Holy Spirit of God. . . . Reflection on what? *History in the light of the Word of God*" [italics added].[11]

Syncretistic Contextualization

Finally, there is the kind of contextualization advocated by M. M. Thomas, John Hick, Wilfred Cantwell Smith, and others. Concerning a meeting of representatives of various major religions in which participants not only discussed religious teachings but also worshiped to-

---

10. Shoki Coe, "Contextualizing Theology," *Mission Trends No. 3*, ed. Gerald H. Anderson and Thomas F. Stransky (Grand Rapids: Eerdmans; New York: Paulist, 1976), 21–22.
11. Kosuke Koyama, *Waterbuffalo Theology* (Maryknoll, N.Y.: Orbis, 1974), 106–7.

Figure 11
The Contextualization Continuum (b)

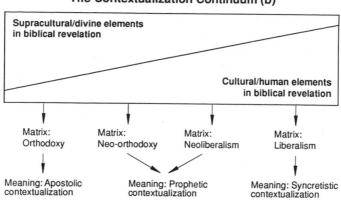

gether, Hick writes, "We live amidst unfinished business; but we must trust that continuing dialogue will prove to be dialogue into truth, and that in a fuller grasp of truth our present conflicting doctrines will ultimately be transcended."[12]

If Hick's quotation is understood in the light of all that precedes it, his meaning is clear enough. He and those of like mind seek to accommodate various cultures, religions, and ideologies by selecting the best insights of all of them and evolving a faith that goes beyond any one of them. Though Hick does not use the term *contextualization* as such and though the method he describes is open dialogue, it seems obvious that he has in mind something similar to what Thomas calls *Christ-centered syncretism*. Classical liberalism not only allows for this; it encourages it.

We can now enlarge our contextualization continuum to include the definitions that emanate from these varied theological orientations (see fig. 11).

Methods of Contextualization

Are the foregoing distinctions merely semantic in the less intensive meaning of the word, or do they represent significant differences in methods and results? We have already intimated that they do. Let us see how that is so by examining liberal, neoliberal, neo-orthodox, and orthodox methods of contextualization.

12. John Hick, "Dialogue into Truth," in *Truth and Dialogue in World Religions: Conflicting Truth Claims* (Philadelphia: Westminster, 1974), 155.

The Liberal Dialogical Method—Pursuing Truth

In March of 1970 the World Council of Churches sponsored a consultation in Ajaltoun, Lebanon. Called a "Dialogue Between Men of Living Faiths," the consultation assembled Christians, Buddhists, Hindus, and Muslims for ten days of conversations. The program included opportunities for joint voluntary worship within the general theme "The Meaning and Practice of Spirituality." Papers were read and discussions were held on significant themes. Meetings were scheduled for Hindu-Christian, Buddhist-Christian, and Muslim-Christian groups. The final two days were spent in unstructured meetings during which the participants discussed ways to bring to bear the perspectives of living faiths on world issues, the lessons learned at Ajaltoun, and the future possibilities for dialogue.

One of the personal reflections offered by a participant at the close of the consultation considered its results:

> The dialogue, functioning as an internal sign of hope, introduced most of us to a new spirituality, an interfaith spirituality, which I mostly felt in common prayer: who actually led the prayer or meditation, a Christian or a Muslim, or a Hindu, or a Buddhist, did not much matter, what actually was said during prayer was not all important, whether a Muslim would say "amen" after a Christian prayer mentioning sonship of Christ, was not the question, what we really became aware of was our common human situation before God and in God.
>
> We were thus led gradually into a new relation with God, with our own selves, and with others, and this new relation was perhaps to what entire human history was moving. . . . Our dialogue was therefore not an end but a beginning, only a step, there is a long way to go.[13]

Notice such phrases as "a new . . . interfaith spirituality," "a new relation with God," and "our dialogue was . . . but a beginning." We have witnessed the beginnings of this approach to contextualization and, quite likely, a new rapprochement between various religions. This is in line with a subsequent WCC conference in Yaoundé, Cameroon, which concluded:

> Elements of the Christian "story" such as the deutero-Pauline idea of the "cosmic Christ" (Col. 1:15–20) could provide a basis for reformulating the doctrine of salvation in such a way that this category, which is common to all religions, could provide the missing link between the many

13. Stanley J. Samartha, "Dialogue Between Men of Living Faiths, the Ajaltoun Memorandum," in *Dialogue Between Men of Living Faiths*, ed. Stanley J. Samartha (Geneva: World Council of Churches, 1971), 114.

"stories" of the peoples, whether they be told as African myths or Indian Philosophies, and the one gracious revelation of the only God. In Africa, we are told, he was already recognized before the missionaries came, and was already given many names.[14]

These words are certainly reminiscent of (in fact, may have been informed by) the contextualized theologies of Thomas and John S. Mbiti who, as we have seen, speak in almost identical terms. Perhaps even more extreme in his liberal view is a Methodist minister from Sri Lanka who says that we have sinned in absolutizing Christian religion and philosophy, implying that all other religions are false. He argues for the contextualization of a radical, existential understanding of Christianity.[15] New books such as *Religions in Dialogue: East and West Meet*[16] propose that we consider dialogue as mission and move on to construct a world theology.

This is radical contextualization. The *context* is the interfaith meeting of religious progressives seen as a microcosm of the world of diverse cultures and faiths. The *method* is to pursue (new) truth by means of nondisputational dialogue. The *result* is a new syncretistic "gospel" which is supposed to eventuate in a new day of relationships between God and humanity and among people.

The Neoliberal Dialectical Method—Discovering Truth

As an example of the neoliberal method of contextualization, look again at the liberation theology of Gustavo Gutiérrez. Though we may agree with some of the concerns that occasion liberation theology, we categorize Gutiérrez's expression of it as neoliberal because it does not start with the Bible (or even tradition) but with an enlightened response to the human predicament. Its objective is world improvement rather than human regeneration.

Gutiérrez agrees with Yves Conger when he says that if the church wants to respond to the real issues of the world it must abandon the method of classical theology which starts with revelation and tradition. Rather it must begin with the questions and facts that are derived from the world and from history. He goes on to say,

14. "Religious Experience in Humanity's Relationship with Nature," *Dialogue with People of Living Faiths and Ideologies* (Geneva: World Council of Churches, 1978), 133.

15. S. Wesley Ariarajah, "Towards a Theology of Dialogue," *Ecumenical Review* 29 (1977): 3–11.

16. Zacharias P. Thundy, *Religions in Dialogue: East and West Meet,"* eds. Kuncheria Pathil and Frank Podgorski (Lanham, Md.: University Press of America, 1985).

Theology thus understood, that is to say as linked to praxis, fulfills a *prophetic function* insofar as it interprets historical events with the intention of revealing and proclaiming their profound meaning. . . . The theologian . . . will be someone personally and vitally engaged in historical realities with specific times and places. He will be engaged where nations, social classes, people struggle to free themselves from domination and oppression by other nations, classes, and people. In the last analysis, the true interpretation of the meaning revealed by theology is achieved only in historical praxis. "The hermeneutics of the Kingdom of God." observed [Edward C.] Schillebeeckx, "consists especially in making the world a better place. Only in this way will I be able to discover what the Kingdom of God means." We have here a political hermeneutics of the Gospel [italics added].[17]

What could be more clear? The *context* is provided by the dialectical struggle between nations, classes, and peoples in the contemporary spacetime world, a Marxist interpretation of history. The *method* is to discern truth by participating in that struggle, and perceptively and prophetically dealing with the world's agenda. The *result* is a "political hermeneutic of the Gospel" which calls men to make the world a better place (establish the kingdom of God?).

The Neo-orthodox Dialectical Method—Discovering Truth

Closely related to neoliberalism methodologically, and yet distinct from it, is neo-orthodoxy. The similarity between the two approaches is epistemological. Both place a primary emphasis on the contemporary historical context in which we theologize. The biblical revelation of yesterday is a kind of compass, as it were, but we must chart our specific course on the basis of contemporary history. A seemingly basic difference between neoliberalism and neo-orthodoxy, however, is that the former gives more credence to the spirit of the theologizer while the latter gives more credence to the Spirit of God who illumines the theologizer.

Koyama's waterbuffalo theology and his discussion of the "beginning of faith" exemplify this.[18] The biblical case in point was the amazing faith of the Gentile woman who came to Jesus out of concern for her demon-possessed daughter (Matt. 15:21–28). Koyama says that the "mother's love for her daughter—a universally valid and relevant factor (*eros* or natural love)—was transformed and sanctified and resulted in a profound confession of faith in the presence of the Son of David." He concludes that the beginning of faith must contain some universally

---

17. Gustavo Gutiérrez, *A Theology of Liberation* (Maryknoll, N.Y.: Orbis, 1973), 13.
18. Koyama, *Waterbuffalo Theology*, 73–75.

valid and relevant factor that can erase religious, cultural, and political demarcations. And he says, "My interest in this *beginning* of faith did not come from myself but was forced on [me] by my Thai neighbours."[19] It is important to note this, because the idea that faith must emanate from a "universally valid and relevant factor" did not and does not stem from an exegesis of the biblical text itself.

The contextualized theologies of both Gutiérrez and Koyama find their aegis in the context of human need. But in the case of Gutiérrez it would seem that human need is interpreted in Marxist terms and is the controlling factor. In the case of Koyama it would seem that human need is interpreted in Kierkegaardian terms and is the occasioning factor. In both cases, the *context* is history as it is being lived out in various cultures. The *method* is to discern truth in the dialectical tension between living history and the Scriptures as one is illumined by the Holy Spirit. The hoped-for *result* is that the Word of God will "come through" the biblical text.

The Orthodox Didactic Method—Teaching Truth

The approaches to contextualization of Bruce J. Nicholls, Byang H. Kato, Tim Matheny, Norman L. Geisler, Morris A. Inch, Phil Parshall, Samuel Escobar, Don Richardson, and others grows out of a commitment to a fully authoritative Bible and to evangelize the world in accordance with Christ's command to disciple the nations and teach them to obey all that he has commanded (Matt. 28:16–20).

Geisler, for example, writes of the necessity to understand and adjust to the worldviews of respondents. But at the same time he maintains that the Christ of "historical-biblical Christianity" must be communicated as opposed to the "mythical 'Christ' of liberal or existential theology." He reminds us that, though "dialogue presupposes common ground for meaning, it does not presuppose that one view must accept the truth of the other before dialogue is possible. For not more than one world view can be truth; the others *as systems of truth* are wrong."[20] Speaking of proclaiming the gospel, he insists that the New Testament evangelists not only proclaimed it as true; they also provided an *apologia* or defense when it was challenged.[21] Geisler makes a case for the apologetical theology of the first-century apostles.

Returning to the models of part 2, we recall that Bruce J. Nicholls does not hesitate to call for a contextualized *dogmatic* theology and

19. Ibid., 75.
20. Norman L. Geisler, "Some Philosophical Perspectives on Missionary Dialogue," *Theology and Mission*, ed. David J. Hesselgrave (Grand Rapids: Baker, 1978), 249.
21. Ibid.

proceeds to point the way to its achievement. As Emil Brunner says, there are many who object to dogmatic theology. He gives four reasons for this.[22] The first objection comes from those who espouse a "simple faith in Christ" and are chilled by the idea of massive learned tomes. The second objection is raised by people who feel that the biblical gospel calls for action, so dealing with intellectual questions is a waste of time. The third objection is to the idea of dogma which for many connotes coercion and is in opposition to the freedom of faith. The fourth objection is that dogmatics resurrects the divisions that have plagued the church for centuries. Presumably, what is needed today is the kind of thinking that engages contemporary questions and makes the gospel intelligible to modern man.

Brunner, nonetheless, makes a strong case for dogmatics, which he roots in three sources in the life of the church.[23] The first source is the struggle against false doctrine. The second source is the need for catechetical instruction. The third source is the search for an exegetical theology which enables the church to penetrate more deeply into the meaning of the Bible so that provisional knowledge can be replaced by an understanding of biblical doctrine as a whole. From this it is possible to reconstruct an "apostolic doctrine."

Though Brunner would likely take issue with some of Nicholls's conclusions, he is in complete agreement with Nicholls's goal. All churches need a doctrinal basis which, while suited to the struggles and questions peculiar to their particular existential situation, is nevertheless profoundly biblical and goes beyond more speculative and provisional statements. This is precisely what Nicholls is striving for. Moreover, this is precisely what the first-century apostles provided.

The key terms in the orthodox method—dialogue, gospel, faith, doctrine, and so on—derive their meaning from the Scriptures. The *context* of contextualization is the arena of non-Christian belief systems. The *method* is to establish a common ground or a communicational bridge so that unbelievers can be convinced of the truth of the biblical gospel and to teach the Scriptures to those who are so convinced. The anticipated *results* are the spiritual transformation of those who place their faith in Christ and the discipling of the nations. Our diagram can now be completed (see fig. 12).

The meanings and methods assigned to contextualization fall along a theological continuum determined by various theological consider-

22. Emil Brunner, "The Necessity for Dogmatics," in *The Necessity of Systematic Theology,* 2d ed., ed. John Jefferson Davis (Grand Rapids: Baker, 1978), 75–78.
23. Ibid., 79–82.

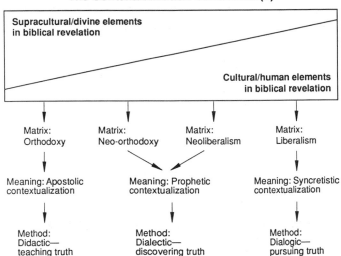

Figure 12
The Contextualization Continuum (c)

Supracultural/divine elements
in biblical revelation

Cultural/human elements
in biblical revelation

| Matrix: Orthodoxy | Matrix: Neo-orthodoxy | Matrix: Neoliberalism | Matrix: Liberalism |

| Meaning: Apostolic contextualization | Meaning: Prophetic contextualization | Meaning: Syncretistic contextualization |

| Method: Didactic— teaching truth | Method: Dialectic— discovering truth | Method: Dialogic— pursuing truth |

ations. Those considerations largely reflect the relative weight assigned to supracultural/divine elements of biblical revelation as against cultural/human elements. As a consequence, understandings of contextualization lend themselves to familiar theological categories (liberal, neoliberal, neo-orthodox, and orthodox).

Another way of analyzing contextualization questions, then, is to find the theological roots of the contextualization understanding and attempt in view. This kind of analysis is not offered with a view to affixing theological labels. Indeed, theologians and contextualizers may sometimes embrace meanings and methods which *logically* adhere to theological orientations with which they would prefer not to be identified. Our concern here is not to categorize persons theologically, but to relate contextualization meanings, methods, and models to a framework of theological orientations which is already in place, recognized by the informed Christian public, and intimately associated with differing understandings of contextualization.

12

An Anthropological Perspective
Language and Meaning

The Parameters of Context

One of the more obvious elements of contextualization is the concept of context. The parameters of the cultural context in which communication takes place can be defined in terms of the relationship between culture and language.

Culture

For the purposes of this discussion culture can be defined as the body of knowledge shared by the members of a group.[1] That knowledge takes the form of rules[2] which govern the way in which individuals relate to and interpret their environment. The utilization of such knowledge leads to culturally specific forms of behavior, patterns of communication (not language per se), sets of values, and types of artifacts.

---

1. James P. Spradley, *Participant Observation* (New York: Holt, Rinehart and Winston, 1980), 6. Compare R. Daniel Shaw, *Transculturation: The Cultural Factor in Translation and Other Communication Tasks* (Pasadena, Calif.: William Carey Library, 1988), 24–25.
2. On the concept of rules see James P. Spradley, "Foundations of Cultural Knowledge" in *Culture and Cognition: Rules, Maps and Plans*, ed. James P. Spradley (Prospect Heights, Ill.: Waveland, 1987), 3–35.

This definition of culture emphasizes two basic concepts. First, it refers to shared knowledge. At the root of this idea are the dual concepts of learning and enculturation (transmission). The collective pool of knowledge which governs behavior in a given culture is something which can be transmitted, that is, passed on to succeeding generations or even to expatriates who are willing to learn.

Second, the definition focuses attention on the fact that this shared knowledge is used to interpret and evaluate the ways in which individuals and groups relate to one another and to their environment. On the basis of this learned set of rules both the individual and the group are able to evaluate the appropriateness of behavior, patterns of communication, and even emotions. How does one know that a certain reaction is appropriate? Only by comparison with the existing catalog of guidelines.

Language

The other component of context is language. Edward Sapir defined language as a "purely human and non-instinctive method of communicating ideas, emotions, and desires by means of voluntarily produced symbols."[3] If we agree, then language is not primarily an expression of ethnicity but rather a convenient, perhaps even arbitrary, means of expressing the content or thoughts of a given culture. Sapir reasons that because cultural and linguistic content are derived from the "science of human experience" the latent content of all languages and cultures can be considered universal. Furthermore, since it is impossible to show that the form of language has even the slightest connection with national temperament no causal relationship between the development of language and culture exists. "Culture may be defined as *what* society does and thinks. Language is a particular *how* of thought."[4]

Nevertheless there is a correlation[5] between the structure (constant ways of arranging data) of a language and the way in which its users interpret their environment. According to Sapir, it is an illusion to imagine that one can adapt to reality without the use of language or to assume that language is merely a means of solving specific problems of communication or thought. "The fact of the matter is that the 'real world' is to a large extent unconsciously built up on the language

3. Edward Sapir, *Language* (New York: Harcourt, Brace and World, 1921), 8.
4. Sapir, *Language*, 215–17.
5. The apparent discrepancy in the Sapir-Whorf hypothesis has been pointed out by a number of researchers. See, for example, Jane O. Bright and William Bright, "Semantic Structures in Northwestern California and the Sapir-Whorf Hypothesis," in *Cognitive Anthropology*, ed. Stephen A. Tyler (Prospect Heights, Ill.: Waveland, 1987), 66–78.

habits of the group. We see and hear and otherwise experience very largely as we do because the language habits of our community predispose certain choices of interpretation."[6]

This phenomenon can be demonstrated at both the behavioral and conceptual levels. For example, Benjamin Lee Whorf reports the case of some distillery workers who were surprised by the fact that heat ignited a protective covering known as "spun-limestone" which had been applied to a metal still. The "behavior that tolerated fire close to the covering was induced by the use of the name 'limestone,' which, because it ends in '-stone,' implies non-combustibility."[7]

Whorf's research also verified the effect that language can have on one's worldview. He showed, for example, how the differences between the grammatical structure of SAE (Standard Average European) languages and Hopi speech determined the way in which time, space, substance, and matter are perceived. Within the SAE context reality is analyzed primarily in terms of objects plus "modes of extensional but formless existence that it calls 'substances' or 'matter.' " As a result existence is viewed as a "spatial form plus a spatial formless continuum" analogous to the outline of a container and its contents. This approach to reality is largely a result of the three-tense system of SAE verbs. At the heart of this structure is an objectification of time which enables us to arrange units of time sequentially. As a result we can "construct and contemplate in thought" a system of past, present, and future as an "objectified configuration of points on a line."

Hopi verbs, on the other hand, have no tenses, but rather "validity-forms (assertions), aspects, and clause-like forms (modes), that yield even greater precision in speech." The validity-forms denote that the speaker (not the subject) simply reports the situation. The aspects are used to denote different degrees of duration and tendency. The result is that Hopi language favors an analysis of reality in terms of events, which are referred to either objectively or subjectively. Objectively "events are expressed mainly as outlines, colors, movements, and other perceptive reports." Subjectively events are viewed as an expression of invisible intensity factors, upon which their stability and duration depend. This "implies that existents do not 'become later and later' all in the same way; but some do so by growing like plants, some by diffusing and vanishing, some by a procession of metamorphoses, some by enduring in one shape till affected by violent forces." This "growth" cycle is

6. Edward Sapir as quoted by Whorf in John B. Carroll, ed., *Language, Thought and Reality: Selected Writings of Benjamin Lee Whorf* (Cambridge, Mass.: M.I.T. Press, 1956), 134.

7. Whorf, *Language, Thought and Reality*, 135–36.

inherent in every existent. Thus everything is already prepared for the way in which it has been, is now, and will be manifested.[8]

These studies seem to support the conclusion that the context of any communicative event is determined by the use of a specific language within the matrix of the culture with which it is associated. Language is a means of expressing and disseminating the content of culture. As such it functions as the key to, and primary vehicle of, the reflective processes which generate the pool of shared knowledge that defines a given culture. Language is also a determining factor in the way in which its users perceive the world. As such it is the interface between individual thought and the "real world."

In spite of its obvious importance most of the models we have discussed simply assume the existence of context without attempting to define it and, in some cases, without so much as mentioning it. This deficiency creates two major problems. One problem is that evaluation of these models becomes extremely difficult. If the meaning of a piece of information is tied to the context in which it was initially formulated, and if it may be modified to fit a second or third context, how will we know whether a message has survived transplantation unless we understand the nature, roll, and function of the contexts involved? The second difficulty is that the lack of a clear definition gives the contextualizer too much latitude in transculturating the message. It is reasonable to assume that the context of the source culture may modify a message in a way similar to an analogous context within the receiving culture. Thinking in terms of the contextualization of the gospel, unless care is taken to identify and match context levels and functions, syncretistic distortions will be touted and defended as authentic contextualizations of the gospel. For these reasons it is advisable to add to our list of analytical perspectives a carefully defined understanding of context which will help us determine whether a contextualization is faithful to Scripture.

We tend to think of context in terms of a clearly defined set of factors outside of and therefore influencing the receptor. It might be more accurate to view context in terms of the interplay between a universal frame of conceptual reference (semantic fields), the nested layers of contexts of the receptor's life, and an internal template within the receptor. All of these determine how communication is interpreted.

The Universal Frame of Conceptual Reference

Recent anthropological research has contributed significantly to our understanding of the nature of language. One of the more interesting

8. Ibid., 138ff.

developments is the idea that human knowledge can be understood in terms of fields of lexical/semantic relationships.

A Universal Set of Semantic Relationships

Our assumption is that, although lexical/semantic units differ among languages, the lexical/semantic relationships which build the internal structure of every language are universal.[9] In other words, a shared function of each language is to allow its users to understand and communicate definitions—all the meanings which are possible in its lexical units.

In its most general form "a definition can be regarded as a statement of a semantic relationship between a concept (X) being defined and one or more other concepts (Y), presumed to be known to the hearer (reader), and having properties considered relevant to the term being defined."[10] The interesting thing about this scheme is that it points out a recurring pattern of semantic relationships used to construct definitions which appear to be universal. Joseph B. Casagrande and Kenneth L. Hale have suggested fourteen such relationships.[11] They can be summarized as formula-like statements describing their nature and the questions which could be used to elicit each relationship (see fig. 13).

Casagrande's and Hale's initial conclusions were based on a preliminary study of only one language, Papago. However, subsequent studies have shown that these and other relationships are evident in all languages and can be reduced to more basic sets. Oswald Werner and G. Mark Schoepfle, for example, have suggested a three-part schema: taxonomy (T), modification (M), and queuing (Q).[12] To understand their approach two basic terms have to be defined. *Intension* (connotation) is the number of discriminations that need to be or can be made in order to recognize the applicability of a lexical unit. The *extension* (denotation) of a lexical unit is the set of examples which have the same intension. If the intensions of the term B are included in the intensions of A, it can be maintained that B is a kind of A, that is, the terms are related taxonomically (T). If the intensions and the extensions of two lexical units A and B are taxonomically identical, the terms are synonymous. Modification (M) implies that the intension of a term is increased by adding attributes. Queuing (Q) shows the relation of a term

---

9. See Oswald Werner and G. Mark Schoepfle, *Systematic Fieldwork*, vol. 1, *Foundations of Ethnography and Interviewing* (Beverly Hills, Calif.: Sage, 1987), 104.

10. Joseph B. Casagrande and Kenneth L. Hale, "Semantic Relationships in Papago Folk Definitions," in *Studies in Southwestern Ethnolinguistics*, ed. D. Hymes (Berlin and New York: Mouton, 1967), 167.

11. Ibid., 168, 190–91.

12. Werner and Schoepfle, *Systematic Fieldwork*, 1:111–16.

Figure 13
Semantic Relationships

1. Attributive:	X is defined with respect to one or more distinctive characteristics of Y. What does X (God) have that is distinctive?
2. Contingency:	X is defined with relation to a usual or necessary antecedent or concomitant Y. What usually proceeds from or follows X (repentance)?
3. Function:	X is defined as the means of affecting Y. What is X (lamb) used for?
4. Spatial:	X is oriented spatially with respect to Y. Where is X (church) located?
5. Operational:	X is defined with respect to an action of Y of which it is a characteristic goal or recipient. What does one do with X (Bible)?
6. Comparison:	X is defined in terms of its similarity and/or contrast with Y. What is X (sin) similar to?
7. Exemplification:	X is defined by citing an appropriate co-current, Y. What is an example of or has the quality of X (love)?
8. Class inclusion:	X is defined with respect to its membership in hierarchical class Y. Is X (Christian) a member of a class?
9. Synonymy:	X is defined as being equivalent to Y. Is there another way of saying X (faith)?
10. Antonymy:	X is defined as the negation of Y, its opposite. Is X (truth) the opposite of anything?
11. Provenance:	X is defined with respect to its source Y. Where does X (salvation) come from?
12. Grading:	X is defined with respect to its placement in a series or spectrum that also includes Y. What comes after (or before) X (conversion)?
13. Circularity:	X is defined as X. Is X (unbelief) an X (sin)?
14. Constituent:	X is defined as being a constituent part of Y. What is X (the Gospel of John) a part of?

Adapted from Joseph B. Casagrande and Kenneth L. Hale, "Semantic Relationships in Papago Folk Definitions," in *Studies in Southwestern Ethnolinguistics,* ed. D. Hymes (Berlin and New York: Mouton, 1967), 190–91. Used by permission.

to the larger world in serial order or sequence. This relationship may be spatial, chronological, or logical.

The three atomatic relationships (MTQ) clarify a number of complex semantic relationships. Of particular importance to our study is not so much relationships between identical (synonymous) terms but the equivalence of two or more terms (double implications). A term may be used by two languages to refer to the same or a similar object or person but have vastly different intensions (folk theories/definitions). The term *God*, for example, may have the same referent but very different intensions for various African tribes (Shona, Karanga, Zambesi, and Ila) as noted by John S. Mbiti (see p. 100). Equivalence or referential identity could be established only if one were able to say that X in language 1 means Y in language 2 *and* Y in language 2 means X in language 1.[13] For this reason it is highly unlikely that data taken not only from several tribes, but also from various strata of each tribe's

13. Ibid., 115.

religious experience (shamanism, spirit worship, sacrifice) would have sufficient intensional similarity to justify the conclusion that all of these tribes worship the same "supreme God."

Deep Structures

These schemes are similar to Noam Chomsky's deep structure theory. Chomsky concluded that each language draws upon a universal set of phonological and semantic features for its own internal, deep structures. The deep structures express the semantic content of a given language. Each language, then, has an inner, context-free set of rules used to rearrange the words and sounds or phonemes to generate speech patterns which can be recognized as standards of correct usage in English, French, or whatever language is involved.[14]

Linguistic Context

Both the deep structure and the universal set of semantic field play a significant role in organizing or partitioning knowledge within an individual or culture. Partitioning of knowledge into specific domains of discourse is absolutely necessary if interpersonal communication is to remain consistently accurate. Partitioning determines how to interpret a sentence such as "The truth will set you free." This sentence means one thing in a political context (partition), such as is described by Gutiérrez, and quite another thing in the biblical/theological context of John 8:32. This kind of partitioning functions as a metalinguistic modifier not only of specific words, but also of entire verbal events. It creates the "context" for a given verbal exchange.

Implications

This research has several implications for our discussion of useful perspectives in the evaluation of contextualization attempts. First, the evidence seems to verify at least the possibility of a universal paradigm or conceptual frame of reference (see p. 162). If all languages use universal semantic relationships certain basic categories of meaning must exist. Second, each language has within it the basic structures which make communication (translation) possible. All languages share a sufficient number of semantic relationships to allow for the same semantic/lexical meaning to be expressed even though the units of expression differ. For that reason we need not be overly pessimistic about the prospects for accurate cross-cultural transmission of information. Third, some form of categorization or partitioning is required to

14. See John P. B. Allen and Paul van Buren, eds., *Chomsky: Selected Readings* (New York: Oxford University Press, 1971), 55–68.

efficiently manage the sheer vastness of human knowledge. It is this partitioning which helps establish the context of any given linguistic situation.

Contexts within Contexts

Anthropologists often refer to several kinds or layers of context—cultural, social, and situational.

Contexts of Culture

"Contexts are nested within contexts, each one a function of the bigger context, and all . . . finding a place in the context of culture."[15] Our understanding of context at this level assumes an integrating body of knowledge and language behavior shared by a number of groups or communities. It embodies the total system of cultural principles, inter-community communication patterns, and forms of acceptable behavior of that culture. Thus, one can speak about Mexican, Japanese, or even Asian contexts.

Although we should never overlook this wider dimension, the problem is its scope, at least in the relationship between context and the process of contextualization. At this level the number of variables required for adequate description and understanding has been multiplied until only general phenomena can be predicted and described.

Imagine, for example, a description of "the typical Frenchman." Such a composite sketch might serve usefully as an orientation, only as long as we keep in mind that the person thus described likely does not exist. Similarly, Mbiti's description of African culture is a generalization which will require considerable fine tuning if it is to be applied to specific peoples of Africa. This type of overgeneralization can be quite misleading. Thus, Mbiti's observations about the "African" concept of time may well apply to certain groups, but it hardly has pan-African validity.

Social Context

The concept of social context is complicated by the various ways in which it can be used. Generally it refers to the individual's member-ship in a community. It implies familiarity, often unconscious, with cultural values and beliefs, institutions and forms, roles and personali-ties, and the history and ecology of the community. When applied to communicative events and social situations, this knowledge enables

15. J. R. Firth, "On Sociological Linguistics," in *Language in Culture and Society*, ed. Dell H. Hymes (New York: Harper and Row, 1964), 70.

the individual to behave in a socially appropriate manner. This can be viewed as the effect of a regulatory matrix in which certain variables limit the behavioral options open to the individual in any given situation. These sociological variables include differences in sex, status, and relatedness to a group. They are constantly being updated by the process of social change, which itself is subject to rules that define what changes can occur under what conditions. The variables also determine the structure or organization of society. Accordingly, social organization can be described as "a network of partial or complete understandings between members of organizational units of every size and complexity . . . which is being re-animated every day by particular acts of a communicative nature."[16] It can be seen that speech is the primary means by which an awareness of social structure becomes part of the individual's experience.

Although an understanding of the dynamics of this contextual layer ties much together and helps put such experiences as conversion into perspective, it still lacks the power to adequately describe individual behavior in a given situation.

Context of Situation

The most specific layer of context is the individual's relationship to the immediate situation in which he is involved. It has been suggested that "a statement in real life is never detached from the situation in which it is uttered."[17] In that case, context functions as a mechanism of reference, that is, the participants learn a given situation and reuse its major components by recalling from memory the physiological, intellectual, and emotional experiences of that situation. Here the focus of contextual function begins to shift from the general dynamics of the cultural matrix to the deliberate and conscious action of the individual. Obviously "one cannot speak of any aspect of human behavior without talking about culture, social organization, etc. Context, to be operative, must pervade all levels."[18] But it is this lowest level—the individual's internal view of his own cultural context, both past and present—which is the ultimate key to cross-cultural understanding, communication, and contextualization (see fig. 14).

16. Edward Sapir, "Communication," in *The Psychology of Language, Thought, and Instruction,* ed. J. De Cecco (New York: Holt, Rinehart and Winston, 1967), 75–78.

17. B. Malinowski, "The Problem of Meaning in Primitive Languages," in *The Meaning of Meaning,* ed. Charles K. Ogden and Ivor A. Richards (London: Kegan Paul, Trench, Trubney, 1923), 450–51.

18. Oswald Werner and Gladys Levis-Pilz, "Memory and Context: Toward a Theory of Context in Ethnoscience," *Language and Logic in Personality and Society,* ed. Harwood Fisher (New York: Columbia University Press, 1985), 65.

Figure 14
Layers of Context

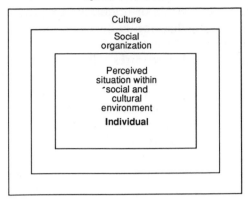

Internal Template

Based on the concepts of lexical/semantic fields and nested layers, context could be defined as an internal template in the mind of a human being. Such a network contains everything the individual knows about his world, and is best conceived of as memory. The long-term memory is almost limitlessly expandable and is therefore never applied in its entirety to any given situation. That is, no context is broad enough to require all of a person's permanent memory. However, in order to interpret and respond to a situation properly the short-term memory which processes that information has to find the correct long-term memory partition. The intermediate memory processes, partitions, and integrates the components of the long-range memory and functions as a restricting mechanism which interprets language and behavior. Therefore, "contextualization means recognizing the criteria for the application of a particular rule of context by measuring perception against a template in memory."[19]

Aspects of Memory

For contextualization to take place context overlap or match will have to be achieved at one or all the levels we discussed. In the case of conversion, for example, information has to be inducted into the permanent memory of the listener, which in turn is integrated into the intermediate memory's template for future reference and application. The first part of this transaction assumes (1) a universal set of semantic

19. Werner and Schoepfle, *Systematic Fieldwork*, 1:118.

relationships making basic communication possible, (2) a universal paradigm of conceptual reference, which for our purposes means that every human being is capable of understanding the basic concepts in the kerygma, and (3) the distinction between identity and equivalence or referential identity.

Effective communication requires what could be called a matching of semantic/lexical fields. Thus, it is not only not necessary for the missionary to unilaterally substitute local terminology for biblical objects of reference which do not naturally occur in the host culture, but to do so invites distortion. If, for example, the listeners are not familiar with the "Lamb," explanatory information can be provided and received by the short-term memory and ultimately be added to a knowledge partition in the long-term memory. Several stages of instruction may be needed to refine the concept, but there is less risk of the listener identifying Christ with an animal which may be referentially equivalent but not identical.

Once the information is transmitted (and explained), the act of conversion, which may well be participated by the communicator's appeal, is concretized within the framework of the recipient's own culture. Thus, it is the confluence of the newly expanded memory (now focused on God's offer of salvation, kerygma) and the convert's inner template which becomes the actual context of the conversion experience. That being the case, the communicator has, and should have, only limited influence on the way in which the experience unfolds. It becomes superfluous to try to measure the authenticity of the experience in terms of impact. Anything short of absolute template overlap would render the standard of measurement nothing more than a figment of the source's imagination. Rather than passing judgment on the nature of the experience, it would be more appropriate to continue the process of supplementing the recipient's permanent memory with biblical data.

This scheme could be used to evaluate the degree of faithfulness to Scripture achieved by various models of contextualization. Consider, for example, Matthew 2:1–6 according to Clarence Jordon's *Cotton Patch Version of Matthew and John:*

> When Jesus was born in Gainsville, Georgia, during the time that Herod was governor, some scholars from the Orient came to Atlanta and inquired, "Where is the one who was born to be governor of Georgia? We saw his star in the Orient, and we came to honor him." This news put Governor Herod and all his Atlanta cronies in a tizzy. So he called a meeting of the big-time preachers and politicians, and asked if they had any idea where the Leader was to be born. "In Gainsville, Georgia," they

replied, "because there is a Bible prophecy which says: 'And you, Gainsville in the State of Georgia, are by no means the least in the Georgia delegation; from you will come forth a governor, who will wisely guide my chosen people.' "[20]

From our perspective this "contextualization" fails in all three areas of context discussed in this chapter. First, no semantic set match is achieved. Certainly we can speak of referential identity in the case of the two governors. However, in light of the vastly different sets of intensions (tizzy, big-time preachers, politicians, and delegation) equivalence is simply out of the question. Second, no context level match is achieved. The relationship between an elected governor to his autonomous state and the United States is altogether different from the imposed governor of a subjugated and insignificant province of the Roman Empire. Equally faulty is the decontextualization of the prophecy. By dehistoricizing the event this "translation" robs the incarnation of its very essence—God with us in a particular time and place. Third, no template match is achieved or even pursued. The intermediate memory rules which enable the first-century Palestinian to interpret or choose the appropriate partition for the relationships and events reported in the biblical text are quite different from those being used by the twentieth-century Georgian.

In this chapter we have suggested that recent anthropological and linguistic research can aid us in our attempt to evaluate the degree of biblical fidelity achieved by the various models of contextualization. Our analysis of the term *context* led to an evaluative framework which focuses on semantic fields, nested layers of contexts, and the internal template of the receptor.

20. Clarence Jordon, *The Cotton Patch Version of Matthew and John* (New York: Association, 1973).

13

A Hermeneutical Perspective
Basic Assumptions and Patterns

Crossing the Meaning Gap

Judging from recent missiological literature,[1] evangelicals have taken seriously at least one of the issues raised by the proponents of the new hermeneutic. They accept the notion that one's preunderstanding necessarily affects the way in which we understand, interpret, and communicate the meaning of a given biblical text.[2] Accordingly, the interpreter's initial task is to seek to span the gap between the horizon of his own culturally bound mode of understanding and the horizon of understanding established by the cultural context in which the text was formulated. The gap must be crossed in such a way as to meet the demands of the interpreter's horizon without violating the intention emanating from the horizon of the text. Once this text-informed understanding has been achieved the interpreter may attempt to communicate that understanding across contemporary cultural boundaries. The complexity of the interpretive and communicative challenge involves three cultures—

1. See, e.g., Donald A. Carson, *Biblical Interpretation and the Church* (Nashville: Thomas Nelson, 1984).
2. Anthony C. Thiselton, *The Two Horizons: New Testament Hermeneutics and Philosophical Description* (Grand Rapids: Eerdmans, 1980).

170

that of the source (the ancient Near East), that of the interpreter/ communicator (in our case North America), and that of the listener (e.g., the North American Eskimo). How effectively can someone brought up in the asphalt jungle of New York City communicate the meaning of the agrarian parable of the sower to an Eskimo?

Any attempt to communicate biblical content cross-culturally will involve us in an initial stage of contextualization, the process of minimizing intercultural meaning-discrepancy[3] as well as the interference occasioned by our own search for transcultural understanding. Once the gospel has been successfully implanted in a given culture, as individuals are converted and incorporated into a new and developing church, contextualization assumes an added dimension. It must be unfolded with appropriate meanings for that culture. Ultimately this is the theological responsibility of the church embedded in the cultural matrix to which the gospel has been applied. In many cases these will be the so-called younger churches which have developed out of the cross-cultural missionary outreach of European and North American churches. In other cases it will involve established churches in their struggle to maintain relevancy in an ever-changing world. Although expatriate missionaries should not be charged with the development of appropriate forms and theologies, they are directly involved in both and for that reason have a responsibility to at least help evaluate the outcome of this process of maturation. We are being called upon to observe and help evaluate our fellow believers' attempts to bridge the gap between their own horizon of understanding and the horizon of Scripture and to do so from the vantage point of a third, our own, horizon.

Our task, then, is one of hearing, understanding, and encouraging rather than of merely passing judgment. However, this advisory role is not without its special dangers and pitfalls. It would, for example, be all too easy for the missionary to insist, directly or indirectly, on maintaining some "proven truths or methods" assumed by his own organization and thereby overlook or even reject indigenous developments which are not at variance with Scripture. On the other hand, the Third World believer's desire for independence may cause him to reject as Western certain ideas or concepts which are required by Scripture. In either case, it is the authority of Scripture which is both appealed to and subsequently abandoned in favor of the interpreter's preunderstanding. If the normative basis of scriptural authority is rejected, such discus-

---

3. Mathematical theory of communications which measures the amount of information transferred in terms of the decrease or elimination of ambiguity. See Claude E. Shannon and Warren Weaver, *The Mathematical Theory of Communication* (Urbana, Ill.: University of Illinois Press, 1964).

sions will devolve to the level of an exchange of opinions in which personal preference and cultural givens are used to determine the meaning of Scripture. Certain basic hermeneutical assumptions and patterns should be considered to provide a more stable, scripturally determined framework for discussion. Such tools facilitate the evaluation of attempts at contextualization and avoid, at least to some degree, the potentially introverting effects of unchecked preunderstandings.

Basic Assumptions

The Supracultural Validity of the Truth of the Gospel

According to the Book of Acts we have every right to assume the supracultural validity of the Christian gospel. The gospel was presented to Parthians, Medes, Elamites, and a host of other nationalities (Acts 2:5–13) on the day of Pentecost. It was later conveyed to Samarians (8:4–8), to Romans (chap. 10, esp. vv. 34–35, 45), and to Greeks (11:19–21). Without denying or violating the cultural trappings in which it was couched, the truth of God's revealed plan of salvation was presented to and understood by representatives of an amazingly diverse group of cultures.

Although few would question the fact of the gospel's validity, there has been considerable difference of opinion as to the sphere or extent to which the elements of the gospel are valid cross-culturally. Little is to be gained by attempting to identify supracultural elements of the gospel and its culturally bound parts. Cultural conditioning affects us as we formulate and present these elements. Our own preunderstandings always tend to skew the results of that screening process. The evaluative responsibility to which we have referred does demand that a framework be established for making decisions about the degree of faithfulness to Scripture achieved or maintained in any contextualization attempt. For that reason it may be more useful to our view of the truth of the gospel if we distinguish two types of validity—categorical and principial—each equally true but each differing from the other in its scope and modus of actualization.

1. *Categorical validity* can be ascribed to those aspects of the Christian message which are absolutely nonnegotiable. They can be grouped into two broad types.

First, consider those aspects of the truth *necessary for justification by grace,* such as the sacrificial death of Christ, faith, repentance, and conversion. Certainly these truths have to be presented in culturally relevant terms. But however presented, the sacrificial death of Christ must be shown to be a vicarious death which is the sole source of salvation within any culture. As Bruce J. Nicholls puts it, "the distinct work of the Creator-Savior must be maintained." Che Guevara, who, according to José Míguez-Bonino's report, may indeed have resembled Jesus in some respects, was nevertheless not *the Christ*.[4] To allow or encourage an understanding of these essential truths of the gospel which vary significantly from the meaning prescribed by the horizon of the biblical text would make impossible an active participation in the work of Christ.

This, it would seem, is precisely what is being proposed by some Latin American contextualizers. Rather than starting theological investigation with the horizon of Scripture it is being suggested that socioanalytical tools of Marxism can be used as the interpretive horizon of departure. Biblical exegesis is relegated to the status of second step, is dominated by contemporary preunderstanding, and yields results which compromise the categorically nonnegotiable validity of the gospel. The concept of salvation is redefined by modern sociopolitical jargon as humanity's newfound freedom to transform the world and participate in God's saving activity by struggling against "sinners" on behalf of the "sinned against." Surely every believer should be sensitive to sociopolitical injustice. But this reinterpretation leads (a) to an offer of a salvation which requires faith in the implementation of political theory rather than in the salvific work of Christ, (b) to an aggressive (if not violent) grasping for what is perceived to be one's right rather than humbly accepting undeserved grace, and (c) to a perpetuation of the evils denounced since salvation is offered to only one segment of society, the oppressed, leaving the oppressors to their own devices.

Second, consider that which, by nature of its form or symbolism, *cannot be altered without losing its meaning.* The sacraments offer a good illustration. In the case of baptism the use of water is tied to the meaning which the sacrament seeks to convey and must be retained unaltered throughout the process of contextualization. In the Lord's Supper, however, the form of the elements could conceivably be altered without changing the basic meaning of the ordinance. For example, a legitimate celebration of communion, if not otherwise altered, might be possible if strawberry juice were substituted for wine and yams for bread. This would be possible in a cultural setting in which neither of the biblically prescribed elements were available and in which strawberry juice and yams were not already associated with concepts or practices which would trivialize or violate the gospel. Although we might concede some latitude of expression, the original form of the sacrament dictates the limits of possible contextualization. Substitut-

4. José Míguez-Bonino, *Doing Theology in a Revolutionary Situation* (Philadelphia: Fortress, 1975), 2–3.

ing cola and chips for the traditional elements in a North American college dormitory celebration would hardly be acceptable. In other words, there may well be something sacred about the form—in spite of what Charles H. Kraft has suggested—depending on how closely related form and meaning are in a given text.

2. *Principial validity* can be ascribed to those aspects of revealed truth which grow out of the implications of new life in Christ. Again they can group into two broad subcategories.

First, we encounter those elements of the truth of the gospel which have *explicitly stated and logically necessary implications* for godly living, walking worthy of our calling, separation from the world, and keeping the moral law. Nothing should be taught or changed to undermine the basic moral and ethical implications of the gospel. Our concern for the oppressed, although valid, cannot be allowed to develop into a theologically anchored hatred of the rich or the oppressors. That would violate an explicit command of our Lord to love our enemies (Matt. 5:44). Yet this concept does give us the freedom to retain biblically supported practices already present in the receptor culture. On this basis Tim Matheny rightly suggests that Arab (Muslim) practices such as honoring one's parents, hospitality, and giving to the poor be incorporated into the new believer's expression of faith.

Second, we have to deal with those aspects of the gospel's truth which, although clearly outgrowths of the believer's life in Christ, *are not explicitly stated* and for that reason allow considerable latitude of expression. The particular form or mode of expression could be changed or determined by the respective culture in which it has been implanted. Here we are aided by the principialization or the universalization of the concepts presented in Scripture. In the case of certain parables, for example, the connection to Palestinian culture is obvious. To convey their meaning we have to determine the principle involved through careful exegesis and channel that meaning along a culturally relevant path. Similarly we are encouraged by Scripture to worship but are given little explicit instruction as to how this is to be done. Matheny is again within this latitude when he advocates the incorporation into Christian worship of certain Muslim practices such as sitting on the floor, removing one's shoes in the place of worship, and bowing prostrate when praying.

The Cross-Cultural Communicability of the Gospel

That the gospel can be communicated cross-culturally assumes that the interpreter can bridge the gap back to the horizon of the text and accurately understand its intended meaning. If this were not the case, the commands to keep Christ's teaching and to proclaim the gospel to all nations would be both meaningless and impossible. It further assumes that the interpreter/communicator can fuse his own horizon with the horizon of his cross-cultural listener sufficiently to enable an accurate transmission of an understanding of the text. If this cannot be maintained, then, by implication, no meaningful communication of any kind can be expected. It also assumes that the listener, when properly instructed, can himself reach back to the scriptural horizon and thus validate or complement the initial interpreter's understanding, that is, contextualize it. This also provides the framework for the cross-fertilization of contextualization attempts.

Additional assumptions can be made about the communicability of the categorical and the principial aspects of the gospel. First, in the case of the categorically valid aspects, we assume that they can be understood by all men in all cultures. Since there is one God, and since the plight of man is the same in all societies, and since his yearning for release is answered in the sacrificial death of Christ, these essential elements of the gospel will correspond to universally known elements of the human dilemma. On the basis of this fundamental continuity it seems reasonable to assume that all men possess the thought categories which will enable them to understand and accept at least those elements of the Christian message which have salvific import.

Second, with regard to the principially valid aspects of the gospel, we assume that genuine faith has the same ethical implications for daily life in any society in which one lives. The moral law, keeping the commandments, and certain ethical principles are universally applicable. Certainly one will have to determine who one's neighbor or enemy is in each respective society, but the command to love both does not lose its applicability when communicated cross-culturally.

Hermeneutical Patterns

To determine which category of validity a specific scriptural command or teaching fits we will first have to determine the meaning of the words as used in a given text (context). This involves the spectrum of meaning of which a word is capable (public meaning), as well as the specific sense prescribed by its use in the text (user's meaning). If the interpreter (hearer) ascribes to the text a meaning which generally accepted usage does not include, or favors one possible meaning over the author's intended meaning, the text ceases to communicate anything other than what is foisted upon it by the interpreter.

Public Meaning

The effective use of any language depends on a "latitude of correctness," that is, the correct or generally accepted use of speech. One is free to insist that he rides to work in a sardine can. But this arbitrary redefinition of a term not usually used of transportation wrecks the communication process. Some meaning could be salvaged if the redefined term were in some way related to the broad limits of acceptable usage. "Sardine can" could refer to a very crowded bus, in which case the speaker would have to give clear indication of that figurative use. Another possibility would be for the user of such private language to carefully explain his terms. But how can we be sure of the meaning of the explanation? And how could this private redefinition be presented as the meaning intended by anyone else?

It is this kind of arbitrary redefinition of key theological terms that has made much recent deliberation so frustrating and fruitless. For example, Kosuke Koyama's discussion of the "beginning of faith" (see p. 84) is based on the assumption that the German term *Anfechtung* in Luther's commentary on Matthew 15:21–28 could be translated by the English word *assault*. However, this meaning of the word usually translated *temptation* breaks out of the latitude of correctness prescribed by the German language. It would appear that Koyama has based his contextualization on a contrast which is generated by his own redefinition (translation) of the term *Anfechtung*.

Recent interest in conversion within ecumenical circles serves as another case. "Having recognized the necessity of rethinking conversion as a goal of mission" ecumenical scholars determined to "redefine the term and fill it with new theological content."[5] And that is precisely what has happened. The redefinition has taken the following form:

1. Conversion is a "personal reorientation towards God."
2. Since this has social implications, turning to God necessarily entails a simultaneous turning towards humanity.
3. That in turn binds one to participation in the movement towards God's ultimate goal, his kingdom.
4. The authenticity of conversion can thus be measured by the individual's willingness to assume political responsibility and to actively participate in society's problems, as well as in the struggle for liberation.[6]

The first statement certainly falls within the generally accepted biblical use of the word. And since conversion does have an effect on one's

---

5. Johannes Triebel, *Bekehrung* (Erlangen: Verlage der lutherischen Mission, 1976), 150–52.
6. Ibid.

relationship to other men, the second statement could be related to the broad limits of acceptable usage. The third and fourth statements, however, explode the limits of correct usage by referring to the conversion, not as a gift or new creation, but as a binding responsibility or law and by introducing the word *kingdom*, itself redefined in sociopolitical terms. Conversion is no longer a result of God's grace but participation in God's historical dealings with humanity.

The User's Meaning

Although a word's meaning must be limited to that of which it is capable, its actual meaning in speech is controlled by the user. "Within the latitude of correctness marked out by public usage, or even slightly beyond it, he determines the sense of the words he uses. . . ."[7] To ignore this principle is to fall into the trap of the intentional fallacy, supposing that a writer meant something other than he has actually written.

Context, tone, and referent show, for example, that Jesus intended as exclusive and absolute his claim to be "the way" (John 14:6). When injected into the debate on Christianity's relationships with other religions this can be quite distasteful to our tolerant, secular contemporaries. For many the apparently intended meaning is untenable. There are, of course, ways to justify rejection of the obvious meaning. One can argue that the intended sense falls outside the latitude of correctness. Ernst Troeltsch argued that Christianity, being historical and thus relative, can make no absolute claims.[8] One can appeal to the complexity and grandeur of the non-Christian religions which make the traditional and exclusive attitude inadequate.[9] After all, "in Hinduism men explore the divine mystery and express it both in the limitless riches of myth and the accurately defined insights of philosophy. The Muslims worship God, who is one living and subsistent, merciful and almighty, the creator of heaven and earth, who has also spoken to men."[10]

Once the perspicuous meaning is rejected the attempt to explain the "real" meaning begins, that is, something has to be invented to put in the place of what is rejected. John Hick, for example, claims that since truth is emotive (and personal) and not cognitive, Jesus is indeed the Christ, just as Gautama is the Buddha, Ramakrishna the Avatar, and

7. G. B. Caird, *The Language and Imagery of the Bible* (London: Duckworth, 1980), 49.

8. Ernst Troeltsch, *Die Absolutheit des Christentums* (Munich: Kaiser, 1969), 64ff.

9. Lothar Litpay, "Christianity and Other Religions," *Communio Viatorum* 22 (Spring/summer 1979): 60ff.

10. Karl Rahner and Herbert Vorgrimler, *Kleines Konzilskompendium* (Freiburg: Herder, 1967), 356.

Muhammad the Prophet. This is so to the extent that they all stimulate feelings of worship and belongingness.[11] Karl Rahner, while admit-
ting that Christianity claims to be the only true religion, allows for
legitimate religion outside Christ and for anonymous Christians who
cannot be approached as though they had not been touched by the grace
and truth of God.[12]

It is our right to reject the author's intended meaning "but if we try,
without evidence, to penetrate to a meaning, more ultimate than the
one the writers intended, that is our meaning, not theirs or God's."[13]
What then remains of God's revelatory communication?

Principles Involving Changes of Meaning

We have already seen that meaning is determined in part by the
limits of correct definition which, in turn, are delineated by current
usage. But since usage is subject to change, latitude of correctness and
ultimately meaning are themselves in a constant state of flux. Failure
to keep pace with these changes, which either broaden or narrow a
word's scope, undermines our ability to understand and communicate
with others. If, for example, one insists on using the term *secularization* in its original sense (the transfer of clerical rule and administration
to worldly powers) in a current debate where it refers to the process
whereby ideas and behavioral patterns are loosed from their religious
context and derived on the basis of logic, then misunderstanding is
inevitable.

Since the presentation of the gospel depends so decisively on an
accurate understanding of certain key terms, we are well-advised to
trace any shifts in their meaning (usage). The following is a brief description of such changes in the German language:

1. *Repentance* was used in the New Testament to describe the total
   reorientation of a person's thoughts and life, involving a turning
   away from evil and a turning toward God. Later it was used to
   refer to the reparation of a religious transgression. It is currently
   understood as a quittance for some misbehavior which, after re-
   mitted, frees the offender from all guilt and allows him to proceed
   on his original path. The original meaning is thus lost, putting
   repentance on the same plane as paying a parking ticket.
2. *Sin* originally referred to a state of rebellion and separatedness

11. John Hick, ed., *Truth and Dialogue: The Relationship Between World Religions*
(London: Sheldon, 1974), 77–95.
12. Karl Rahner, *Schriften zur Theologie*, 136–58.
13. Caird, *Language and Imagery*, 61.

from God, having totally missed his standards for life. It is currently thought of in terms of isolated misdeeds which are easily corrected, as opposed to a state of being.

3. *Faith,* which first was used to describe the total trust awarded a knowable Savior and thus the prerequisite for inclusion in that salvation, has deteriorated to an acquiescent admission of ignorance. It is that which one cannot know cognitively and may, but not necessarily, come to know experientially. In the absence of rational and empirical evidence one simply believes and so has faith.

4. *Conscience* at one time denoted man's ability to make moral judgments about himself in the light of Christ's redeeming sacrifice and in accordance with his standards of right and wrong. Modern usage has divorced this ability from any outside influence, making it totally individualistic and subjective.

Since a presentation of the gospel using the terms of sin, repentance, and faith is liable to be misunderstood or not comprehended at all, the communicator will have to define his terms carefully or develop a new supplementary vocabulary. This involves choosing an understandable but neutral word and filling it with new meaning. The term *course correction* is understandable and is not burdened or loaded with too specific a meaning. It could, therefore, be used to explain the biblical idea of repentance. *Misbehavior,* again a very broad and perhaps vague term, could be useful in presenting the concept of sin. Current usage has not confined the term *conscience* to a religious corner and lends itself to the idea of programing. Our ability to make moral judgments has to be *reprogramed* by a relationship to Christ if it is to function properly.

The search for new supplemental terminology is an endeavor fraught with danger. It requires precision and creativity. It is, however, necessary in light of the shifts in meaning, which have made so much of our communication of the gospel incomprehensible.

Faithfulness to Scripture is our primary standard for evaluating contextualization. This raises the question of what aspects of the truth of the gospel have cross-cultural applicability. We have suggested that the gospel can be viewed in such a way as to enable us to distinguish between its categorically valid and principially valid aspects. To determine which type of validity applies to a given biblical teaching we have proposed the use of several hermeneutical principles which involve public meaning, the user's meaning, and changes in meaning.

14

A Communication Perspective
The Semantic Problem and the Communication Process

A Complex Inquiry

To some it seems that communication must be a simple thing because we communicate all the time. After all, experts reduce the number of basic elements involved in the communication process to three (Eugene A. Nida)[1] or to no more than five (Robert G. King).[2] These include the context, the source or sender, the message, the delivery system, and the receptor or receiver. But peruse even the most elementary introduction to communication and it will be apparent that the process is exceedingly complex. The supposed simplicity quickly evaporates as one encounters such notions as signs and symbols; encoding and decoding; linguistic and nonlinguistic codes; vehicles, channels, and media; and feedback. Even that is but the beginning.

Whatever else contextualization may entail it certainly has to do with communication. Because the communication process is complex

---

1. Eugene A. Nida et al., *Style and Discourse* (Cape Town, South Africa: Bible Society, 1983), 145.
2. Robert G. King, *Fundamentals of Communication* (New York: Macmillan, 1979), 37.

it has been the focus of a great deal of attention down through the centuries and never more so than today. Inquirers into the subject have framed a variety of questions for which they have proposed a multiplicity of answers. Many of these questions have to do with cultural contexts, but some of the most basic of them involve the communication elements. These fundamental questions have great impact on contextualization meanings and methods.

In this chapter we deal with some of these basic questions: How valid is language? What is meaning and where is it to be found? What happens when we communicate? To be authentic and effective, contextualization must be based upon answers to these questions that both take into account communication theory and are consonant with the Scriptures. Not all proposals measure up.

Inquiries into Semantics and Symbolization: A Thumbnail Sketch

Plato's Realm of Forms and Aristotle's Chain of Being

From very early in the Western world great minds wrestled with the nature of meaning and the validity of language. As an idealist Plato anchored his theory in a realm of forms. "Real reality" was to be found in the forms, so the world of sensory objects and verbal symbols could be no more than dim reflections of reality. More empirical in his approach, Aristotle accepted the world of particulars as a real world and considered linguistic symbols to be fairly reliable indicators of both the sensory and unseen worlds. A word such as "angel" (and similar words having to do with the upper reaches of his chain of being) can be meaningful because angels are in some respects analogous to observed beings which are lower on the chain of being.

Aquinas's Proofs and Occam's Razor

Soon after Thomas Aquinas developed his proofs for the existence of God in the mid-thirteenth century, William of Occam insisted that the existence of God could not be proved and that all universals and absolutes are no more than mental conveniences. Aquinas distinguished between supernature and nature and recognized that we do not name things as they are in themselves but as they are to our minds. He also recognized that the meaning of word symbols such as "God" may not be easily arrived at. But with help from Aristotle he concluded that meanings in such cases are arrived at analogically, that is, by reference to meaning in another sense. William of Occam discounted all of this. His basic principle (*praeter necessitatem non sunt multiplicanda*— "entities should not be multiplied more than necessary") was aimed at dispensing with terms having to do with the nonsensory world and intangible universals. It became known as Occam's razor.

The Scientific Method and the Theologians' Response

Early contributors to the scientific method such as Galileo, Francis Bacon, and Sir Isaac Newton retained both the existence of God and the meaningfulness of absolutes, but as the scientific method developed through the centuries nature became increasingly dominant, and to use Francis Schaeffer's phrase, "supernature was eaten up." The language of scientists and theologians became increasingly diverse. The Reformers pointed the way to restoring a single universe of discourse. They recovered meaning for supernature by insisting upon the *biblical* teaching concerning God and people, and the relationship between God and people and God and the world.

Later on, existentialist theologians took another approach. They said that the Bible may indeed be a mixture of truth and error when viewed from a historical perspective, but though a Bible passage may be *objectively* false, it may at the same time be *subjectively* true. What is nonsense historically may be meaningful religiously. For their part, the general trend among scientists was to view any proposition which could not be tested empirically with suspicion. Knowledge came to be identified more and more with sensory experience and its implications.

The Ethnolinguists and the General Semanticists

Enter the twentieth century with its intensified interest in linguistics, ethnolinguistics, and semantics. Edward Sapir and Benjamin Whorf challenged the ideas that language reports reality as we see it and that language reflects a kind of natural logic. On the contrary, language is the means by which we acquire a worldview and logic. Noam Chomsky and others of the generative transformational grammar school of thought objected to this accentuation of the differences between people and languages. They attempted to show that similarities at the deep-structure level greatly outweigh differences at the surface level.

Meanwhile semanticists challenged communication thinking by reexamining some of the classical questions in the light of contemporary disciplines. Jeremy Bentham's interest in the formulation of law led him to inquire into semantic problems. He greatly influenced his student, Charles K. Ogden, who coauthored *The Meaning of Meaning*.[3] Albert Einstein overturned the mathematic and verbal symbolism of

3. Charles K. Ogden and Ivor A. Richards, *The Meaning of Meaning*, 8th ed. (New York: Harcourt, Brace, 1946).

physics and in the process influenced Alfred Korzybski's *Science and Sanity*[4] and Percy W. Bridgman's *Logic of Modern Physics.*[5] It is the work of these and still other semanticists that has largely informed modern communication theory and has left naturalists with the kind of unsolvable dilemma expressed by Susanne K. Langer:

> That man is an animal I certainly believe; and also, that he has no supernatural essence, "soul" or "entelechy" or "mind-stuff" enclosed in his skin. . . .
> Now this is a mere declaration of faith, preliminary to a confession of heresy. The heresy is this: that I believe there is a primary need in man, which other creatures probably do not have, and which actuates all his apparently unzoological aims, . . . and his awareness of a "Beyond" filled with holiness. . . .
> The basic need . . . is the *need of symbolization*. This symbol-making function is one of man's primary activities, like eating, looking, or moving about. It is the fundamental process of his mind, and goes on all the time.[6]

Indeed it is. Indeed it does. To say that the need is there, and the process goes on, without reference to an Intelligence above our mental machinations, a world beyond our sensory experience, and a revelation beyond our flashes of insight is to say in the end that the primary need of man is of no more eternal significance than the dust which is the destiny of animality. Alas, that is what is being said.

Some Conclusions of the General Semanticists

Not all general semanticists agree on every point, of course. Every theorist approaches semantic problems from an individual perspective, but, as we shall see, there is a basic consensus among Korzybski, Ogden, Ivor A. Richards, Bridgman, and other pioneers in the field. This consensus has profoundly influenced modern communication theory.

Alfred Korzybski

Writing concerning Korzybski's views, Stuart Chase says:

> Our remote ancestors, when language was in its infancy, gave words to sensations, feelings, emotions. Like small children, they identified

4. Alfred Korzybski, *Science and Sanity* (Lancaster, Pa.: Science Press, 1933).
5. Percy W. Bridgman, *The Logic of Modern Physics* (New York: Macmillan, 1932).
6. Susanne K. Langer, *Philosophy in a New Key* (New York: New American Library, 1948), 44–45.

those feelings with the outside world, and personified outside events. They made sensations and judgments—"heat," "cold," "bad," "good,"—substantives in the language structure. Though not objects, *they were treated like objects.* The world picture was made anthropomorphic. Sun, moon, trees, were given feelings like men, and a soul was assigned to each. In the old mythologies, gods or demons in human shape made everything with their hands. (The world was created in six days.) These remarkable concepts became rooted in the structure of language and the structure, if not the myth, remains to plague us to this day.[7]

And thus we are introduced to Korzybski's view of the kind of problems that stem from our supposed linguistic past and accrue to the study of language and meaning even today. Along with our linguistic symbols and language structures we have inherited certain ways of viewing ourselves and our world—ways that often promote misunderstanding and occasion communication breakdown.

Korzybski says, for example, that almost all languages—German, Japanese, or English—present us with the "equating verb 'is,' " and "is" causes us to identify the word with the thing. (He says that we need to handle the word *is* like a stick of dynamite.) He insists that abstract nouns occasion the mistaken idea that they actually refer to something in space and time. We should employ high-level abstractions only consciously and with full knowledge of the abstraction level involved. And yet again our languages, particularly Indo-European languages, promote the one- or two-valued judgments of Aristotelian logic instead of the multivalued judgments that accord better with the actual world. Korzybski encourages the modification of language usage in accord with his non-Aristotelian, non-Euclidian, non-Newtonian system.[8]

That the language of mathematics informs Korzybski's approach becomes apparent when we examine more of his recommendations:

1. Use a "structural differential," a continuum that stretches from an event or object to a word or label to an inference or abstraction. This continuum helps identify clearly what is being talked about in any given instance.
2. Find the object or referent to which a word refers and then discover its attributes and relationships.
3. Use mathematical symbols like dog_1, dog_2, dog_3, etc., to remind ourselves that all dogs are not the same, nor are all whites, all blacks, or all Chicanos.

7. Stuart Chase, *The Tyranny of Words* (New York: Harcourt, Brace, 1938), 75.
8. Korzybski, *Science and Sanity,* chap. 7.

4. Append dates to statements (such as "synapses as understood in 1989") to show that new understandings may yet emerge.
5. Make liberal use of hyphens (as in "psycho-linguistics") and et ceteras (etc., etc., etc.) to underscore the fact that much information is omitted in most instances of communication.

Charles K. Ogden and Ivor A. Richards

In *The Meaning of Meaning* Ogden and Richards analyze semantic problems from perspectives supplied by their interest in literature. From an outside stimulus or a process inside of us we receive a *sign.* The sign calls up an object or *referent,* such as a tree, a car, or a house. Attempting to interpret or find meaning in the sign, we reflect on it and file a *reference* in our brain. Then we verbalize or assign a *symbol* to the reference. In short, we move from *sign* to *referent* to *reference* to *symbol* (see fig. 15).

The fundamental semantic problem is that there is no *direct* connection between the symbol and the referent (unless the symbol is simply a pointing gesture in the direction of the tree, car, or house). The word is not the thing.

In the case of symbols such as "the eternal" and "angel" the problem is even greater. The referents do not exist. Therefore it makes no difference how comforting such symbols may be, meaningful communication is impossible if we insist on using them.

In the face of such problems Ogden and Richards propose various canons for the governance of language. We note but two of them here.

Figure 15
The Semantic Triangle

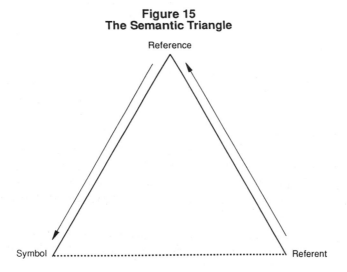

Figure 16
A Continuum of the Genres of Language

Reference

| (No referents; references only) | Poetic Language | Mixed Language | Scientific Language | (Referents and references) |

1. One symbol stands for only one referent, whether a simple one like "my Chevy" or a complex one like "all Chicanos in Chicago."
2. A symbol refers to what it is actually used to refer to. It does not refer to what the receptor thinks it refers to or to what good usage indicates, but rather to what is in the source's head (the reference).

Richards further analyzed semantic problems and solutions in other works such as *Practical Criticism*[9] and *The Philosophy of Rhetoric.*[10] One of his primary suggestions is that we recognize differences in language types (see fig. 16). By locating any specific instance of communication on this continuum we can know how to go about interpreting it. The songwriter says, "Ole Man River, he jus' keeps rollin' along." The scientist says, "At the place where the Mississippi River enters the city of New Orleans it is X number of feet wide." The song is not right or wrong; we cannot check it out. On the other end of the continuum the scientific statement is testable. However, most instances of communication represent a mixture of poetic and scientific language, so we must sort them out.

Where does religious language fit on this continuum? As far as Richards is concerned almost all religious language is poetic and therefore its truth or factualness is not worth quibbling about.

Percy W. Bridgman

One of the most influential early books on semantics was Bridgman's *Logic of Modern Physics.* In it Bridgman explains that in the broadest terms, science is concerned with two basic techniques: *instruments* with which to conduct experiments and *language* with which to explain those experiments. These experiments (and the development and use of instruments and language) must be approached without any absolutes or a priori principles whatsoever. Nothing but experience can judge experience. And the fact of the matter is that we do not experience absolutes and abstractions. Eternity, for example, is never experienced; time is not

---

9. Ivor A. Richards, *Practical Criticism* (New York: Harcourt, Brace, 1935).

10. Ivor A. Richards, *The Philosophy of Rhetoric* (London: Oxford University Press, 1935).

experienced either. It is only as we experience and measure a certain time period or "kind of time" that we can arrive at a definite meaning for the concept *time*. And that meaning is determined by the operations involved in the measurement. The meaning of a term, therefore, is the meaning of the operation by which it is measured.

Bridgman's operational approach to meaning has had a profound effect on logical positivists among others. Logical positivism has not shown a great deal of resilience because of its reductionism and impracticality. But Bridgman reinforced the fundamental conclusions of other semanticists, so his influence lives on.

Semantics and Communication Theory

Modern Communication Theory

Turn to almost any basic textbook on communication theory and you will find that, however the communication process is diagramed and explained, the conclusions of the general semanticists are almost invariably deeply embedded in the concepts. This is so whether one examines standard textbooks such as David Berlo's *Process of Communication*[11] and Robert G. King's more recent *Fundamentals of Communication*[12] or popularizations such as Don Fabun's *Communication*.[13] (Fabun, for example, puts great stress on the distinction between "inside your skin events" and "outside your skin events." He caps off his discussion of the "problem of 'isness' " with the boldfaced dictum: **"Stamp Out Isness!"**).

However expressed, amidst and underlying discussion of signs and symbols, linguistic and nonlinguistic codes, perception, and transmission, certain ideas are almost axiomatic in the literature:

1. The very structure of language is rooted in prescientific world-views and myths, in our human nervous system, and in our particular environment. It is not rooted in the world as it really is.
2. Language is cast in a subject-predicate form in which the "is" of identity is fundamental. Thus the word tends to become the thing. This is the chief cause of communication breakdown.
3. Language reflects and reinforces a one- and two-valued axiology in which things, people, and events are good or bad, fair or unfair,

11. David Berlo, *The Process of Communication* (New York: Holt, Rinehart and Winston, 1960).

12. King, *Fundamentals of Communication*, 37.

13. Don Fabun, *Communications: The Transfer of Meaning* (Belmont, Calif.: Glencoe, 1968).

desirable or undesirable. A multivalued axiology corresponds much better with the actual world.

4. Our symbol systems make it all too easy to employ (and confer an objective quality on) abstractions. We begin by labeling a behavior or an event as bad or good and end up by talking about badness and goodness as though these labels referred to something that has independent existence. It is important to remember that a statement can be true or false, but there is no such thing as truth per se.

5. The widespread employment of absolutes disguises the fact that they are nothing more nor less than the unwarranted objectifications of our subjective experiences and feelings. To say that a waterfall is beautiful is really to say, "*To me* the waterfall is beautiful." Beauty is in the eye of the beholder. There is no objective, empirically discoverable standard of beauty which enables us to say that all people should react to the waterfall in the same way.

6. Meaning is in people, in sources and receptors, not in words or events or things. Words as such have no meaning. The source of a message entertains an idea which he or she then expresses in the words and phrases of a language code, but the meaning stays in the source's head. The receptor is stimulated by the words and phrases (the message) that he or she decodes into a certain meaning which, in turn, corresponds more or less to the meaning entertained by the source. But the meaning is to be located in the two minds, not in the message.

7. The communication process is dynamic, not static. To understand what is happening in any given instance of communication, the interpreter must "get into" the context, understand the worldview, and examine the give and take (and much more) of the communication event in question.

Of course, this list is incomplete. But perhaps it is sufficient to alert us to the fact that while modern theories serve to clear up some old problems, they also introduce us to some new ones. One does well to take some of this kind of semantic medicine, but only in carefully measured doses. Otherwise the new cure may prove to be more debilitating than the old disease.

The Plus Side

Faith in Christ saves us from all sin but does not save us from all delusions. Believers as well as unbelievers can benefit from some of the semanticists' insights.

First, if we Christians are not blinded by the charge that the Genesis account is pure myth and the assertion that myths such as this are reflected in language structures, we will be prepared to see another side of the relationship between myth and language. While semanticists such as Korzybski deem such myths to be a plague, that is not the final word on the subject. As Chomsky, anthropologist Claude Levi-Strauss, and others insist, surface structures of language and culture vary greatly among peoples, but at the deeper levels languages tend to be remarkably similar. This deep-level similarity has been proposed by Robert Longacre and others as an argument for the fact of creation and the existence of the *imago Dei* in humankind. More than that, linguists such as Nida and missiologists such as Harvie M. Conn argue that a study of myth and a shift of focus from surface to deep structures holds great promise for the missionary cause. For instance, the older indigenization approach focused on such surface forms as national leadership and local support. A better understanding of what lies beneath the surface would enable the contextualizer to get closer to the heart of a culture—closer to its center of change.[14]

Second, semantics and communication theory also remind us that language is not the solid, rock-ribbed communication vehicle we often assume it to be. How easy it is to suppose that when we have delivered our message we have also communicated our meaning. Were we to inquire as to how the receptor(s) actually understood our message, the shock might be devastating but the experience would be enlightening. After all, word symbols are not independent of word users. *Persons* attach meaning to words, *persons* change those meanings, and *persons* determine whether a symbol is actually a word, that is, whether it has meaning. To say that a word is used or understood incorrectly is to say that it is not being used or understood according to convention. But that should not be the end of the matter. It is important to inquire of the source exactly how the word is being used or to ask the receptor exactly how it is being understood.

Third, modern theory helps us remember that to lay hold of a symbol is not to lay hold of the referent for which it stands. It is entirely possible to know all about the symbol *God* without knowing God himself. It is possible to know the theology of salvation without being saved.

Fourth, contemporary theorists do well to remind us that if high-level

14. Regarding myth see Harvie M. Conn, *Eternal Word and Changing Worlds: Theology, Anthropology, and Mission in Trialogue* (Grand Rapids: Zondervan, 1984), 324–29. On the significance of deep structures see Robert Longacre, *An Anatomy of Speech Notions* (Lisse, Netherlands: Peter de Ridder, 1976).

abstractions are economical in that they encompass a great deal of information within a small linguistic package, they also mislead because they cover up differences in reaching for similarities. Thus "salvation" is a good word, but unless we use it advisedly it may evoke five different meanings in five different receptors, especially if they do not possess a biblical background. The phrase *born again* used to be confined largely to the fundamentalist and evangelical subcultures. In the last generation, however, evangelists have been so successful in conveying the imagery of the new birth to a larger audience that the phrase is much more widely used. Studies show that it is now applied to a variety of spiritual, psychological, and even physical experiences. Some people are "born again" by looking at a sunset. Automobiles are "born again" when they get a new paint job. The phrase has become ambiguous.

Fifth, and especially germane, semantic theory has resulted in greater attention to the meaning of meaning itself. In writing about the language of the Bible, G. B. Caird, for example, recognizes the difficulty of "pinning down" a meaning for "meaning." He resorts to the index numbering system of the semanticists to distinguish between types of meaning. He writes, "Meaning is a highly ambiguous term, and the only safe way of handling it is to identify by indexing the various senses in which it is commonly used. [There is a] vital distinction between meaning (referent) and meaning (sense), i.e. between what is being spoken about and what is being said about it."[15] Caird proceeds to index other uses of the term *meaning,* such as value in the sentence "This means a lot to me" and entailment in "Nationalism means war." Distinctions such as these are not only helpful; they are essential.

The Minus Side

But if positive insights for Christian contextualization emanate from semantic and communication theory, they must be weighed against that which is negative. Some of the minuses are obvious. Others are subtle. Consider a few of them.

First, absolutes now tend to be viewed with great skepticism. Christians will retain God as an absolute no matter what semanticists might say. Even Christians, however, may be tempted to question absolutes that have to do with orthodox doctrine and with ethical and moral standards of good and evil, to say nothing of esthetic judgments of what is beautiful. Beginning with a British grade-school textbook that makes "beautiful" and "ugly" (with reference to a waterfall) nothing more than expressions of individual taste, C. S. Lewis makes a strong case

15. G. B. Caird, *The Language and Imagery of the Bible* (Philadelphia: Westminster, 1980), 37.

against this kind of relativism. He argues convincingly that to the extent that man succeeds in abolishing absolutes he also "succeeds" in abolishing himself.[16]

Second, if we concur too readily with modern theory, then the more we use language to describe the really important aspects of our world the greater the suspicion with which we will employ religious language. Think for a moment of the kind of statement that is *most* meaningful to general semanticists: "I have a fever today," "My dog's name is Rover," and "The Mississippi River is X feet wide at the point where it enters New Orleans." Then think of the kind of statement that is *least* meaningful (or meaningless) to them: "In the beginning God created the heavens and the earth," "Salvation is of the Lord," "Jesus was the virgin-born Son of God," and "Heaven is my home." Millions of Christians have died for such truths, but they are hardly worth contending for in the view of general semanticists and even in the views of some who are engaged in the work of the church and its missions.

Third, when the instrumentalistic, functional view of language is taken to its extreme, the emphasis shifts from propositional truths to dispositional attitudes. The focus tends to move from the fidelity of the message to the autonomy of source and receptor, from content to impact, from form to function, from adherence to the conventions of language usage to the convolutions of the receptor's brain. The results of this can be little short of disastrous, especially from a Christian point of view. F. Peter Cotterell shows how important rhetorical form is to the proper interpretation of the conversation between Jesus and Nicodemus.[17] Nida and others underscore the intimate relationship between literary form and author meaning.[18] If it is possible to be too beholden to form, it is also possible to be overly committed to function!

Fourth, the more rigorous one becomes in the application of some of the principles of modern communication theory, the more difficult it becomes to retain consistency and the more impractical its principles become for everyday usage. Semanticists may insist that we never know the world as it really is, but Korzybski cannot resist talking about a multivalued "*real* world." It is all right for him to propose the use of mathematical symbols like dog_1, dog_2, and dog_3 to make a point, but by the time we get to dog_{300} (to say nothing of dog_{3000}), we have had it with his method. It is all right for him to propose a liberal sprinkling of

16. C. S. Lewis, *The Abolition of Man* (New York: Macmillan, 1947).

17. F. Peter Cotterell. "The Nicodemus Conversation: A Fresh Appraisal," *Expository Times* 96 (May 1985): 237–42.

18. Nida et al., *Style and Discourse*, esp. chap. 11.

et ceteras in our writings, but the first ones to object will be our English teachers.

Something similar is true of communication and contextualization theories as proposed by some Christians. They can take us so far afield that we must break with what we say to the student in the classroom in order to be intelligible to the man in the street.

Communication Theory and Contextualization Proposals

Many, if not most, Christian contextualizers make use of the insights of contemporary semantic and communication theory but relatively few do so explicitly. Among those whom we have considered in some depth, Charles H. Kraft is the most forthright in this regard. Not only does he deal with basic communication theory in *Christianity in Culture*, but also he has given us a separate work, *Communication Theory for Christian Witness*,[19] which consists almost entirely of communication theory rewritten for the Christian communicator. We should, therefore, briefly evaluate some of his ideas.

Some Proposals of Charles H. Kraft

Kraft is at his best when he warns us that many of our long-held ideas about Christian communication are best categorized as fiction, not fact. Consider a sampling of his suggestions:

1. Christian communication should be receptor-oriented.[20] Very often Christian communicators attend to the message and to delivery systems while failing to realize that receptors are not just "sitting there." They are active participants in the communication process, processing the message in accordance with their needs, interests, and values.

2. Christian communicators, therefore, should become aware of the *interpretational reflexes* of their respondents—their predispositions and prejudices (largely culturally determined) that go a long way toward determining how they will interpret and respond to a given message.[21]

3. Christian communicators should employ the *specificity principle*. Their message will have a greater impact if, rather than using

19. Charles H. Kraft, *Communication Theory for Christian Witness* (Nashville: Abingdon, 1983).

20. Ibid., 89–108.

21. Charles H. Kraft, *Christianity in Culture: A Study in Dynamic Biblical Theologizing in Cross-Cultural Perspective* (Maryknoll, N.Y.: Orbis, 1980), 131–34, 138.

generalizations and abstract propositions, they employ narratives, illustrations, parables, and descriptions that are true to the life of respondents.[22] The Lord Jesus was a master communicator in this regard.

Suggestions such as these draw upon the best insights of communication theory and commend themselves to careful consideration. However, in the light of our previous discussion we must ask whether Kraft takes us too far down the path of contemporary theory. Consider some of his most cherished ideas which led inexorably to Kraft's "dynamic-equivalent transculturation." We will number them to facilitate reference.

Idea 1. We must always distinguish between "reality as it is" and any human perception of reality. Kraft calls this *critical realism*. It is the awareness that our perception of reality is always more or less subjective and distorted.[23]

Idea 2. Meaning is not in words or things, but only in persons.[24] Communication, therefore, is the transmission of a message, not the transfer of meaning. Meaning exists only in the minds of sources and receptors.

Idea 3. The crucial problem in Christian communication is not a lack of the knowledge of the gospel but a lack of the motivation to accept it.[25] Contextualization is foremost a matter of providing an effective stimulus, not of providing adequate information. People already know enough facts to be saved, but they are not ordinarily inclined to act upon those facts.

Idea 4. The constants of Christianity are in the functions and meanings behind the doctrinal and behavioral forms rather than in the forms themselves.[26] The forms (words, creeds, theological statements, rituals, rules) are therefore dispensable and changeable. It is the function and the meaning that must be maintained.

Such theorems accord well with much of modern semantic and communication theory. We may agree that they contain important elements of truth and to that extent can be helpful to Christians. But, as

22. Ibid., 140–41.
23. Kraft, *Communication Theory*, 233–34.
24. Ibid., 110–15.
25. Ibid., 53.
26. Kraft, *Christianity in Culture*, 118–19.

Kraft defines them, are they reasonable? Are they practical? And, more important, are they scriptural? Unfortunately, all three questions must be answered in the negative.

As for reasonableness, these ideas project the problems inherent in modern theory into the Christian sphere. Idea 4 leads Kraft to say that, while Jesus was sinless, the Bible autographs cannot be errorless. By what logic can one say that the omnipotent, omniscient Holy Spirit of God can miraculously use the body of Mary as a vehicle to bring the sinless Lord Jesus in the world while insisting that the same Holy Spirit cannot use the vehicle of prophetic and apostolic language to give us an errorless Scripture?

Something similar can be said in terms of practicality. There is a sense in which Idea 2 is correct. God and man give meanings to words. We know that meaning is not engendered by words themselves nor does meaning adhere to words like iron to a magnet (though onomatopoeic words such as "buzz" and "hiss" do resemble natural sounds). Do not all of us, however, including the linguists, often speak of the meaning of words and phrases even though we know all of this? Pressed too far, to say that there is no meaning in words is like saying that there is no value in stocks or bonds or a one-thousand-dollar bill. There is no inherent, intrinsic value in them, but they have an imputed, invested value. Otherwise people would not rob banks.

It is in fidelity to Scripture that Kraft's proposals become most problematic. He speaks rather vaguely about the "meaning behind the forms" of Scripture (Idea 4).[27] But what kind of meaning is he talking about—authorial intent or receptor response? His primary concern seems to be with the latter, but we have little more than studied (primarily anthropological and psychological) conjecture upon which to base receptor response—little more than the precise words of Scripture, that is. When we go to Scripture it is imperative that we first attempt to discover the *author's* intent. This endeavor does not disparage but rather necessitates careful attention to Scripture forms! In discussing this relationship between form and meaning, Eugene A. Nida and William D. Reyburn place formal elements such as transliteration, morphological structures, phrase structures, rhetorical devices, measured line, figurative language, discourse structures, and literary genres on a continuum. They note that in transliteration the structures are almost entirely arbitrary. The amount of meaning carried by the formal structures is minimal. Rather radical adaptations are therefore admissible. As one proceeds to the other end of the continuum, however, the forms become increasingly important to meaning:

---

27. Ibid., 118.

When one reaches the areas of discourse structure and literary genre, the need for or possibilities of adaptation are greatly reduced. Extensive alterations or transpositions must generally be rejected, because they inevitably involve significant shifts of meaning and violate the larger units of form that embody the intent of the original communication.... The fundamental principle remains valid: as one proceeds from the most restricted and least meaningful structures to the most inclusive and most meaningful ones, the extent to which formal changes are advisable and necessary diminishes significantly.[28]

Idea 4 also yields the conclusions that the Christian faith is not a system of teaching but a relationship with God and that this is what Jude, for example, is writing about when he urges Christians to contend for "the once-delivered-to-the-saints faith" (a literal translation of Jude 3).[29] But few exegetes so understand it. In any case, the New Testament continually emphasizes the importance of sound doctrine.

Idea 3 leads to the dubious conclusion that a person such as Cornelius did not need additional information to be saved. But Scripture is clear that he needed to know what God had commanded (Acts 10:33) and that he required words by which he and his household could be saved (Acts 11:14).

Idea 2 runs counter to the biblical teaching that God has invested meaning in the things that he has made so that, by virtue of God's creation, man knows important truths about God and is obligated to act upon them (Ps. 19; Rom. 1).

Idea 1 leads Kraft to accuse Carl F. H. Henry, Francis Schaeffer, Harold Lindsell, and others of "naive realism" because they claim to see reality as it is, to understand revelation clearly, and to categorize those who disagree with them as wrong.[30] But these men do not claim that *human* perception is undistorted or that *human* formulations are infallible. What they claim is that *divine* disclosures and formulations are undistorted, authoritative, and true. Even though mediated through fallible, human, and limited linguistic instruments and even though we "see through a glass darkly," what we are looking at is *divine*. The Lord Jesus insisted on precisely that when he said that the Scriptures cannot be broken (John 10:35) and that even the smallest markings in the text of the law would not pass away until all has been fulfilled (Matt. 5:18). Kraft's analogy should be turned around. Even though our Lord Jesus had a human body with the limitations that that body im-

28. Eugene A. Nida and William D. Reyburn, *Meaning across Cultures*, American Society of Missiology Series 4 (Maryknoll, N.Y.: Orbis, 1981), 47.
29. Ibid., 133.
30. Kraft, *Communication Theory*, 233–34.

posed, nevertheless he was the sinless and perfect Deity. So it is that even though Scripture is in the human language of human authors, nevertheless it is the inerrant Word of God.

The Proposals of Other Contextualizers

It would be beneficial to analyze the proposals of still other contextualizers considered in this book in the light of semantic and communication theory. Were we to do so we would likely retain reservations with the contextualizations, for example, of Brunner, Thomas, and Koyama. But we would likely see more clearly how Rudolf Bultmann can claim to retain the message of the cross while dispensing with the historicity of the Bible. We would be in a better position to assess how M. M. Thomas translates religious symbols into secular ones and how he derives Christian meanings from Hindu religious symbols. We would learn something positive from Kosuke Koyama's consummate ability to manage old symbols and create new ones in his attempt to communicate the Word of God which needs to "come through" the words of Scripture. And finally, we might wish that Byang H. Kato were still with us and that Nicholls would give greater attention to semantic and communication problems in his attempt to preserve a theology that is both contextualized and biblical.

Contextualization draws deeply from the wells of modern communication theory, which, in turn, depends heavily upon modern semantic theory. As might be expected, semantic theory entails a philosophy of language and indeed of the nature of reality. There is, therefore, both a positive and a negative side in modern communication theory. If contextualizers do not learn from semanticists and communicologists they dull the Christian message at its cutting edge. But if they learn too well, they "stamp out isness," and their trumpets give an uncertain sound. When that happens, they become very unlike the apostle Paul, and they part company with the greatest Communicator of them all!

Authentic and Relevant Contextualization: Some Proposals

Introduction to Part 4

We have looked at contextualization backgrounds, a variety of proposals, and tools for analyzing those proposals and their results. Though it has been impossible to exhaustively treat such broad subject matter, we have tried to avoid oversimplification. In any event, many of our readers may be thinking, "Well and good; but exactly how would the authors go about contextualization? What methods do they espouse? What do authentic, effective contextualized products look like?"

Preliminary answers to these questions have been implicit in the preceding chapters. In part 4 we will describe and illustrate contextualization. We will provide some contextualizations of different kinds of materials for a variety of cultural contexts. We have purposely decided to abbreviate theory in order to include the examples. Both the advantages and disadvantages that accrue to this approach will be obvious. We are especially sensitive to the likelihood that some will think that what we set out to do here is overly ambitious and even somewhat arrogant. Therefore we urge readers to take note of two important caveats.

First, we recognize that no contextualization can lay claim to authoritative finality. We claim that our views are worthy of consideration only in that we believe them to be in accord with orthodox presuppositions and commitments.

Second, we recognize that contextualization is best done within the receiving cultural context by qualified indigenes. Both expatriate missionaries and native evangelists and teachers, however, sometimes require practical prods to action and theoretical hooks on which they can attach ideas (and which they can refashion and improve). We are quite satisfied if we can make a contribution to that important process. In any event, by virtue of the need to communicate the gospel in an understandable and compelling way, all cross-cultural Christian workers are required to adjust their message to new contexts amd peoples. In view of the importance of that effort, a consideration of even imperfect models may be superior to having no models at all.

15

Contextualization That Is Authentic and Relevant

Balancing Faithfulness and Meaningfulness

It has become clear that a wide variety of meanings, methods, and models attach to the word *contextualization*. Some of them are more consistent with Scripture and the historic Christian faith, and therefore are more authentic, than others. The Theological Education Fund (TEF) originators of the term did not hesitate to speak of "authentic contextualization," but it seems that for most of them authentic contextualization had to do with contextuality—correctly reading, and relating to the context. Authenticity should have to do with God's revelation first of all, with faithfulness to the authority and content of the will of God as revealed in his creation, in man's conscience, and, especially, in his Son and his Holy Spirit–inspired Word. We say especially because though all men already share in the testimony of creation, it is the particular task of the church to share the Christ of whom the Scriptures testify (John 5:39). Of course, in and of itself, authenticity does not assure us that the message will be meaningful and persuasive to our respondents. Therefore we must also speak of effectiveness—of the kind of communication that grows out of an understanding of our respon-

Figure 17
Contextualization—A Three-Culture Model

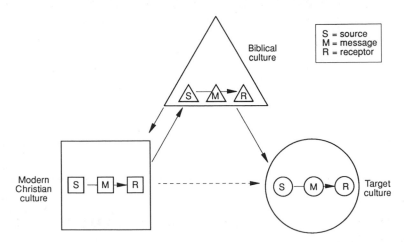

Adapted from Eugene A. Nida, *Message and Mission: The Community of Christian Faith.* Copyright ©
1960 by Eugene A. Nida. Reprinted by permission of Harper and Row, Publishers, Inc.

dents in their particular context and out of the active ministry of the
Holy Spirit in us and in them.

From this point of view Christian contextualization can be thought
of as the attempt to communicate the message of the person, works,
Word, and will of God in a way that is faithful to God's revelation,
especially as it is put forth in the teachings of Holy Scripture, and that
is meaningful to respondents in their respective cultural and existential contexts. Contextualization is both verbal and nonverbal and has
to do with theologizing; Bible translation, interpretation, and application; incarnational lifestyle; evangelism; Christian instruction; church
planting and growth; church organization; worship style—indeed with
all of those activities involved in carrying out the Great Commission.
Something of what is involved can be seen by resorting to the use of a
diagram proposed by Eugene A. Nida and modified somewhat for our
purposes (see fig. 17).

In simple and succinct terms the explanation of the "three-culture
model" in figure 17 illustrates that the biblical message came in language and concepts meaningful to sources (prophets, apostles, and Bible authors) and receptors (their hearers and readers) in the Hebrew and
Greco-Roman cultures of Bible times. Consciously and unconsciously
it has been contextualized to be meaningful to people in cultures to
which the Christian message spread, in which the church developed,

and from which it sends out its cross-cultural missionaries. Their task and the task of the churches that grow out of their work is to interpret (and decontextualize) the biblical message to limit the intrusion of materials growing out of their own culture. They then must contextualize the message to communicate it effectively to respondents in a target culture. The principles and activities involved are complex, and they have already been illustrated in the course of our discussion. Now we will summarize some of the more salient principles before concluding our study with some examples.

Contextualization and the Biblical Text

The adequacy of an attempted contextualization must be measured by the degree to which it faithfully reflects the meaning of the biblical text. Thus, the contextualizer's initial task is an interpretive one: to determine not only *what* the text says but also the *meaning* of what has been said. It may be useful to think of contextualization as a process with three distinct elements, revelation, interpretation, and application, throughout which a continuity of meaning can be traced.[1]

Revelation

The process begins with God's revelation of his truth in language. Under the guidance of the Holy Spirit, a human author, using linguistic symbols to convey the meaning of that revelation, produced a text. Since the inscripturation of revealed truth took place under the direct inspiration of God's Spirit, the correspondence between that which was revealed and the resultant text is guaranteed.

From the interpreter's vantage point, it must be recognized that the range of possible interpretations which legitimately can be ascribed to the text is limited. Clues to that range of meaning are provided by the generally accepted use of the linguistic symbols at that time (latitude of correctness), by the author's particular use of linguistic conventions, and by the original audience's response, that is, the publicly observable aspect of language of which the author was certainly aware. These factors do not themselves generate meaning. However, they do indicate and limit the specific meaning assigned to the text by the author.

1. Percy B. Yoder, *Toward Understanding the Bible* (Newton, Kans.: Faith and Life, 1978), 22–23.

Interpretation

The second element is the reader's or hearer's perception of the intended meaning. The formation of this perceived meaning is affected by the two horizons of the interpretive task—the horizon of the interpreter's own culture and that of the text. The interpreter's own enculturation leaves an indelible stamp on his thought patterns and will certainly affect the way in which he interprets a given message. But in spite of the limitations imposed by the interpreter's ethnocentrism, human language, and the distorting effects of sin, the student of the biblical text is able to gain a more or less accurate understanding of its author's intended meaning. This is possible since the perspicuity of the text and the analytical tools of exegesis, theology, and history work to keep the meaning which takes shape in the mind of the interpreter within the scope of meaning prescribed by the text itself.

Application

The third element involves two steps. First, the interpreter formulates the logical implications of his understanding of the biblical text for the culture in which it is to be lived out. Second, the interpreter consciously decides to accept the validity of the text's implications or to reject it (or some part of it) and superimpose his own meaning. If he rejects the claims of the text, the continuity of meaning is broken, and he loses touch with the truth embodied in the text. An acceptable contextualization is rendered impossible. If, on the other hand, the interpreter accepts the claims of the text, he will be able to appropriate its meaning to his own sociocultural environment. The continuity of meaning of the text is unbroken, and Scripture takes on significance in a specific situation. This is not to imply that biblical content *becomes* true. Rather, because it *is* true it can, if properly understood, be repeatedly applied to specific contexts in an everchanging, multicultural world. At this point the interpreter already will have begun to classify biblical content according to its categorical and principial validity (see pp. 172–74). The interpreter may now distinguish between culture-bound aspects of the Christian message which are open to modification from revelatory content which has nonnegotiable supracultural validity.

Thus, acceptable contextualization is a direct result of ascertaining the meaning of the biblical text, consciously submitting to its authority, and applying or appropriating that meaning to a given situation. The results of this process may vary in form and intensity, but they will always remain within the scope of meaning prescribed by the biblical text.

Contextualization and Respondent
Peoples and Cultures

In part 2 of this book we saw that contextualizers approach contextualization tasks in a variety of ways. The paradigms that they use for doing contextualization for peoples in other cultures tend to reflect the discipline(s) in which they are schooled (e.g., historical theology, cultural anthropology, comparative linguistics, or cross-cultural communication). When one considers the vast amount of knowledge required to master the relevant communications and social science disciplines, and the diversity of cultural configurations among respondent peoples around the world, one realizes that there is no one correct way of doing contextualization. There are, however, parameters outside of which Christian orthodoxy, and good science and sound logic, will not allow us to go (as we saw in part 3).

In order to understand what is involved in communicating the Christian gospel to respondents in other cultures, consider the following seven-dimension paradigm:

1. Worldviews—ways of viewing the world.
2. Cognitive processes—ways of thinking.
3. Linguistic forms—ways of expressing ideas.
4. Behavioral patterns—ways of acting.
5. Communication media—ways of channeling the message.
6. Social structures—ways of interacting.
7. Motivational sources—ways of deciding.

This can be diagrammed as in figure 18.

All messages must pass through this seven-dimension grid. There is no way they can go around or otherwise escape it. Moreover, as the "funnels" between encoder source and the respondent decoder shows, the greater the differences between the source's culture and the respondent's culture the greater the impact of these dimensions upon the message and the more critical the contextualization task. Of course we must keep in mind that these dimensions of intercultural communication interpenetrate one another. They may be separated for analysis, but they combine to form one reality.

All of this has been explained in considerable detail in *Communicating Christ Cross-Culturally*.[2] Here we can only highlight the process.

2. David J. Hesselgrave, *Communicating Christ Cross-Culturally: An Introduction to Missionary Communication* (Grand Rapids: Zondervan, 1978).

**Figure 18
Dimensions of Cross-Cultural Communication**

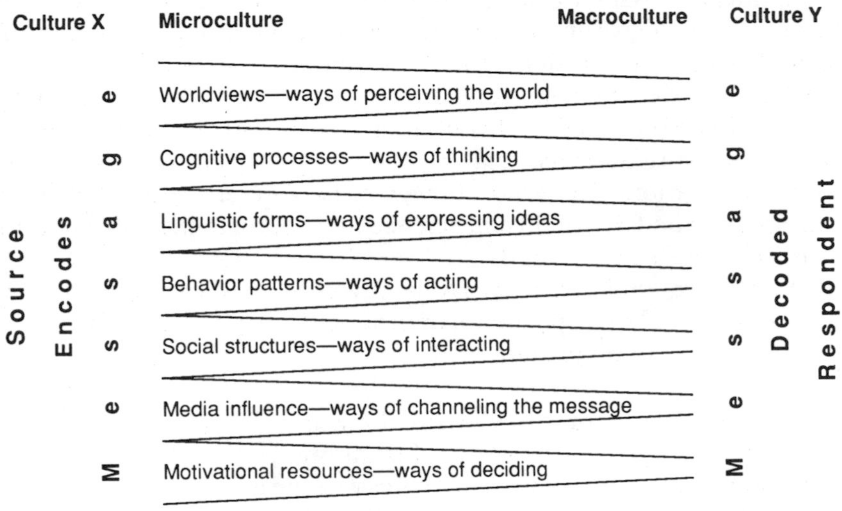

Culture X	Microculture	Macroculture	Culture Y

Source / Encodes

e   Worldviews—ways of perceiving the world   e

g   Cognitive processes—ways of thinking   g

a   Linguistic forms—ways of expressing ideas   a

s   Behavior patterns—ways of acting   s

s   Social structures—ways of interacting   s

e   Media influence—ways of channeling the message   e

M   Motivational resources—ways of deciding   M

Decoded / Respondent

From David J. Hesselgrave, *Communicating Christ Cross-Culturally: An Introduction to Missionary Communication* (Grand Rapids: Zondervan, 1978), 412. Used by permission.

The contextualization attempts with which we conclude this volume will illustrate practical implications.

Worldviews—Ways of Perceiving the World

The concept of worldview has become commonplace in anthropological, theological, and communication materials. Worldview has been defined as the way we see the world in relation to ourselves and ourselves in relation to the world.[3]

Though much more is involved, perhaps it can be simplified in terms of a person's understandings of supernature, nature, humanity, and time.

The monistic worldview of much of Hinduism and Buddhism offers examples. Hinduism (particularly the Vedanta of Shankara) insists that the only reality is the indescribable Brahman. The phenomenal world is illusory (*maya*); the inner Self (*Atman*) is identical with the Brah-

---

3. Robert Redfield, *The Primitive World and Its Transformations* (Ithaca, N.Y.: Cornell University Press, 1957), 85–86.

man; the human problem is ignorance (*avidya*), and a person is caught in an extended cycle of births and rebirths (*samsara*) dependent upon his karma. Through enlightenment he can be reabsorbed into Brahman. Buddhism developed in the Indian context and adopted much the same worldview with its ideas of karma, cycles of birth and rebirth, and ignorance of the true nature of the world. It replaced the idea of Self with "no-self" (*anatta*) and the idea of Brahman with that of Nirvana. The differences between this understanding and the Christian understanding make it apparent that effectively communicating the gospel to a Hindu or Buddhist requires contrasting Hindu-Buddhistic and Christian understandings of God, the origin of the universe, the human problem, grace, the meaning of salvation, the importance of history, the nature of spirituality, and the destiny of humanity and the universe. Not to do so would invite misunderstanding and syncretism.

Analyses of tribal, Chinese, naturalist, and other worldviews reveal a similar necessity of "worldview contextualization." We begin to appreciate the wisdom of Hans-Reudi Weber when he uses the larger biblical narrative to catechize and evangelize in Indonesia (see pp. 215–18). If he did not the Indonesians might simply fit bits and pieces of Christian information into the worldview picture of their own myth.

Cognitive Processes—Ways of Thinking

About the time of World War II, the anthropologist Franz Boas wrote *The Mind of Primitive Man*.[4] After the war, the philosopher F. S. C. Northrop contrasted Eastern and Western ways of knowing in *The Meeting of East and West*.[5] They were not alone in highlighting the different ways in which people think and "know." Works emanating from various disciplines converged to demonstrate that while all cultures have their logic, the logic of the various cultures is not entirely the same. F. H. Smith explained those differences by elaborating three ways of knowing: the conceptual (corresponding to Northrop's cognition by postulation); the psychical (corresponding to Northrop's cognition by intuition); and the concrete relational in which "life and reality are seen pictorially in terms of the active emotional relationships present in a concrete situation" (more or less corresponding to Boas's "primitive" thinking).[6]

Smith's approach dispelled the naive notion that there is one "proper" way of thinking and even the more sophisticated idea that there are only two ways of thinking. He not only elaborated three ways

---

4. Franz Boas, *The Mind of Primitive Man* (New York: Macmillan, 1938).
5. F. S. C. Northrop, *The Meeting of East and West* (New York: Macmillan, 1953).
6. Cf. Edmund Perry, *The Gospel in Dispute* (New York: Doubleday, 1958), 99–106.

of thinking; he clarified the relation between them and insisted that people of *all* cultures think in these three ways. Differences among cultures in this regard, Smith said, are due to the *priority* given to one or another type of thought. Since all peoples think in these three ways mutual respect is in order and cross-cultural understanding can be achieved.

Insights such as these constitute the stuff of which authentic and effective contextualizations are made! Armed with an understanding of the penchant for concrete relational thinking among Africans, Chinese, and various tribal peoples, the contextualizer will give more attention to the importance of history, myths, stories, parables, analogies, aphorisms, pictures, and symbols in communicating within these contexts. Understanding the psychical thought processes of Indians, the contextualizer will adjust to an approach to thinking and knowing that invests a kind of authority in the enlightenment experience that it refuses to invest in any product of postulational thinking, whether it emanates from science or Scriptures. Thus the emphasis on the nature of biblical revelation in the contextualized commentary on Galatians 2. Knowing the classical Muslim mind, the contextualizer will be better prepared for Muslim willingness—and even desire—to engage in debate concerning the relative merits of the claims of Christ and Muhammad or the integrity of the Koran versus that of the Bible.

The Linguistic Form—Ways of Expressing Ideas

Arguments having to do with the degree to which languages differ from each other and the significance of those differences is a crucial one. If Sapir and Whorf are correct in concluding that linguistic differences are deep and abiding, cultural gaps become more difficult to bridge, and the common origin of man and culture in the Divine tends to be obscured. If Chomsky and Longacre are correct that deep structures of languages betray significant similarities, cultural gaps can be crossed more readily, and the Divine origin of man and culture is more readily seen. The debate, therefore, is most significant to the Christian believer. We assume that there is something to be learned from both emphases, and we will underscore several practical lessons that can be learned from them.

First, a simple truism: People everywhere like to communicate in their own "heart" language, in the language in which they were enculturated.

Second, though individual differences result in varying aptitudes for language learning, almost anyone can learn another language.

Third, in learning a receptor language we should remember that there is no one-to-one correlation between languages. For example, among students of Japanse it is often said that there is no word for sin in the Japanese language though many Christian communicators in Japan often use the word *tsumi* as though in merely articulating it they convey biblical meaning! But it is also (increasingly) true that we do not communicate the biblical meaning of sin and related concepts (for example, *hamartia, adikia, anomia,* and *kakia*) in North America simply by resorting to the words *sin, injustice, lawlessness,* and *evil.* No two words in different linguistic contexts mean exactly the same thing. That is as true in translating from the first-century New Testament Greek to contemporary American English as it is in translating from either of these into modern Japanese.

Fourth, not only can we learn a receptor language; we can learn *from* it. European languages reflect the primary importance of time in Euro-American cultures. A person was, is, or will be sick. Languages which do not require this distinction between past, present, and future may seem strange to us, but they are instructive at the very point of their strangeness. Many tribal languages are almost devoid of abstract nouns. Concepts such as goodness, honesty, and beauty are not communicated apart from the concrete circumstance or particular thing, person, or action to which they relate. This does not mean that tribals are not philosophers. Rather, it indicates that they have a different way of philosophizing and theologizing. Communication which majors on abstractions will be foreign to them and, at times, incomprehensible.

The Behavioral Pattern—Ways of Acting

An entirely new dimension is added to our understanding as we examine examples of the many behavioral conventions through which people of the world communicate. The ideas of Edward T. Hall are now common fare among cross-culturalists, and the title of one of his books, *The Silent Language,* is now a part of common parlance when speaking of nonverbal communication.[7] Concerning the "silent language" William S. Howell writes that "the norms of non-verbal interaction involve kinesics, the purposeful use of the body to transmit meaning; proxemics, the use of space and the physical relationship of those communicating; and paralanguage, vocal elements other than those integral to the spoken words, e.g. quality, volume, etc. Interwoven, they constitute the non-linguistic codes of a culture."[8]

---

7. Edward T. Hall, *The Silent Language* (Greenwich, Conn.: Fawcett, 1966); *The Hidden Dimension* (Garden City, N.Y.: Doubleday, 1966); *Beyond Culture* (Garden City, N.Y.: Doubleday, Anchor Books, 1977).

8. William S. Howell, "The Study of Intercultural Communication in Liberal Education," *Pacific Speech* 2, 4 (1967).

Other specialists refer to still other types of nonverbal communication, but kinesics, proxemics, and paralanguage are perhaps the most important. Contextualized communication, then, involves not only what we say but how we say it. Beyond that, it involves what we communicate when we say nothing or do anything. Even though, as we have said, the contextualization models with which we conclude this book will focus on verbal communication, that should not be construed to mean such behavioral patterns as those involved in gestures, rituals, positioning, tone of voice and the like stand apart from the contextualization process. In fact, when one *reads* Luther one can almost *hear* the tone of voice and *see* the intensity of the man who communicated Reformation truth to sixteenth-century Europe (see pp. 231–35). And when debating with a Muslim one must know too much agitation or any display of rancor or disdain will undermine the argument of the Christian advocate.

Media Influence—Ways of Channeling Communication

Though he held to stipulated definitions of "media" and "message" (the change of pace occasioned in human affairs), Marshall McLuhan shattered forever the notion that messages can be "put into" any medium and "come out" intact, untainted, and untouched. Not only do media affect the message; in McLuhan's view they constitute the "message." "The medium *is* the message," said McLuhan.[9] Literacy made it possible to communicate without the involvement of face-to-face involvement. Moveable type promoted sequential learning and government by law. Electronic media, especially television, are remaking the world into a global village.

But in less grandiose ways, attention to the predispositions and preferences of a respondent culture can help all of us to develop sensitivity in media selection and use. Initiators of programmed textbooks for theological education in Africa discovered that even highly motivated African pastors dropped out of the program after several lessons. For one thing the approach used in the textbooks did not "make sense." Students were required to work out certain problems before looking in the back of the book for the correct answers. From their point of view (concrete relational thinking) it was illogical to have to work out the problems if the answers were already known. For another thing, the books were singularly uninteresting because they contained no pictures!

To include pictures and illustrations would seem a simple thing, but a variety of studies indicate that this is not so. Bruce L. Cook did extensive research in Papua, New Guinea, designed to answer the ques-

9. Marshall McLuhan, *Understanding Media* (New York: McGraw-Hill, 1964).

tion, "What kinds of pictures communicate most effectively with people who can't read?"[10] He states his conclusion as "rules of thumb," and his very first "rule" flies in the face of the Western tendency to overlook cultural differences in order to reach a mass audience. It is this: "Sociological and educational differences have the most effect on picture understanding."[11] Picture content is more important than picture style, and pictures of people are most easily understood in nonliterate cultures.[12] He concludes that color is very important and that, apart from color, realistic art (detailed black-and-white line drawings) seem to be best.[13] Other findings are equally important. For example, Cook said, it cannot be assumed that ". . . viewers automatically recognize a cause and effect relationship between two pictures."[14]

To take one more illustration, Charles H. Kraft, Eugene A. Nida, and others have criticized the almost exclusive focus on the spoken sermon as the medium for the communication of the gospel among many Christian groups. One need not denigrate the importance of the sermon to admit that they have a point. Those who attended the Conference on World Evangelization held in Pattaya, Thailand, in 1980 will vividly remember the dramas put on by a Thai drama group even though they could not understand the Thai language. It is doubtful that many of them remember even one of the well-prepared and passionately delivered sermons delivered on that occasion by internationally known speakers.

The Social Structure—Ways of Interacting

People not only have ways of *acting* in accordance with culturally determined rules of conduct and meaning, they also have ways of *interacting* with each other on the basis of social conventions and understandings. The conventions of social structure dictate which channels of communication are open and which are closed, who talks to whom and in what way, and what kind of messages will be most prestigious and persuasive.

Lucian Pye tells of an election campaign in Jahore State, Malaya, involving two Westernized political candidates.[15] One of them took his

10. Bruce L. Cook, *Understanding Pictures in Papua New Guinea* (Elgin, Ill.: David C. Cook Foundation, 1981).
11. Ibid., 79–83.
12. Ibid., 80.
13. Ibid., 81–82.
14. Ibid., 83.
15. Lucian Pye, "Communication Operation in Non-Western Societies," in *Reader in Public Opinion and Communication*, 2d ed., ed. Bernard Berelson and Morris Janowitz (New York: Free Press, 1966), 612–20.

message to the people via rallies which attracted large crowds in village after village. Since his reception was so enthusiastic it was assumed by many that he would defeat his opponent by a wide margin on election day. The election, however, was won by his equally Westernized opponent who had engaged in little direct campaigning. Why? Because in conducting his campaign the popular candidate had bypassed the opinion leaders in the villages he had visited. This omission resulted in distrust and cost him the election. Obviously, success in politics in Malaya is more than "taking your case to the people" or "competing in the open marketplace of ideas."

Perhaps the classic case of a society where social conventions rule verbal and nonverbal communication is traditional China. About two and one-half millennia ago Confucius articulated the idea of the "rectification of names" and the ways in which rulers and subjects, fathers and sons, husbands and wives, and others should relate to each other. To this day, contextualized communication in Chinese culture either takes these conventions into account or runs afoul of them. This helps to explain why a tract written for individualistic Americans and given a gloss translation for Chinese with their emphasis on family relationships and obligations becomes more of an embarrassment to the gospel than an embellishment of it (see pp. 223–24).

The Motivational Dimension—Ways of Deciding

One reason for communicating interculturally is to encourage people to reach certain decisions which grow out of information and motivations which will be reflected in changed attitudes, allegiances, and courses of action. To a great degree the missionary task can be summed up in Paul's words, "Since, then, we know what it is to fear the Lord, we try to persuade men" (2 Cor. 5:11). But who is qualified to make decisions? What kind of decisions can they make? How are decisions made? What bases for decision-making are legitimate? The answers to such questions are largely dictated by one's culture. In many cultures the decisions of children and even older "students" are not really taken seriously. It is only when young people have finished their education and are prepared to settle down and support a family that they are considered ready for serious decision-making. Even then their decisions will tend to be consensus decisions, not simply individualistic ones.

To return to the context of traditional China once again, consider the case of an American missionary who presses a Chinese for conversion. Once the decision has been made the missionary is elated. But some days (or weeks, or months) later the Chinese "convert" does an about-face and gives evidence of a lapse of faith. The response of the missionary is almost automatic. Having been so quickly let down he becomes immersed in the slough of despond and unthinkingly cries out, "That's the way it is with these Chinese (Orientals). They decide for Christ and the next thing you know they have gone back on their decision. You just can't count on them." It never occurs to the missionary that his or her "disciple in the rough" may be reflecting the philosophy of Confucius (not because he is a Confucianist but because he is a Chinese) who explained that the "Superior Man" goes through life without any one preconceived course of action or any taboo. The Superior Man delays making a decision until it becomes absolutely necessary and then he makes it in such a way that he can reverse it if he becomes uncomfortable. True, motivational contextualization that is Christian does not immediately yield to Chinese "wisdom" at this point, but of necessity it takes it into account by focusing on the nuclear and extended family and in a variety of other ways.

Christian contextualizations that are both authentic and effective are based on careful attention to both the biblical text and the respondent culture. Authenticity is primarily a matter of interpreting the text in such a way as to arrive, as closely as possible, at the intent of the author through the application of sound hermeneutical principles. Through this process interpretation biases occasioned by the interpreter's own culture can be gradually overcome and, in that sense, the message can be decontextualized. Effectiveness is primarily a matter of contextualizing or shaping the gospel message to make it meaningful and compelling to the respondents in their cultural and existential situation. Both the decontextualization and the contextualization tasks are best accomplished by persons who are expert in the cultures and languages involved, who understand cultural dynamics, and who are themselves bicultural. But both tasks are so important that all who labor in biblical interpretation and all who undertake to minister cross-culturally should make an effort to understand the cultural dimensions of these tasks.

16

A Contextualized Christian Worldview
A Catechism for Tribals

The Shape of a Worldview

Recent studies emphasize the importance of communicating a Christian worldview in missionizing. Worldview has been characterized by Robert Redfield as the structure of the universe as the people of a culture see it or "know it to be." It is how people see themselves in relation to all things and all things in relation to themselves.[1] Norman L. Geisler has likened a worldview to the eyeglasses through which a person looks out upon the world.[2] Worldview colors and shapes all of a person's experiences. It provides the perspective from which he processes all new information. Therefore, even though a person or a people embrace certain truths of the gospel, if their non-Christian worldview is not exchanged for a Christian one, those truths and subsequent experiences will be interpreted from a non-

---

1. Robert Redfield, *The Primitive World and Its Transformation* (Ithaca, N.Y.: Cornell University Press, 1957), 85–86.
2. Norman L. Geisler, "Some Philosophical Perspectives on Missionary Dialogue," in *Theology and Mission*, ed. David J. Hesselgrave (Grand Rapids: Baker, 1978), 241ff.

Christian perspective. Consciously or unconsciously they will tend to fashion a syncretistic worldview.

There is reason to believe that this is the situation of churches in many parts of the world and that it presents a fundamental obstacle to carrying out the Great Commission around the world (to say nothing of evangelizing unbelievers and instructing new believers at home).

Worldview and Theological Types

Differentiating Theological Types

Making an impact on a worldview begins after we differentiate the various types of theology. B. B. Warfield defined the types this way:

> Apologetical theology prepares the way for all theology by establishing its necessary presuppositions without which no theology is possible—the existence and essential nature of God, . . . the possibility of a revelation and its actual realization in the Scriptures. . . . [We should note here that apologetical theology differs from dogmatic theology in that the former deals primarily with questions emanating from without the church while the latter deals with questions raised within the church.] Exegetical theology receives these inspired writings from the hands of apologetics, and investigates their meaning. . . . Historical theology investigates the progressive realization of Christianity in the lives, hearts, worship, and thought of men. . . .
>
> The task of biblical theology . . . is the task of coordinating the scattered results of continuous exegesis into a concatenated whole, with reference to a single book of Scripture or to a body of related books or to the whole scriptural fabric. . . .
>
> The relation of biblical theology to systematic theology is based on a true view of its function. Systematic theology is not founded on the direct and primary results of the exegetical process; it is founded on the final and complete results of exegesis as exhibited in biblical theology. Not exegesis itself, then, but biblical theology, provides the material for systematics.[3]

Warfield goes on to explain that exegesis is like the recruiting officer who selects those who will constitute the army. Biblical theology organizes the recruits into companies and regiments, arranges them in marching order, and readies them for service. Systematic theology combines these into an army—"a single and unitary whole, determined by its own all-pervasive principle."[4] It is this element of "all-inclusive

---

3. B. B. Warfield, "The Idea of Systematic Theology," in *The Necessity of Systematic Theology*, 2d ed., ed. John Jefferson Davis (Grand Rapids: Baker, 1980), 142–45.
4. Ibid., 146.

systematization" which determines the spirit and method of systematic theology and which "along with its greater inclusiveness, discriminates it from all forms of biblical theology, the spirit of which is purely historical.[5]

Warfield does not expand here on the nature of the discipline of practical theology, but he goes to some length to insist that systematic theology has not been the work of "cold, scholastic recluses, intent only upon intellectual subtleties" but rather has been the work of "the best heart of the whole church driving on and utilizing in its practical interests, the best brain."[6] Moreover he insists that we do not know religious truths in the abstract but in a systematized relationship to other religious truths. What we do not know in this systematized sense is robbed of half of its power to change our conduct.[7]

In line with this, systematic theologians Bruce Demarest and Gordon R. Lewis have tried to develop an *integrative theology* which explicitly relates theological truths and Christian life and ministry in both Western and non-Western contexts.[8] Despite the limitation of not having experienced extended ministries in non-Western cultures, the authors have had an encouraging response from foreign nationals who appreciate the effort to make theology relevant to life and work.

The Importance of Biblical Theology to Change in Worldview

If we follow Warfield's reasoning we are perhaps better prepared to discover a fundamental weakness in the traditional way of discipling the nations. Worldviews are made of thousands of pieces of myths and stories and narratives which purport to have historical connections. These have logical connections which could be (but seldom are) put together in a systematized whole. Now the way to supplant non-Christian worldviews with a Christian worldview is to replace false stories with the true story *as it is unfolded in the Bible.* To attempt to supplant a worldview by removing pieces from the false stories and replacing them with pieces from the true story is to err. The pieces of the Christian story can be expected to make sense logically only in the context of the larger biblical story. Both the method and content of *biblical* theology must precede the method and content of *systematic* theology when discipling the nations.

Traditionally missionaries have introduced Christianity and cate-

---

5. Ibid., 147.
6. Ibid., 156.
7. Ibid., 161.
8. See Bruce Demarest and Gordon R. Lewis, *Integrative Theology*, vol. 1 (Grand Rapids: Zondervan, 1987).

chized new believers in piecemeal fashion—translating this or that New Testament Gospel, preaching on this or that Bible passage, and teaching from one or another book of the Bible as has seemed best at the time. Even when they have attempted to be systematic they have usually dealt with topics that seem most important to them, but not necessarily to indigenes. The result has often been a failure to deal meaningfully with polygamy, witchcraft, ancestral and other spirits, power encounters, and the like until these concerns have been forced upon them. They have also dealt with such matters as the nature of God, sin, salvation, and Christian duty in ways endemic to Western instruction but not necessarily well suited to the Great Commission objective.

One of the authors recalls how impressed a number of early postwar missionaries to Japan were with a series of lessons put together by a colleague. At the expense of many hours of painstaking effort he prepared the lessons on basic topics he believed to be of critical importance if Japanese were to understand the Christian faith. The lessons were on the nature of God, revelation and the Bible, the deity of Christ, sin and salvation, and other topics of equal importance. To acknowledge the superiority of his approach and materials to most of the available alternatives required some measure of humility but no extraordinary amount of intelligence. Nevertheless, in retrospect, even his way of teaching left something to be desired.

Traditional evangelism and catechism communicate a more or less truncated systematic theology—Christian truths logically organized into some sort of unitary whole. The problem with this becomes apparent when we realize three things. First, in the missionary situation the historical data of biblical theology upon which systematics must be based are almost invariably lacking. Second, the development of systematic theology as we know it in the West is inextricably bound up with problems posed by Western philosophy, not by problems posed by tribal, Hindu-Buddhistic, Chinese, or various other worldviews. Third, systematic theology is the crowning, not the foundational, theological type. It comes after, not before, the fabric of biblical theology is in place.

This points to a superior way of discipling the nations, a way so obvious that we have tended to pass it by with scarcely a moment's consideration. It is the way God communicated his truth to mankind in the Bible in the first place. Let us first illustrate how it has been done and then briefly analyze it.

An Indonesian Case Study

In a tremendously insightful little book, unfortunately now out of print, Hans-Reudi Weber shows how Christian communicators can go about the business of teaching the Bible in a way that provides non-Western believers with a Christian worldview.[9]

The Assignment

Located in a remote area of Indonesia, Banggai was almost untouched until this century. Then in 1912 Muslim traders tried to convert some of its one hundred thousand scattered natives to Islam. Partly in response to the pleas of the Dutch government, the Reformed State Church sent a minister to the area. Over a few years he baptized thousands and left them without proper instruction or follow-up.

Converts were of three types: some were sincere, some felt under obligation to adopt the religion of their rulers, and some became Christians in order to remain pagan. Those in the third category thought they had to accept either Christianity or Islam and only the former would allow them to keep the pigs and dogs that were so important to their animistic sacrifices.

After World War II there were thirty thousand nominal Christians in numerous churches in the Luwuk-Banggai area. They were Christians and congregations without the Word of God, and most of them were nonliterate. In 1952 Weber, an experienced missionary, was asked to go and teach them the basics of the Bible. He was given no money and no helpers except indigenous personnel.

The Plan

The church was already divided into seven districts. It was decided to hold short Bible courses in each district. A team of district evangelists and ministers was chosen, and each congregation was invited to send some leaders to a five-day Bible course in a centrally located village. They were to pay for this in money or kind. The leaders had, on the average, three years of elementary education.

The format of the Bible course was simple but profound. By way of introduction, the importance of the Bible in the life of the Christian and the congregation was stressed. The first evening, the "travel route" to be taken through the Bible was sketched: creation to the kingdom of God in Revelation with Christ at the center of the whole and including the fall, the covenants with Israel, the church, and the second coming.

---

9. Hans-Reudi Weber, *The Communication of the Gospel to Illiterates: Based on a Missionary Experience in Indonesia* (London: SCM, 1957). This brief but pioneering work has been supplemented by Weber's *The Cross: Tradition and Interpretation*, trans. Elke Jessett (Grand Rapids: Eerdmans, 1979); and *Experiments with Bible Study* (Geneva: World Council of Churches, 1981).

The four succeeding days highlighted Genesis 3:1–9; Exodus 19:1–6; Luke 2:18–41; and Acts 1:6–11.

Each day began with worship, the reading of the Scripture passage of the day, and a prayer for guidance. Then the passage for the day was studied in small groups, making sure it was linked with preceding studies. Each group reported its findings, and a summary was drawn up. Later this summary was given to each student to help him as a cate-chist. Afternoons were spent in discussing community life, the mean-ing of baptism and communion, evangelism, and similarly important topics. The evenings were devoted to a discussion of Christians in a tribal community, modern Islam, and the world.

On the last evening the witnessing theme was put into action. The whole village was invited to a special gathering. The temple in Jerusa-lem was created, and Psalms 24 and 100 were recited antiphonally by "priest" and "Levite" and a chorus of men and women. Parables such as the good Samaritan (Luke 10:30–37) were mimed, and people were asked to guess the meaning. Then the parable was read from Scripture, explained, and a challenge was given. This was followed by hymns and teatime. Finally, the Genesis 1 lesson of the first evening was balanced with Revelation 21 with its vision of a re-created world of peace and righteousness.

The Lessons

Weber himself made a great discovery as time progressed. He kept hearing about tremendous Christians who would like to attend the stud-ies but could not do so because they were *buta huruf* ("blind with regard to letters," that is, nonliterate). Realizing that the great majority were in that category Weber started talking to more of the nonliterates and dis-covered that, though he spoke their language, communication was very difficult. When he asked the meaning of a word, they would not respond with a synonym or an abstract description. Instead they would use words to "paint a picture" that gave the exact meaning. When describing a person they would not talk about his character but rather would tell a few experiences that described the kind of person he was. Weber began to look upon the nonliterates as artists. He began to see himself as a stunted intellectual with but one method of communication—pallid abstract ideas. He became a pupil in order to learn how to communicate picturesquely and dramatically rather than intellectually and verbally.

Weber tried out his discovery in the nonliterate village of Taulan. The whole village assembled. Weber asked the heathen priest to tell the story of creation as the tribe know it. Then he used simple draw-ings on a blackboard to illustrate the Genesis story. He did the same with the fall and other biblical events. Finally, Weber conducted his

Bible study courses, modified to use the word-picture artistry of nonliterates. Later, in Java and Bali, he added the use of symbols, contrasting the Buddhist zoetrope, the Taoist sign, and the hammer and sickle with various Christian symbols such as the cross and crown.

It is impossible to do justice to Weber's methods in a brief space, but figure 19 will give some indication of the thoroughness of his approach and the capabilities of his learners.

Observations on Contextualized Evangelism and Catechisms

There is little to suggest that Weber gives sufficient attention to the fact that the encounter with tribalists often entails a power encounter that is at least as important as the truth encounter. Tribalists live with a variety of spirits, demons, gods, and goddesses—a galaxy of spirit beings who occupy a kind of intermediate range between humanity and a "high god" who is often considered to be too remote to be of immediate concern. Western missionaries are primarily concerned with God the Father, Son, and Holy Spirit. Because of the influence of naturalism they tend to give little attention to angels and evil spirits though they believe in their existence. As Timothy Warner has reminded us in his telling diagram, missionaries seldom come to grips with the beliefs and practices associated with supernatural personalities and powers that are of the greatest importance to tribal peoples (see fig. 20).

Christian cross-culturalists are beginning to see the importance of biblical theology in discipling the world's peoples. One of the most significant examples is the series of studies being developed for the New Tribes Mission by Trevor McIlwain after his experience with the Palawano tribesmen of the Philippines. Appropriately, McIlwain has entitled the first book in the series *Building on Firm Foundations*[10] because, like Weber, he constructs a biblical theology upon which to build a contextualized understanding of the Christian faith.

Again happily, certain contemporary scholars are pointing to the significance of biblical stories and the larger story of the Bible for Christian instruction within the Western context as well. Narrative theology uses biblical narrative as a point of departure for theologizing and teaching, not just as illustrative of biblical themes. There are limitations to this approach, but it does have significant positive and largely untapped potential. Though not ordinarily thought of as narrative theology, the course of instruction offered in *A Walk Through the*

10. Trevor McIlwain, *Building on Firm Foundations* (Sanford, Fla.: New Tribes Mission, 1987).

Figure 19
Weber's "History of the People of Israel"

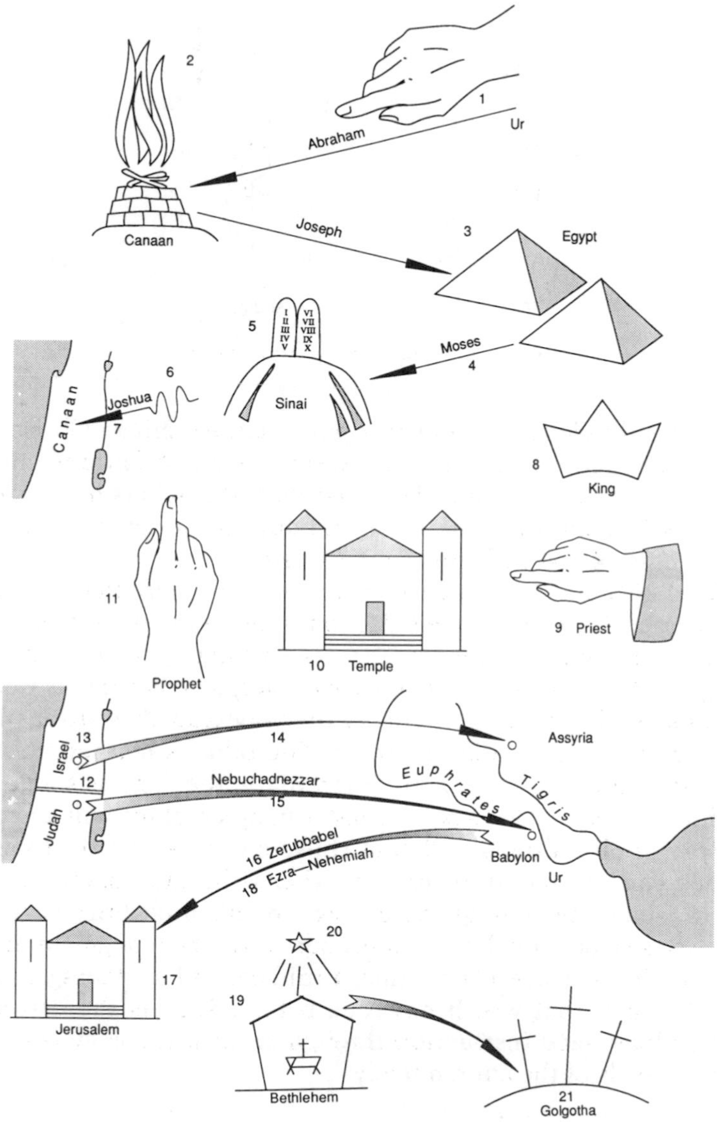

H.-R. Weber, *The Communication of the Gospel to Illiterates* (London: SCM, 1957), 85. Used by permission.

Figure 20
The Animistic Worldview
(creator/god)

Spirits: nature
ancestor
good/evil
Impersonal spiritual power

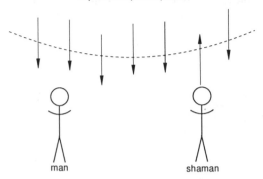

man   shaman

Timothy Warner, unpublished diagram. Used by permission.

Bible[11] exemplifies something of this potential. American Christians, some of whom have logged ten or twenty years of faithful church attendance, have testified that their pastors and teachers have not always provided them with the understanding of Scripture that they gained in a brief period with this course of study.

This kind of Bible knowledge adds up to much more than a collection of historical facts. It is knowledge that follows the pattern of God's unfolding revelation; knowledge that is intimately related to life; knowledge that comes through stories, parables, and pictures as well as propositions. Such instruction reflects the way God chose to instruct his children when he gave us the Bible. The Bible is neither a hodgepodge of data about God, nor is it a systematic theology as such. It is the unfolding record of God's person and principles, of his will and way. In it people of all cultures will find those episodes and truths with which they can intimately relate—whether it be the unbelief of the children of Israel, the consequences of Solomon's mixed marriages, or the steadfastness of Daniel and his friends in the face of government-mandated idolatry. It has a beginning, a middle, and an ending. Everything builds upon that which has gone before. Such is the nature of biblical theology—and instruction through biblical theology is one of the greatest needs of the church today.

11. Walk Through the Bible Seminars, 61 Perimeter Park, NE, Atlanta, Ga. 30366.

Most of us have had the experience of putting a jigsaw puzzle together—not just a simple one designed for children but a complex one designed to challenge adult ingenuity for seemingly endless hours. We have probably discovered that the saving factor in the situation was the small reproduction of the completed picture on the cover of the box. By observing the subject, outline, and shadings of the completed picture we were aided in discovering how to fit miniscule pieces into the whole. Ultimately we were able to put them in just the right place and experience a significant degree of satisfaction in doing so.

So it is in life, whether it be life in an Indonesian tribal culture or in the Hindu culture of India. Before becoming Christians, our animistic, Hindu, Buddhist, or Confucianist friends made sense out of world affairs and were able to cope with their crises and tragedies because they were able to fit them into one of those worldviews. As Christians they will be able to see where the smaller pieces fit to the degree that they grasp the larger picture which emerges when they are taught all that Christ has commanded.

17

A Contextualization
of the New Birth Message
An Evangelistic Tract for Chinese People

The Case of the Two Tracts

They were side by side on the tract rack of a Christian hospital in Hong Kong—two colorful tracts, one in Chinese and one in English. On both the orange-and-white cover pictured a Caucasian man with furrowed brow, resting his head on his hand in a contemplative mood. Above him where the words in bold letters, "How Can a Man Be Born Again?" and below were Jesus' words, "I say unto you, except a man be born again, he cannot see the kingdom of God" (John 3:3). On the next page the text started with the words, "A man named Nicodemus asked Jesus Christ this most challenging question recorded in the Bible (John 3:4)." The same page ended with the statements, "It is not membership in a church or a denomination. It is not personal (self-generated) righteousness or morality!" and the words of Isaiah 64:6. The two tracts were as identical in format and content as any two tracts in two languages as different as English and Chinese could possibly be.[1]

---

1. *How Can a Man Be Born Again?* (Hong Kong: World Outreach, Assemblies of God, n.d.).

222

This indicates a problem that has yet to be resolved by many Christian publishers of evangelistic materials. We have looked on as thousands of evangelistic tracts have been destroyed in lands where gospel tracts were sorely needed. Why were they burned? Because they constituted nothing more nor less than uncontextualized translations of English tracts. Expatriate evangelists and missionaries had dutifully distributed them by the thousands, but believing nationals were too embarrassed by the foreign format, style, and content to distribute them!

The Uncontextualized Tract on the New Birth

For comparative purposes it is necessary to summarize the content of the tract. Most of our readers will be able to fill in the details.

Using an arresting variety of type sizes and fonts, the text of the tract is as follows (throughout the tract are to be found numerous proof texts not given here):

How Can a Man Be Born Again? The Nicodemus conversation.

What "Born Again" Is Not! It is not membership in a church, self-generated righteousness, "Holy Communion," "water baptism," or confessing sins to a priest, minister, or rabbi.

Why Must a Man Be "Born Again"? Because of sin, an evil heart, death, and a need for transformation. God promises a new heart, spirit, mind, life, joy, peace, and hope.

How to Be "Born Again." By repenting of sin, believing that God sent his son, confessing one's sin to God through Jesus Christ, and receiving Jesus into your heart as your personal Savior.

Do It Now. Tomorrow May Be Too Late! No one can be sure of tomorrow.

The text is followed by a page which can be clipped off and mailed to a Hong Kong address. The page includes an invitation to receive Christ (a commitment section) and an application for a Bible correspondence course.

Investigation revealed that, in lieu of something more appropriate, this tract was being given to new Chinese parents by a missionary obstetrician. She believed that its message is true and that it could be used advantageously in certain cultural contexts. But in Hong Kong and for her purposes she felt that it simply did not fit. And in this feeling she was correct. The Chinese would be the first to point out its defects for their culture:

1. Its format is foreign. The Caucasian face on the cover (chosen so as to eliminate the cost of additional artwork?) is particularly problematic.
2. Its theme is ill-chosen. The "born-again" theme carries overtones of Buddhist reincarnation with no comparison of the radical differences between reincarnation and new birth.
3. It asks questions very few Chinese are asking, and it does not ask questions which they are asking. In communication terms, it does not reach felt needs.
4. It assumes a certain familiarity with the Bible by multiplying proof texts—a familiarity which the vast majority of Chinese do not possess.
5. It is too direct in its approach. The tract exhibits none of the subtlety with which the Chinese characteristically approach such questions.
6. It is totally lacking in local color.
7. It is too abstract. The Chinese are concrete-rational thinkers. That is, they tend to think in terms of particulars, of pictures, of stories, parables, and analogies. In this tract even the new-birth analogy is blunted by numerous generalizations and abstractions.
8. It carries an information overload. When one stops to consider all the background information that is essential to an understanding of the major ideas which appear in rapid-fire order in this tract, one is simply overwhelmed by all that is taken for granted. Perhaps it is this penchant on the part of Westerners (particularly Americans) for reducing the great mysteries of the universe into a short, simple formula and then repeating that formula over and over that accounts for a certain Chinese expression in Hong Kong. When they are particularly bored in a conversation the Chinese say, "*gong yeh son*," which means to "talk about Jesus" and carries the connotation, "Oh, there you go talking about Jesus again!"

A Proposed Contextualized Tract: "New Life"

Our obstetrician friend wanted a new, more appropriate and personalized tract that would appeal to the understandings and interests of new Chinese parents and that would elicit opportunities for further and more in-depth personal interaction throughout postnatal care. In response to her request we provided a contextualized tract entitled "New Life" with the understanding that *before publication the tract would be evaluated by several competent Chinese Christian leaders* and revised or replaced in accordance with their counsel.

What follows is the English text of the proposed tract. We have numbered the paragraphs here so we may refer more easily to its sections later.

1. It's happened! . . . You and your husband—and families and friends—have been waiting for this day. . . . Waiting for the new baby who would bear your name and link the past with the future. For nine months you as mother were the source of nourishment to this developing baby. Then there was the cry and the rhythmic pattern of breathing. We cut the umbilical cord. He (she) had arrived! There was NEW LIFE—independent of you, existing on its own!

2. Did I say "independent"? That's not quite true, is it? The responsibility of a mother and father does not end with the cutting of the umbilical cord. In fact, compared to babies in the animal world, a human baby is dependent upon its parents for what seems to be an inordinately long period of time—depending on them for food, clothing, shelter, and daily care.

3. It's hard work. And there are problems too. And once in a while the responsibility of parenthood seems almost too great. But at such times, parents remember how much they owe to their fathers and mothers, and grandparents, and others before them, and they also look ahead to the days when their child will assist them in old age, perpetuate the family name, and support the larger society. And suddenly the small hurts, the demands for love and attention, and the worry and work involved in meeting a child's needs seem insignificant in view of the potential of this small child with its NEW LIFE.

4. The hope that is wrapped up in this small baby makes us realize that parents have a responsibility that does not end with the cutting of that temporary lifeline we call the umbilical cord. Nor does it end with supplying those essentials of life without which a baby could never develop a strong body and mind. Nor will it end with planning for a child's education. Parental hopes for their children involve character and personal qualities that come only from careful spiritual training.

5. Perhaps that is why God—the Creator God who is the Author of all life—arranged that human babies would have a longer period of dependence and parental guidance. God made our human kind as more than just flesh and blood and bone. He made us as spiritual creatures in his own image—to have a modest beginning as babies, but also to grow and live on into eternity (after our body has perished) in his own presence. It is in this area of SPIRITUAL LIFE that man has failed. That's why men remember the ancestors but not the true God of heaven. That's why men are selfish and, thinking only of themselves, bring sorrow to others. That's why men ultimately face death with uncertainty and fear. And that's why many face eternity without hope.

6. Do you realize that the Creator God sent his only Son, Jesus Christ, into the world to give NEW SPIRITUAL LIFE to all who follow him? The

central message of the Christian Bible is that of Jesus Christ. In the Bible Jesus says, "I am come that you might have life and that you might have it more abundantly" (John 10:10). The Bible says concerning Christ, "As many as received him, to them gave he power to become the children of God, even to them that believe on his name" (John 1:12), and "He that hath the Son of God hath life, and he that hath not the Son of God hath not life" (1 John 5:12). Of course this is the NEW SPIRITUAL LIFE that Jesus himself spoke of when he used the interesting phrase "born again"—"Marvel not that I say unto you, you must be born again; that which is born of the flesh is flesh and that which is born of the spirit is spirit" (John 3:6–7). That is what all men need—you and I, and, when he (she) grows old enough to understand, that new little baby—the NEW SPIRITUAL LIFE that Jesus Christ alone can give.

7. Yes, when we have brought our brand new little baby into the world and the umbilical cord is cut, our responsibility still goes on. We must nourish and clothe and provide daily care. But even that is not all. Faithful parents who want the best for their children in this life and the life to come, will want them to know and follow Jesus Christ as their Savior and Lord.

8. Do you have a Bible from which you can learn about Christ? Do you need a spiritual counselor who can help you? This, after all, is now our primary concern . . . that you as a mother and your husband as father, and this son or daughter, may have not only healthy bodies and a hygenic home, but also NEW SPIRITUAL LIFE!

The "New Life" Tract: The Sequel

The contextualized and personalized tract was subsequently printed and distributed to new parents by our obstetrician colleague. Its front page features a picture of her with a newborn baby in her hands. The text is almost identical with that of the proposal but with a few revisions. The changes suggested by Chinese leaders and incorporated in the published tract are as follows:

1. In paragraph 1, "who would bear your name" has been changed to "who would become one of your family members."
2. In paragraph 6, "Just as your newborn baby is received into your family, in the same way a born-again Christian is received into the family of God" is added after the reference to 1 John 5:12.
3. At the end of paragraph 6 two Bible references have been added: Romans 8:17 and Proverbs 14:26.

Additional, less significant changes have also been made. Unfortunately we have not had opportunity to consult with the Chinese editors themselves, but current Chinese contacts indicate that the first change is more appealing to Chinese and that the additional sentence in the sixth paragraph reinforces the new-birth analogy (an analogy that we had suspected might be omitted altogether). They are at a loss to explain the additional Bible references at the end of paragraph 6. Overall, they evaluate the "New Life" tract as being far more relevant and compelling to new Chinese parents than "How Can a Man Be Born Again?"[2]

2. Paper submitted by Min-Fu Hsu for a class in cross-cultural communication at Trinity Evangelical Divinity School, Deerfield, Illinois, 13 June 1988.

18

The Doctrine of Justification by Faith Contextualized
Commentaries on Galatians 2 for Sixteenth-Century Europe and Twentieth-Century India

The Contextualization of Grace

Let us return to Bruce J. Nicholls's suggestion that contemporary India needs the truth of justification by grace through faith as much as did sixteenth-century Europe, but that a contemporary commentary for India would be contextualized differently than Martin Luther's commentary on Galatians 2.[1] He might have added—though it would have been superfluous in view of his purpose—that Galatians 2 itself constituted a Holy Spirit–inspired contextualization greatly needed by the church of Galatia in the middle of the first century. Those who have never really heard the truth of the gospel of grace need to hear it in contextualized form. So do those who have heard the truth of the gospel of grace but are confused and have surrendered it or are in danger of surrendering it.

---

1. Bruce J. Nicholls, *Contextualization: A Theology of Gospel and Culture* (Downers Grove: Inter-Varsity, 1979), 54.

The Doctrine of Justification by Grace Through Faith in Three Cultural Contexts

Consider, then, the need for the contextualized truth of justification by grace through faith in first-century Galatia, sixteenth-century Germany, and twentieth-century India.

First-Century Galatia

Advocates of the biblical approach to contextualization turn to Paul's missionary message to Jews, proselytes, and pagan peoples in Pisidian Antioch, Lystra, and Athens for models. It is entirely appropriate, however, that we take the Epistle to the Galatians, especially chapter 2, as a case in point. Soon after hearing and embracing the gospel, the churches in Galatia formed by new believers were invaded by Judaizers who insisted that true faith had to be accompanied by adherence to the law. Faith was deemed to be good but insufficient. One must be a Jew ritually to be a Christian truly.

Much was at stake in that challenge to the gospel. If the Judaizers had prevailed Christianity would have become little more than a sect within Judaism. The pure gospel would have been surrendered. The mission would have been aborted. In view of these potentially dire consequences, it was imperative that the confused believers and seekers of Galatia get a firm grasp on the meaning of grace and faith and their efficacy for salvation.

Sixteenth-Century Germany

Many factors lay behind the Protestant Reformation, but two stand out as most relevant to Luther's commentary on Galatians 2. First was Luther's own encounter with the truth of Romans 1:17. We are made righteous through faith in the promises of God as revealed and fulfilled in Christ. This negated any thought of works-righteousness. Second was the indulgence issue which grew out of an arrangement between Pope Leo X and the archbishop of Mainz whereby it was agreed that the archbishop would share in the profits of indulgences sold in his lands. Thus church and state shared money which accrued to the sale of merits presumably made possible by the superabundant merits of Christ and the saints. When Johann Tetzel preached these indulgences in the area near Wittenberg, Luther registered his protest. Subsequently the wrath of the pope and the full authority of the church came down upon the head of Luther. Sustained politically by the secular government of Frederick the Wise and spiritually by the testimony of Scripture, every fiber of Luther's being became dedicated to conserving and communicating the truth of *sola Scriptura, sola gratia,* and *sola fide.*

Twentieth-Century India

The background in first-century Galatia and sixteenth-century Germany are generally well known and require little review. The Indian case is different. Behind the Indian need for a contextualization of Galatians 2 lies the entire worldview and religious culture of India as expressed in the central ideas and practices of Hinduism and Buddhism. At the heart of both religions (and a primary motivation for Nicholls's statement) is the Indian idea of *kamma* (karma).

Daniel T. Niles says that, "stripped of all embroidery," the doctrine of *kamma* is:

> That I am responsible for what I am, since life is not haphazard but is determined by a principle of justice, each condition of life being the result of its own deserts.
>
> That *kamma* is produced by action consciously willed, so that while *kamma* is a cosmic law, it is also the law of my own being. It means I am master of my destiny.
>
> That also I share in the *kamma* of others, and they share in mine. In being born into a particular environment, I become part of the result of the *kamma* of others as they are part of mine. Thus the kammic law includes the fact that I can share my deserts, others partaking of the results of my action.[2]

In the *Sanyatta Nikaya* the essence of *kamma* is revealed in the following words:

> According to the seed that's sown,
> So is the fruit ye reap therefrom,
> Doer of good will gather good,
> Doer of evil, evil reaps;
> Sown is the seed, and thou shalt taste
> The fruit thereof.[3]

Man, therefore, has responsibility within a situation that is ethical, given, personal, and shared. Karma is inexorable. In this existence no one can be free from it. Bad karma cannot be forgiven.

At the same time, it is the message of Indian Buddhism that this situation is not "really real." The *dhamma* (Buddhist message) is that karmic existence is false existence and that when rightly understood we are free from it. True and final enlightenment, however achieved,

---

2. Daniel T. Niles, *Buddhism and the Claims of Christ* (Richmond: John Knox, 1967), 33–34.

3. From *Sanyutta Nikaya*, quoted in ibid., 33.

frees one from *samsara* (the wheel of birth and rebirth) in which karma operates.

Contextualizations of Galatians 2

With this abbreviated introduction to the cultures and conditions of the people of first-century Galatia, sixteenth-century Germany, and twentieth-century India in mind, we will reflect on how Paul and Luther communicated justification through grace by faith and how Luther might do so if he were a missionary to India today. Though Luther would remain Luther, he most likely would change the polemic tone of his commentary to one that is more apologetic. Whether he would give attention to critical exegetical issues in the text of his commentary could be debated, but we suggest that he probably would not.

Compare, then, Luther's actual contextualization for sixteenth-century Europe with a hypothesized Luther commentary for twentieth-century India.[4] (Note: We use the New International Version in order to facilitate the Indian contextualization. The English translation of Luther's Scripture references is based on the King James Version.)

Galatians 2

Vv. 1–2. Fourteen years later I went up again to Jerusalem. . . . I went in response to a revelation and set before them the gospel that I preach among Gentiles.

Luther's Commentary	Commentary for India
If God had not ordered Paul to Jerusalem, he would never have gone there. . . .	Here is a case of an apostle getting divine revelation. There is no indication that he waited in meditation. This was a day in which the true God—the God of Israel, the Jehovah of the Old Testament—sovereignly revealed his will, sometimes directly, to his special messengers the apostles, and sometimes indirectly through the church. The apostle Paul went by divine appointment to meet with the other apostles in Jerusalem to

---

4. See Martin Luther, *A Commentary on St. Paul's Epistle to the Galatians*, 2d ed., trans. Theodore Graebner (Grand Rapids: Zondervan, 1939).

verify that they were all preaching
the same good news of Christ Jesus.

Vv. 4–5. This matter arose because some false brothers had infiltrated
our ranks to spy on the freedom we have in Christ Jesus and to make us
slaves. We did not give in to them for a moment, so that the truth of the
gospel might remain with you.

Now the true gospel has it that
we are justified by faith alone, without the deeds of the Law. The false
gospel has it that we are justified
by faith, but not without the deeds
of the law. The false apostles
preached a conditional gospel.

So do the papists. They admit
that faith is the foundation of salvation. But they add the conditional
clause that faith can save only
when it is furnished with good
works. This is wrong. The true gospel declares that good works are
the embellishment of faith, but
that faith itself is the gift and work
of God in our hearts. Faith is able
to justify, because it apprehends
Christ, the Redeemer.

There they were—spies representing traditional religion. For
them faith was good but insufficient. Christ was the great Teacher
but not the incomparable Savior.
Even apart from the Old Testament law, there is a law written on
our conscience by the Creator
which says that a man sows what
he reaps. It is well that this is so
lest people think that evil brings
no punishment and good brings no
reward. That is justice. But for sinners before a holy God that is not
gospel, it is not good news. When
one understands that in the Bible
sin refers not alone to evil deeds
we do by choice, but also to what
we are by nature and in our very
attitude toward the true God himself, then we realize that the holi-
est man in India still needs forgiveness and a new life in Christ. This
is what the gospel offers. That is
why it is, indeed, good news.

V. 6. God does not judge by external appearance. [God is no respecter of
persons.]

Paul is quoting Moses. "Thou
shalt not respect the person of the
poor, nor honor the person of the
mighty" (Lev. 19:15). This quotation from Moses ought to shut the
mouths of the false apostles.
"Don't you know that God is no
respecter of persons?" cries Paul.
The dignity or authority of men

Paul is quoting Moses, the great
leader and lawgiver of the Old Testament times, who wrote, "Thou
shalt not respect the person of the
poor, nor honor the person of the
mighty" (Lev. 19:15). For the Jews
there was no one greater than Moses except God himself. The law
itself had been given through Mo-

means nothing to God.

I would honor the Pope, I would love his person, if he would leave my conscience alone, and not compel me to sin against God. But the Pope wants to be adored himself, and that cannot be done without offending God. Since we must choose between one or the other, let us choose God. The truth is we are commissioned by God to resist the Pope, for it is written, "We ought to obey God rather than men" (Acts 5:29).

ses. *But so had this principle: God does not judge by appearances.* In some cultures such as India, people have accorded great respect to those who have the "appearance of poverty." In some cultures people practically worship power. But neither poverty nor power matters to God. The question to be asked is this: Who faithfully teaches God's truth? Name the great religious teachers of history, such as Abraham, Moses, Vardhamana, Gautama, Muhammad, and Shankara. Some have been esteemed so highly that they have come to be worshiped. Among them were teachers of truth and good examples. But even the best of them were only men. Truth is greater than personality.

But what of the Christ whose person, work, and gospel Paul defends? Why was he different? To that question Paul will soon turn.

V. 9. James, Peter and John, those reputed to be pillars, gave the right hand of fellowship when they recognized the grace given to me. They agreed that we should go to the Gentiles, and they to the Jews.

It is as if the apostles had said to him: "We, Paul, do agree with you in all things. We are companions in doctrine. We have the same gospel with this difference, that to you is committed the gospel for the uncircumcised, while the gospel for the circumcision is committed unto us. But this difference ought not to hinder our friendship, since we preach one and the same gospel."

The most outstanding of the apostles in Jerusalem gave Paul and his companions the "right hand of fellowship," a symbol in that culture and time—as in many today—of mutual agreement and confidence. The conclusion of the meeting was important for all people of all places and of all times. James, Peter, and John would focus on the Jews—Paul and Barnabas on Gentiles. They were to have different audiences but they were to preach the same gospel. So it must be today. There may be many missions, many churches, many preachers in the world—but there is only one true gospel. And only those are "true" who preach and teach that one, true gospel!

V. 20. I have been crucified with Christ and I no longer live, but Christ lives in me. The life I live in the body, I live by faith in the Son of God, who loved me and gave himself for me.

Let us count the price. When you hear that such an enormous price was paid for you, will you still come along with your cowl, your shaven pate, your chastity, your obedience, your poverty, your works, your merits? What do you want with all these trappings? What good are the works of all men, and all the pains of the martyrs, in comparison with the pains of the Son of God dying on the cross, so that there was not a drop of His precious blood, but it was all shed for your sins. If you could properly evaluate this incomparable price, you would throw all your ceremonies, vows, works, and merits into the ash can. What awful presumption to imagine that there is any work good enough to pacify God, when to pacify God required the invaluable price of the death and blood of His own and only Son?

The order of the words in the Greek language of the original text puts special emphasis on "with Christ." Union with Christ—fellowship in His sufferings—became a central feature of Paul's life from the time of his conversion. Again, some English versions translate the Greek *zō de* as "nevertheless I live" or "yet I live." However, it might better be translated "and I live" because Christ's death was followed by His resurrection. To be joined with Christ in His death is veritably to be joined with Him in His life!

Christ was no ordinary man—in fact, he was not just an extraordinary man. He was the perfect Son of God who had been with God the Father from eternity past. On earth he was the perfect Son who always obeyed the Father. Note this. He was not another *avatar* and this is no myth. Jesus Christ was the only incarnate Son of God, and this is history.

More, he died no ordinary death—in fact, his death was not just a martyr's death. And he did not have to die; he *gave* himself to the cross. For what? A cause? No. "For me," says Paul, implying that it was for sinners everywhere. "He died for our sins," Paul says elsewhere. For our *lawlessness*—when we refused the law itself. For our *lawbreaking*—when we recognized the law but still broke it. *For me*. He *lived* for me—fulfilling the law that I would not, could not, keep. He *died* for me—dying the death which would have separated me from a holy, just God forever.

This is true *pattidana*—"man enjoying the merits of God's living and holy action in Christ." This is true salvation. True salvation is not the denial of the reality of the *kamma* principle or the reality of this world. It is a salvation in which Christ pays the penalty we incurred for breaking God's law and a salvation enjoyed in this world as well as in the next.

V. 21. I do not set aside the grace of God, for if righteousness could be gained through the law, Christ died for nothing!

Who could not detest his own vows, his cowls, his shaven crown, bearded traditions, yes, the very Law of Moses, when he hears that for such things he rejected the grace of God and the death of Christ. It seems that such a horrible wickedness could not enter a man's heart, that he should reject the grace of God, and despise the death of Christ. And yet this atrocity is all too common. Let us be warned. Everyone who seeks righteousness without Christ, either by works, merits, satisfactions, afflictions, or by the law, rejects the grace of God, and despises the death of Christ.

All of this is grace—*charis* in the Greek language. To refuse Christ is to say, "As far as I am concerned Christ died in vain." It is to refuse the only real righteousness available—Christ's righteousness. To believe, to accept, is the only proper response. For, you see, *charis* has a twofold meaning— God's offer *and* man's response. Elsewhere Paul says that when men knew God they did not respond by glorifying and thanking him. So God gave man up to unbelief and idolatry (Rom. 1). Now in Christ he offers his salvation, his righteousness — himself — once again. And our greatest responsibility—our highest privilege—is to accept by faith what he offers in grace.

Summary

Before drawing any conclusions whatsoever, let us allow that this contextualization represents only brief extrapolations and in the Indian case is very tentative. An exemplary contextualization for India must be done by someone who lives and works there (preferably a national) and would have to exhibit more of the "local concreteness" evidenced in Luther's sixteenth-century commentary. Nevertheless, building on these partial contextualizations we offer some principles which seem to us to be of crucial contemporary importance.

First, as is the case with all authentic Christian contextualizations, contextualized commentaries reflect understandings of the receptor culture by comparing biblical truth with cultural ideas in such a way that the truth of the gospel is confirmed and communicated both where that truth is reflected and where it is distorted by the local culture.

Second, the truth of the gospel is preserved by asserting the uniqueness of Holy Spirit–inspired "contextualizations" in Scripture and by sustaining biblical "text as text" insofar as is possible. Invariably, interpretation is involved in both the translation and the application of Scripture. But Scripture authority is maintained (and dogmatic theology à la Nicholls is made possible) only to the degree that the biblical text itself is distinct from commentary on the text. The authentic contextualizer refuses to place private interpretations in the text.

Third, a commentary is the appropriate vehicle for the "context-specific" messages which, in contrast to generalized utterances, result in understanding and impact.

These three principles are evident in the contextualizations we have just reviewed. Cultural and subcultural notions are challenged; biblical authority is maintained; gospel truth is communicated. To some in the first century, Paul must have been thought of as making a big fuss out of little nothings. But Paul knew that the truth of the gospel was at stake. By divine inspiration he wrote to expose heresy for what it was and is. Similarly, Luther's commentary sounds harsh and uncharitable, especially in this day of ecumenical concern, dialogical endeavor, and relational theology. But *as commentary* he preserved the integrity and truth of Scripture in a way that helped ignite the fires of the reformation.

The tone of a commentary prepared for contemporary India, caught as it is between Hindu inclusiveness and gospel truth, is quite different. After all, we are not addressing misunderstandings that are to be found only or primarily in the believing community but in the unbelieving community as well. Nevertheless, the superiority of the biblical text over all competing texts must be sustained, and the truth of the biblical gospel as compared with all competing false gospels must be established.

Contextualized commentaries on Galatians 2 for sixteenth-century Europe and twentieth-century India are so diverse in substance and style that it would be most inappropriate and even incomprehensible if the European commentary were to be translated into Hindi today or the Indian commentary to be translated into German for the sixteenth century. But, beginning with the biblical text and contextualizing its teaching for these two very different contexts, the biblical message becomes understandable and compelling in both contextualizations.

19

A Contextualization for Muslims
A Debate

The Strategy of Public Encounter

Throughout the history of the Muslim/Christian encounter the public debate has played an important role. Pre-Reformation missionaries from Constantine (see pp. 22–24) to Raymond Lull, and modern evangelists from Samuel Zwemer to Josh McDowell, have sought to expose the inadequacies of Islam by means of this vehicle. However, it is interesting to note that the perceived outcome of such debates have often been disputed. The outcome seems to depend on the listener's orientation: A Christian is likely to view the representative of his own faith as the winner, while the Muslim will tend to regard his fellow Muslim's performance as superior.

This discrepancy, however, should not be viewed as somehow rendering the debate strategy without merit. It may well be difficult to declare an obvious winner, but if carefully prepared and presented the debate may encourage a more honest search for the truth. The following hypothetical debate is based upon our own experience,[1] as well as

---

1. One of the authors has been invited to debate Muslims on several occasions. The topics included the general concept of God, the expectations of a true religion, the solution to sinfulness, and the identity of Jesus Christ. Two other debates are drawn

that of other Christian apologetes. It is a composite of several debates dealing with a few major issues which could be useful in preparing for and evaluating such encounters.

The Debate

Moderator: Ladies and gentlemen, welcome to an open dialogue between Islam and Christianity. The Muslim representative is Dr. Mahmood, distinguished Muslim scholar of the Christian Bible. Speaking for the Christian faith is Dr. Jones, experienced missionary and Christian authority on Islam. This evening we will depart from our usual format and encourage an interactive and spontaneous discussion. Rather than fifty-to-sixty-minute opening statements followed by rebuttals we will allow each speaker to make a brief response to the question posed by myself and then direct further questions and comments to his debate partner. Since this arrangement bears the risk of deteriorating into a disorderly exchange, I beg the participants to exercise discipline and courtesy.

Let me direct my first question to Dr. Jones. Islam and Christianity are among the few monotheistic religons of the world. What are the distinctive features of your respective general understandings of God?

Jones: Your question raises the issue of the so-called attributes of God, that is, those permanent qualities which constitute his nature and which cannot be applied to man. Accordingly we are able to speak of God's greatness. This idea includes characteristics such as his spirituality, his personality, and his infinity. Thus, we view God as a personal being bound neither by time nor by space. To this we could add the idea of God's goodness. This concept provides a framework for speaking about his absolute moral veracity, his holiness, justice, love, and mercy.

Moderator: Much of what you say could also be asserted by a Muslim, is that not so, Dr. Mahmood?

Mahmood: Indeed, the concept of an eternal, unlimited, and just God is central to Islam. However, although much of what Dr. Jones has stated sounds familiar—after all such information was revealed by God even to the Jews and Christians—it does not reflect the main emphasis of Islam. You see, a Muslim's first response to the question of the nature of God will be an affirmation

upon: one between Ahmed Dedat and Robert Douglas ("The Crucifixion: Fact or Fiction") and another between Josh McDowell and Dedat on similar issues.

of his unity. As it is stated in the Holy Koran (Sura 112): "Say: He is God, One, God, the Everlasting Refuge, who has not begotten, and has not been begotten, and equal to Him is not any one." So it is that we refuse to compare him with anything human.

Jones: Just a moment. Doesn't the Koran itself use anthropomorphic language with reference to God? In Sura 30:37–38 we read about the "face" of God. Isn't that comparing God with the limitedness of mankind?

Mahmood: No more so than those Old Testament passages which speak about the "hand" of God (Ps. 138:7–8). In such cases, both the Bible and the Koran employ certain analogies in order to aid us in our understanding of God. How else are we humans to recognize him? To use these parallels is not in any way to ascribe to God the limiting characteristics of a human. That would involve us in the most grievous of all sins (*sirk*) and is exactly what the Christians are guilty of when they insist on ascribing to God the fatherhood of Jesus.

Moderator: But why would the concept of fatherhood be any more or less limiting than the terms you have already mentioned?

Mahmood: Because the Christian understanding of that Father/Son relationship is not to be understood as an aid to understanding God but rather the most evil of all sins. It goes beyond ascribing some limiting qualities to God. It even ascribes the eternal attributes of God's divinity to a man and thereby violates the unity of God. He is one, not three. He is eternal and indivisible and cannot share divinity with anyone.

Jones: No Christian would claim to worship three Gods. In fact the kind of tritheism against which Muhammed argued has also been rejected by Christians. In Sura 5:116 we find reference to a "trinity" consisting of Jesus, the Father, and Mary. This understanding of the Trinity may reflect the teaching of the Collyridians, who are reported to have included Mary in the Godhead,[2] but it does not reflect teaching of any orthodox Christian group.

Moderator: Perhaps, but that does not solve the problem raised by Dr. Mahmood with regard to the supposed deity of Christ.

Mahmood: Now I don't want to be misunderstood in this matter. I am not trying to disparage the person of Christ. In fact, Islam is the only non-Christian religion which makes it an article of faith to believe in Jesus Christ. He is viewed as a mighty messenger of God, as

---

2. Epiphanius of Salamis describes the Collyridian sect (*Panarion* 3.2.79).

having had a miraculous birth, as one who has given life to the dead and healing to the sick. However, what we cannot tolerate is ascribing deity to him. He may be the greatest Prophet after Muhammed but he is not God. But Dr. Jones, you are a learned man. Perhaps you can provide us with some reason for this belief of yours.

Jones: The best thing for me to do is refer you to Christ's own words. In John 10:30 he is reported to have said, "I and the Father are one." In John 8:58 he points to his preexistence by saying, "before Abraham was born, I am." He even gives us an answer to the question you raised about how to recognize God. "Anyone who has seen me has seen the Father. How can you say, 'Show us the Father'?" (John 14:9). If these statements are not plain enough, also consider the sign or proof he supplied. In John 2:19 Jesus, in response to the Jews' desire for a sign, said, "Destroy this temple, and I will raise it again in three days." He was, of course, speaking about his own body and in that way ties his identity to his own death and resurrection. In other words, the crucifixion and resurrection of Jesus provides proof not only of what he accomplished but also of who he is, namely the divine Son of God.

Mahmood: Your appeal to the crucifixion proves nothing. As you know, the Prophet—peace be upon him—revealed to us the fact that Jesus was never crucified, that he didn't even die. It was merely the boasting of his enemies who said, " 'We slew the Messiah, Jesus son of Mary, the Messenger of God'—yet they did not slay him, neither crucified him, only a likeness of that was shown to them . . . God raised him up to Him" (Sura 4:156).

Jones: What then of the eyewitnesses, the disciples who saw not only the execution, but also—

Mahmood: Wait, according to your own New Testament, they could not possibly have seen anything. According to Mark 14:50 all disciples fled. Therefore they could not be eyewitnesses. Any information they did have was based on hearsay.

Jones: Certainly they fled, but it is simply an assumption on your part to conclude that they did not return or did not witness any of these events, especially the postresurrection appearances of Christ.

Mahmood: All right, then, just what was it that they saw? Jesus returned after his crucifixion and the disciples were terrified. Why? Ordinarily one would embrace a returning friend. Not so in this case. Why the great fear? Most likely because they assumed that what they saw was a spirit. This assumption was probably based on the fact that they had heard, through hearsay, that Jesus had been hanged on a cross. Thus they were afraid. In order to correct their false perception Jesus said, "Look at my hands and feet. . . ." (Luke 24:39). In other words, it is not as you think; a spirit has no flesh and bones. Jesus himself points this out in one of his answers to the Jews. On one occasion they tried to trap Jesus by asking which one of several men who had been married to a single woman would have her in heaven (Luke 20:27–40). Jesus' answer was that there will be no marriage in heaven because we will be like angels, that is, we will be spirits with no physical bodies.

Jones: But again you read too much of your own understanding into the text. Yes indeed, we are told that the disciples were afraid. In fact, Luke (24:37) seems to go out of his way to underscore the terror they experienced at seeing Jesus. But the reason for their fear was a result of their not having grasped the nature of the resurrection. They thought that they were seeing a phantom, that is, a ghost. To their way of thinking a ghost or spirit was an independent being which was to be distinguished from normal beings which can be perceived by the physical senses. The same thing happened when Jesus approached them on the water during the night (Matt. 14:26). They were not afraid because they thought he had been killed, but rather because they falsely identified the being coming toward them. In that case, as well as after his resurrection, Jesus does not have to show them that he is alive, but rather he alleviates their fear by identifying himself. During the post-resurrection period the most obvious form of positive identification was the clear evidence that he had indeed been crucified, his very wounds.

Mahmood: If you choose to speak of clear evidence, let us turn to Jesus' own statement concerning the sign he was asked to provide. In Matthew 12:38–40 the Jews ask him to give a sign. In reply Jesus promised them a single sign, that of Jonah. Now the whole point of that sign was the fact that, although one could expect his death, Jonah did not die. Was he alive when he was cast overboard? Yes, and he was still alive after he was put back onto the shore. What makes this a great miracle is the fact that he did not die either in the sea or in the fish. If you were going to take this seriously, you would have to assume, by analogy, that Jesus too did not die. Jesus is thought by the Christians to have been dead. But after the resurrection Jesus never dared to remind them of this sign. In addition to this, we should also expect Jesus to have been in the grave three days and three nights. But, the traditional account places him in the grave Friday evening and out again Sunday morning, only one day and two nights. This does not fit the sign, does it? Who is the liar?

Jones: The New Testament leaves no doubt about the fact that he died. In Matthew's Gospel (27:50) we are told that "he gave up his spirit." Mark 15:37 tells us that they crucified him and that he "breathed his last." There is no question about what is being presented here. He did die. Even the Koran speaks of his death (Sura 3:48) and the "day of his death" (Sura 19:34). How do you explain that?

Mahmood: According to the Koran, Jesus was not crucified but taken up into heaven (Sura 4:156–60) thus ending his earthly life.

Jones: In the case of the sign the issue is not whether he was dead or alive, and not whether he was in the grave three days or one day and a half, but rather the fact that he was entombed and cut off from the living. Dr. Ahmed Dedat also seems to ignore the traditional Muslim interpretation and puts Jesus, alive, in the grave for three days instead of him never having been in the grave at all. Who is right? Why make such a fuss about the time spent in the grave? After all, what does five minutes mean in the Middle East? A little while, right? Then counting days in that way is to ignore the wide range of possible meanings and to trivialize the issue. That is something that should not be done to so meaningful an event, namely, that Jesus consciously sacrificed himself for the world.

Mahmood: But how can you claim that he died for the sins of the world? His behavior seems to be more like that of a man desperately clinging to life. At the Last Supper he told them to buy swords, that is, to arm themselves. Then they went to the Garden of Gethsemane in the middle of the night. Jesus posted eight men to guard the entrance and took two with him into the garden. This was his inner line of defense. Now, according to Christians there was a contract between the Father and the Son before the foundation of the world. Then why did Jesus pray the way he did? Does this sound like a man who is about to willingly sacrifice himself for others? Hardly. He intended to fight off the threat. But the Jews outsmarted him by bringing Roman soldiers with them. Jesus had to capitulate and thereafter he behaved like one who has escaped death by the skin of his teeth and not like one who had been resurrected.

Jones: The biblical texts which you cite give us no reason to conclude that Jesus was setting up guards in the garden, nor preparing
for a fight. No, those conclusions seem to be assumptions you
make in order to support your own opinions. Jesus was not preparing for battle but for the ultimate sacrifice. This is something to
which all to Scripture gives witness. From its beginning the Holy
Book points to the death and resurrection of Jesus. In Genesis 22
the report of Abraham's willingness to sacrifice his own son[3] is an
allegory pointing to the loving nature of God. Exodus 12 provides
the background for understanding Jesus being the Lamb of God,
that is, the Passover Lamb. This idea is echoed in many Old Testament passages. And then in John 12 there is the parable of the seed
falling into the ground, dying, and bringing forth new life. John
9:35 refers to the Son of man, the one who was speaking to the
disciples and who would pour out his blood as a ransom for many
(Matt. 20:28). Not only are we told that he did die, but also why. It
was because of man's sin. Sin is, of course, not just some kind of
mistake—

Mahmood: Just a moment. The whole idea of one man dying for
another is fundamentally unjust. Why would God need to take
one man's life in order to save another?

Jones: That is what I was getting to. Sin is not just a kind of ethical
mistake but a deliberate choice with severe results. How many of
you can overcome self-centeredness and lust on your own? You
cannot. And for that reason the crucifixion is really a matter of
honor. You see, sin brings dishonor to God. How does one deal
with dishonor? With ritual? What about the honor of God? What
is to be done? In John 5:23 we are told that "he who does not honor
the Son does not honor the Father, who sent him." So the crucifixion was necessary because we violated the honor of God, and
without it we have no hope. It was a demonstration of God's love,
and it brought together and satisfied both the justice and the
mercy of God. Jesus' voluntary death on the cross was the most
profound example of this—he laid down his life for his friends.
Perhaps it would be useful to point to a case of substitutionary
death imbedded in Muslim tradition. When Husayn was killed
during a battle on the plain of Karbela (A.D. 680) he is reported to
have said, "I die parched, and offer myself a sacrifice for the sins of

---

3. At this point we could be much more specific and refer to Isaac by name. However,
given the Muslim's conviction that Ishmael was the object of this particular account, it
is probably wise to leave the person unnamed.

my people, that they should be saved from the wrath to come."[4] You see, then, the idea is not completely foreign even in Muslim tradition.

Moderator: Since the allotted time has almost elapsed I want to give each participant a final opportunity to summarize his own position. Dr. Jones . . .

Jones: As I have stated, the substitutionary death and resurrection of Jesus is crucial to the Christian faith. It not only provides the basis for our salvation; it also gives us a direct encounter with God. That is, in Christ God himself has broken into time and space. The final proof of this divine nature was given by Christ himself. He said that he would be crucified and would rise up again after three days and that is exactly what he did.

Mahmood: In closing I would like to point out that even the New Testament writers forsaw the coming of Muhammed. In John 14 Jesus explicitly states that another would follow. This fact is also confirmed by Jesus' own statements in the Gospel of Barnabas (221).

As the reader can see, this type of exchange could be useful in clarifying some of the concerns involved in the Christian/Muslim encounter. Obviously the issues addressed in this debate represent only a few of the questions which could and eventually should be raised. For example, at some point in our dialogue with Muslims the relationship between the Koran and the Bible—including the matter of their respective claims to authority and textual integrity—will have to be raised.[5] There is reason to believe that through the vehicle of a debate the gospel could be presented in such a way to encourage individual Muslims to reconsider traditional answers and positions. One may not necessarily have to think in terms of a live or actual debate. A written account such as has been presented here could be submitted for group discussion, something akin to a case study. As to who won—that we leave up to the reader.

4. Thomas Patrick Hughes, *Dictionary of Islam* (New Delhi: Oriental, 1976), 416. Husayn's martyrdom is celebrated during an annual "passion play" (Muharram).

5. See David J. Hesselgrave, "A Legacy of Enmity," *Moody Monthly* 88 (October 1986): 72–75; and Nathan D. Irwin, "On What Authority—The Quran or the Bible?" *Trinity World Forum* 5, 1 (1979): 6–8.

20

A Contextualized Sermon
for Nominal Christians
in Central and Northern Europe
The Lordship of Christ

Contextualizing the Lordship of Christ

Nominal Christianity can be defined as a secularized form of religious commitment which has been focused either on the formulation of Christian teaching (dogma) specific to one particular denomination or on the institution itself. This reorientation is, of course, the direct result of a rift between the sacred and the secular, a rift which calls the supernatural into question and tempts the individual to abandon the commitment to a personal God in favor of a more concrete ideology or even a material object. The reoriented Christian may focus on a system of doctrinal truth or a specific creedal statement. Commitment then is measured by degrees of orthodoxy. If the separation becomes absolute, a system of ethics, a philosophy, or some cause, such as the struggle for justice, might become the exclusive object of religious commitment. Obviously these objects can never elicit absolute commitment. Public opinion and doctrinal plurality always limit the scope, as well as the derived meaning and sense of purpose.

246

However, as the press of secularization continues to erode the authority of doctrine, the individual may feel compelled to anchor his commitment in something more solid than an invisible God. Institutionalized forms of religion become the focus of attention. Participation—not necessarily regular—in corporate church activities, church-sponsored projects, ritual, and membership are the standards of commitment. Often this will be related to doctrine, but there is no necessary connection between ritualistic practice and understanding or accepting specific beliefs. This kind of segmentation renders total commitment impossible. Secular obligation to a company, government agency, social club, or sports club steps in to take the place of meaningful religious commitment. These functional substitutes for religion become increasingly dominant as secularization advances, and commitment is increasingly limited to that sphere of life dominated by the respective institution.

Effectively directed to the nominal Christian, the gospel message must confront the inadequacy and insufficiency of a religious commitment focused on an institution and the inconsistency of an attenuated Christian commitment. The theological themes emphasized in any presentation of the gospel to nominal Christians should include:

1. *The need for a personal decision.* It is natural that men seek stability and security in systems and traditions that appear firmly anchored in history. Yet no human contrivance can adequately provide the desired benefits, which is why the institutional church is declining in influence, and secular society is unable to ameliorate the ills of modern society. The heightened sense of insecurity encourages the search for alternatives deemed more worthy of commitment, such as the peace movement. Alas, no human invention can serve as an object of absolute commitment. For these reasons, the Christian communicator should reemphasize the need for a personal decision to follow Christ. Rather than being swept along passively by institutional tradition and mollified by minimal requirements, the nominal Christian should be challenged by the radical nature of personal commitment and the cost of discipleship. Only within the context of an intensely personal relationship to a personal God can the individual hope to receive an affirmation of his own worth, God's unconditional love, and inner confidence and peace in the face of humanity's manifold ills.

2. *The lordship of Christ.* It is absurd to claim to adhere to a gospel meant to permeate and correlate all aspects of life while relegating its influence to a single sphere of life and limiting its function to the providing of social standing. Commitment is thereby robbed of rationale. It is moribund and unworthy of even the slightest investment. The gospel should be presented as unified and consistent. The communica-

tor should expose the fallacy of an atomistic orientation and expound the life-unifying nature of truth, life, and the inclusive nature of Christian faith. Submission to Christ's domination over all of existence is the only solution to the sophistic nature of a circumscribed commitment to a comprehensive system of truth.

3. *The empowering of the Holy Spirit.* Societal structures have never provided the means whereby the individual is enabled to comply with institutional demands. Thus, the communicator must emphasize that the gospel is the power of God which will transform anyone who believes. The gospel not only establishes clear norms, but also provides the wherewithal to meet God's demands. The communicator can demonstrate this aspect of the gospel in the effects of Christ's indwelling presence in his own life. The recipient has a right to see the results of personal commitment to Christ. Christian communicator and Christian community thus become part of the message.

One passage of Scripture which speaks powerfully to these concerns (especially the first two) is Hebrews 1:1–4. As has already been shown (see pp. 201–2), the development of a contextualized proclamation and application of the gospel progresses through several meaning-related stages. The communicator must begin by gaining an understanding of the *intended meaning* of the biblical text. This has to be coupled with a *decontextualization* of the communicator's own understanding of the text, that is, an examination of how his interpretation of the text might be affected adversely by a culturally determined, often ill-conceived, understanding or *perceived meaning* of specific concepts and terms. Finally, the *intended meaning* of the text has to be given an *applied meaning* to the listener's context.

Decontextualization: Divesting Ourselves of Culturally-Induced Misunderstandings

Hebrews 1:1–4 presents the North American with contextualization difficulties in at least two areas:

1. *Hebrew socioreligious traditions and institutions.* The historical context into which the Letter to the Hebrews was written presumes a knowledge of institutions which are unknown today. The prophet, for example, is likely to be taken simply as "one who foretells the future." Some of our contemporaries may broaden the meaning to include such dubious activities as palm reading, fortune telling, and the reading of horoscopes.

Similarly, the term *fathers* likely will be viewed as referring to one's own male parent or perhaps several generations of progenitors. The tendency toward this understanding is heightened by recent social developments in our culture, such as the demise of the extended family, the independence and mobility of the nuclear family, and the increase in single-parent homes, usually headed by mothers. These developments may lead to a decidedly negative view of fatherhood. In any case the phrase *the fathers* is not likely to have the religious connotation in our society that it did in ancient Hebrew society.

2. *The meaning of certain Greek (and Hebrew) words in translation.* The way in which the author uses some words in this passage may be difficult for the modern North American to understand. The term *world* may be given a purely materialistic or physical connotation. The word *radiance* may conjure up visions of a completely independent source of light, that is, one light among many. The word *power* may call to mind associations drawn from the modern business world.

Decontextualization is vital to communicating this passage, whether one views it as preliminary to contextualization or a part of the process. The culturally induced tendency to misunderstand and misapply the text must be recognized and corrected by careful attention to the socio-cultural and linguistic context in which the revelation was originally given.

Interpretation: Determining the Intended Meaning of the Text

As a final illustration of our vision and design of the contextualization process we offer the following set of abbreviated notes for a sermon to a German congregation. The first set of notes works through exegetical procedures and highlights aspects of the text relevant to the objectives of the contextualization.[1]

1. **Authorship and date.** The author was probably a second-generation Hellenist Christian who addressed the letter to believers in Rome (?) shortly before A.D. 64.[2]

2. **The text.** Certain observations on significant features and variant readings in the text are important.

Verse 1: Note the alliteration of the *p* throughout the verse,[3] a common literary device.

---

1. Commentaries consulted for this exegesis were F. F. Bruce, *The Epistle to the Hebrews* (Grand Rapids: Eerdmans, 1964) and Otto Michel, *Der Brief an die Hebräer* (Göttingen: Vandenhoeck and Ruprecht, 1975). See also Helmut Feld, *Der Hebräerbrief* (Darmstadt: Wissenschaftliche Buchgesellschaft, 1985) and Mathias Rissi, *Die Theologie des Hebräerbriefs* (Tübingen: JBC Mohr, 1987).

2. Bruce, *The Epistle to the Hebrews*, xxxv–xliv.

3. *"Polumerōs kai polutropōs palai ho Theos lalēsas tois patrasin en tois prophētais."* For an example of this literary device, see Clement of Alexandria, *Stromata* 1.27.1.

Verse 3: phanerōn instead of *pherōn* (the likely original) bears the markings of a scribal error. Of greater significance is the omission of *autou* and the insertion of *di autou* (as in Mss. P[46] and 1739) or *autou di* (as in D, K, and L). *Di autou* may indeed reflect the original reading, *autou* being an easy corruption and *di eautou* the conflation of the other two. This would lead to the translation "Jesus supports the universe by the word of power; through himself he has effectuated the purification of our sins."[4]

Verse 4: Note the omission of *tōn* (supported by P[46]), although *tōn angelōn* probably reflects the original.

3. **Exegetical observations.** Certain exegetical observations will be important to our contextualization for a German audience.

Verse 1: The subject of the sentence which spans verses 1 and 2 is clearly *ho Theos.* The definite article is used to connect with *uiō* (v. 2) and thereby indicate the common source of the revelation.

Patrasin and *prophētais* in the Jewish rabbinical tradition is an expression used to refer to the Jews' historical continuity with their religious past.

The terms *polumerōs* (the various revelational media) and *polutropōs* (the various modes of revelation) are not presented here as an expression of the richness of God's communicative resources but rather to point out the incomplete nature of those resources.

The phrase *lalēsas . . . en tois prophētais* is not to be understood as a specific mystical form of inspiration, but rather is to be taken instrumentally in the sense of the Hebrew use of *bĕyad* or *bĕ.* Philo writes, "A prophet says nothing of his own but is a translator or mediatory. Another gives him that which he brings."[5] In that case the Word of God is perceived to be promise, encouragement, or even salvation, but not an extension of the Law.

Verse 2: The eschatological phrase *ep eschatou tōn hēmerōn toutōn* is a rough equivalent of the Hebrew *b'aḥărît hayāmîm* ("in the last days," as in Gen. 49:1; Isa. 2:2; Dan. 10:14) and refers to the unbroken sweep of salvation history and, in particular, to the time of the Messiah. It may be appropriate to set this off from the first part of the verse with "but now" (*lalēsas*) balanced off against *elalāsen.* The apex of this sentence is reached with the words *en*

---

4. Bruce, *The Epistle to the Hebrews,* 3–4 n. 4.
5. As quoted by Michel, *Der Hebräer Brief,* 93 n. 2.

uiō. The absence of the definite article leads to the rendering "in [one who is] Son." Thus the idea of and the dignity of sonship are emphasized and contrasted with prophethood. This contrast between the prophets and the Son (Christ) implies the completeness and finality of the Word brought by the Son. His Word was not completely uttered until Christ came; but when Christ came, the word spoken in him was indeed God's final word. Seven facts about the Son are then presented to demonstrate both his own greatness and the superiority of the revelation brought by him.

"Heir of all things." There is a close relationship between the idea of Son and that of heir (see Ps. 2:8). *Ethēken* translates as "to make someone something." (See the Septuagint translation of 1 Sam. 18:12). *Klēronomon* designates ownership. However, this is not to be taken in a legal and technical sense but rather in an eschatological sense (the sense suggested in Heb. 2:8), since it embraces not only this present world but also the future world.

"Maker of all worlds." The object *aiōnas* corresponds to the rabbinic use of *'ôlamîm* which includes not only the chronological aspects but also the material, ideological, and religious contents of the world.

Verse 3: This verse takes the form of a liturgical or confessional statement.

The "effluence of God's glory" (*apaugasma*, here used in its active sense) denotes a radiated light which assumes the unity of the source and effluence (Wis. of Sol. 7:25). The writer of Hebrews goes beyond this personification of wisdom to describe One who lived on earth and was at the same time the radiance of God's very nature. *Doxēs* (Heb. *kabôd*) is the form in which God manifests himself (Exod. 24:16; 33:18) and comes close to being a synonym for God himself.

The "image of God's substance" (*charaktēr*, used only here in the New Testament) expresses in even stronger terms than would *eikon* the idea of a stamp or impression which, as in the case of a coin, corresponds exactly to the die used to make it. Thus, what God is is evident in Christ.

He "sustains all things by the word of his power." The Hebrew *nasa* underlies *pherōn* and emphasizes the activity of preserving the world from decay and chaos and thus assuring its appointed course (see Strack Billerbeck 3:637, rabbinic commentaries on Exod. 36:4 and Deut. 33:27). The construction is thought to be an "hebraic adjectival genitive"; thus, "His mighty word or his enabling word."

He has made "purification of sins." This is a priestly function (cf. Job 7:21) which only the Son of God could have made. He "sat down at the right hand of majesty on high." This refers not only to exultation but also to appointment to coregency, sharing in the functions of the throne (Phil. 2:10). The verb implies special privilege. According to rabbinical sources (Chag. 15a) only the *megalōsune* is allowed to sit in God's presence in order to record the deeds of Israel. Christ, however, is not a recorder but rather Judge and Lord. *Megalōsunē* (Heb. *gbûrâ*) is a character trait of God (1 Chron. 29:11; Ps. 145:3, 6) and is to be taken as a periphrasis for God. This term had already taken on a messianic interpretation in the apocalyptic literature (cf. Mark 12:36; 14:62 with Hen 453 51,3 61,8). In Christ the unity of priest and king has been completed and fulfilled.

Verse 4: The greatness of Jesus draws every possible accolade and underscores his special relationship to God, to the world, to history, and to man. His exaltation to coregency distinguishes him as superior to all other beings. His name *Son* (or perhaps "Lord") was given by God from the beginning (1:2), and was ascribed to him in full after he completed his appointed task.

Application: Delivering a Contextualized Sermon

The outline that follows is an attempt, based on the preceding exegesis, to contextualize a sermon for nominal Christians in Central and Northern Europe. The reader should understand that the European worship service—the setting in which this sermon was delivered—is generally characterized by a solemnity and dignity which the average North American would likely interpret as stifling rigidity. The reader may find the sermon to be rather unappealing because of its tightly reasoned theological style and the fact that it is devoid of humor and anecdotes. The difference between North American and German audiences underscores the necessity of contextualization.

Sermon Outline

Subject: The lordship of Christ
Theme: An Object Worthy of Our Faith
Sermon Text: Hebrews 1:1–4

Introduction: Let me begin with a modern parable:

Once upon a time two explorers came upon a clearing in the jungle. In the clearing were growing many flowers and many weeds. One explorer says, "Some gardener must tend this plot." The other disagrees, "There is no gardener." So they pitch their tents and set a watch. No gardener is ever seen. "But perhaps he is an invisible gardener." So they set up a barbed-wire fence. They electrify it. They patrol with bloodhounds. (For they remember how H. G. Wells' *The Invisible Man* could be both smelt and touched though he could not be seen.) But no shrieks ever suggest that some intruder has received a shock. No movements of the wire ever betray an invisible climber. The bloodhounds never give cry. Yet still the believer is not convinced. "But there is a gardener, invisible, intangible, insensible to electric shocks, a gardener who has no scent and makes no sound, a gardener who comes secretly to look after the garden which he loves." At last the skeptic despairs, "But what remains of your original assertion? Just how does what you call an invisible, intangible, eternally elusive gardener differ from an imaginary gardener or even from no gardener at all?"[6]

Explanation: The kind of skepticism expressed by Antony Flew in this parable comes as no surprise in the secularized world in which we live today.

1. There are, of course, many definitions of secularization. For some it represents the welcomed decline of Christian institutions which, after impeding progress for centuries, are now in the throes of their own demise. For others it is the radical separation of the secular and the sacred which will finally free us from the tyrannical tutelage of religion and its nonexistent gods. Thus unshackled, humanity can go about realizing its vision of a world in which technopolitical means will be used to solve ethical and societal issues.

2. The odd thing about all of this is that people, in spite of themselves, have not been able or willing to abandon the religious trappings of society. One almost gets the impression that they are hanging on to some form of belief "just in case."[7] Perhaps the fear of God has been supplanted by a new fear—a fear of the unknown—and the sneaking, unsettling suspicion that human abilities may not be all that they are cracked up to be.

3. This is not to be taken to mean that the secular person has any great interest in maintaining the status quo of the religious past. No, it might

6. Antony Flew, "Theology and Falsification," in *New Essays in Philosophical Theology*, ed. Antony Flew and Alasdair Macintyre (London: SCM, 1955), 96.

7. For documentation of this trend see Edward Rommen, *Namenschristentum* (Bad Liebenzell: Verlag der Liebenzeller Mission, 1985).

be more accurate to suggest that, among other things, even religious commitment has been secularized. Personal devotion has been replaced by a modicum of routinized public practice and external symbols. The content of beliefs and norms has been desacralized, trivialized, and generalized into oblivion. Nevertheless, collective ambivalence has not produced an exodus from the ecclesiastical institution. For some reason, all but the most rash of free-thinkers favor the maintenance of a Christian facade. Gerhard Szczesny has observed that Europeans "are witnessing a most curious performance, in which contemporary man professes himself to be a Christian with a vehemence that increases in direct proportion to his loss of faith. The farther his ideology and mode of living stray from Christianity, the more implacably he declares himself for his lost faith."[8]

4. For this reason most nominal Christians are offended by the assertion that they do not believe. Indeed, it would seem that they do believe in something. But the question is, "In what?" By all indications the object of their faith is some externalized form of institutional Christianity. But, is an institution a worthy object of religious commitment? Can mere tradition, doctrine, and ritual satisfy the human need for orientation? Hardly!

Thesis: The only worthy object of religious commitment (faith) is Jesus Christ.

Transition: That Jesus alone is worthy of our faith can be seen from the three unique relationships described in Hebrews 1:1–4.

I. Jesus' Unique Relationship to God
   A. Jesus is the Son of God (v. 2).
      1. This designation is found frequently in both the Old and the New Testaments. When it is used with reference to Jesus it is designed to point out his messianic office and his divinity.
      2. On the basis of the ancients' use of Hebrew we know that the term *Son* implies not subordination but rather essential identity.

        For example, between A.D. 132 and 135 the Jews rebelled against their Roman rulers. The leader of the rebellion was Bar Kokba who claimed to be the Messiah and referred to himself as the "son of the Star." The reason that he adopted this designation was his desire to be identified as the star which was to "come out of Jacob" to "crush the foreheads of Moab" (Num. 24:17).

        In a similar way, Barnabas, the "Son of Encouragement" (Acts 4:36), was the encourager, and the "Sons of Thunder," James and John (Mark 3:17), were men of a thunderous nature.

8. Gerhard Szczesny, *The Future of Unbelief* (New York: G. Braziller, 1961), 215.

        3. Thus when Jesus referred to himself as the Son of God his contemporaries understood that he was equating himself with God (John 5:17–18).

        4. God not only spoke to us through prophets then, but he also speaks through his own Son. That is the highest and most complete form of communication.

    B. Jesus is the radiance of God's glory (v. 3).

        1. The term *radiance* presents us with a picture of light but not a light which is reflected. No, it is one which radiates of its own accord. That means that Jesus received the light from the Father and brought it himself, undiminished, into our dark world. And just what is this glory which he radiated?

        2. Again we owe our understanding of the term in question to Hebrew usage. On the one hand the term refers to richness and opulence of the kind which brings majesty to its bearer. For that reason Jesus could refer to Solomon who "in all his splendor was [not] dressed like one of these" (that is, like the birds of the air, Matt. 6:29). But the far more important usage of this word always comes within the context of God's self-revelation.

           For example, God reveals his glory to Moses (Exod. 33:18–23). And in Psalm 19:1 we read that the heavens declare the "glory of God."

        3. This glory of God of which the Old Testament so often speaks has shone forth here among us in the person of Christ. "For God, who said, 'Let light shine out of darkness,' made his light shine in our hearts to give us the light of the knowledge of the glory of God in the face of Christ" (2 Cor. 4:6).

    C. Jesus is the exact representation of God's nature (v. 3).

        1. Here we have a second image—that of a stamp, seal, or coin into which a clearly distinct impression has been stamped. Jesus is the imprint which leads to a recognition that there is a God and tells us who he is.

        2. Jesus is also the source of our understanding of the attributes and the character of God. Everyone can look at Jesus and gain an accurate image of God. "Anyone who has seen me has seen the Father" (John 14:9).

II. Jesus' Unique Relationship to the World

    A. Jesus created the world: through Christ God "made the universe" (v. 2).

        1. God created the universe through the agency of Jesus. In the original text one reads "ages" or "eons." Once again we are indebted to Jewish language use for our understanding of this interesting term. The Jew used this word to refer not only to the various epochs but simultaneously to the content of those epochs. In other words, every age has its own content. Thus the term includes both time and space and refers to the whole of the created universe as well as to all of time.

    2. Jesus as Creator is outside of, or independent of, time and space. He created not only that which has material substance but he also initiated time itself. Thus he is timeless or eternal.

    3. To begin to grasp the unfathomable mercy of God one need only reflect upon the fact that this Jesus, who stands above everything, came to earth as a child and voluntarily bound himself to time and space to achieve salvation for people.

B. Jesus sustains the universe: "sustaining all things" (v. 3).

    1. Christ is not only the Creator of the world; he is also the one who now sustains the entire universe and prevents the world around us from devolving into utter chaos. "If it was his intention and he withdrew his spirit and breath, all mankind would perish together and man would return to the dust" (Job 34:14–15).

    2. It is Jesus who provides and controls the energy needed to run the physical world. It is he who represents the middle point of history which he guides to its appointed end. Everything is in some way related to him. He "carries" the cosmos.

C. Jesus owns the world: "appointed heir of all things" (v. 2).

    1. Jesus is the appointed heir of all things. He is the rightful owner of the cosmos. When history reaches its end, he, and he alone, will reign over all of creation.

    2. Even now Jesus exercises that right of ownership, not as though he has had to wrest it from some other power. No, it has always been in his hand, since it is his own creation. All of this gives Jesus incomparable significance, since in him we see and hear that one to whom everything has been entrusted.

III. Jesus' Unique Relationship to Man

A. Jesus is prophet: "God . . . has spoken to us by his Son" (v. 2).

    1. The author of our text presents Christ as the source of divine revelation. Just as the prophets of old he brings the Word of God. However, in contrast to those prophets he lives within the framework of perfect love and flawless unity with God. He has unimpaired insight into God's will and is able to bring us comprehensive, exhaustive revelation.

    2. But his revelation is not only complete; it is at the same time the decisive and concluding disclosure of God's salvific intent. Outside of Christ nothing can or will be done in regard to man's salvation. Christ is the very center of both world history and salvation history.

B. Jesus is priest: "He . . . provided purification for sins" (v. 3).

    1. As truly incarnate man Christ experienced all aspects of human existence. He suffered pain as well as death and was tempted in every way (Heb. 4:15).

    2. Through his death Jesus brought a purification from sin.

    3. The evolution of the term *purification* is interesting. In the Old Testament it usually refers to some ritual practice, such as the

ceremonial washing of the hands. Peter shows us that this can only be acquired through personal faith in Christ (1 Pet. 1:22). John refers to it as a result or fruit of Christ's death (1 John 1:7). In the Book of Hebrews we are told that this cleansing is an unparalleled event in the life of every believer. This implies the forgiveness of our sins.

    4. Thus, Jesus has carried the burden of our sin. He did what we could not do for ourselves.

C. Jesus is king: He "sat down at the right hand of the Majesty" (v. 3).

    1. Having completed his work of salvation Christ took his rightful place at the right hand of God the Father and now shares in his reign. This fulfilled the prophecy: "The LORD says to my Lord: 'Sit at my right hand until I make your enemies a footstool for your feet' " (Ps. 110:1).

    2. We can turn to and trust this sovereign King in all situations of life.

Conclusion: Jesus Christ is the only object worthy of our commitment.

    1. He is the Son of God, who exactly represents God's nature and radiates God's glory.

    2. He is the Creator, Sustainer, and Heir of all creation.

    3. He is mankind's Prophet, Priest, and King.

In this sermon we have sought to present a contextualized message to nominal Christians in Europe. In light of the nominal Christian's need for a worthy object of faith, Christ's unique relationship to God, the world, and man has been emphasized. The style of the sermon represents an attempt to accommodate European expectations. What remains, of course, is an explicit call to commitment. That is, however, best left to the privacy of a personal encounter.

Bibliography

Addison, James Thayer. *The Medieval Missionary*. Philadelphia: Porcupine, 1976.

Allen, J. P. B., and Paul van Buren, eds. *Chomsky: Selected Readings*. New York: Oxford University Press, 1971.

Anderson, Gerald H., ed. *Asian Voices in Christian Theology*. Maryknoll, N.Y.: Orbis, 1976.

Arberry, A. J. *The Koran Interpreted*. New York: Macmillan, 1955.

Ariarajah, S. Wesley. "Towards a Theology of Dialogue." *The Ecumenical Review* 29 (1977):3–11.

"The Authority of the Bible—The Louvain Report." *The Ecumenical Review* 23, 4 (October 1971):419–37.

Bailey, Kenneth E. *Poet and Peasant: A Literary-Cultural Approach to the Parables in Luke*. Grand Rapids: Eerdmans, 1976.

———. *Through Peasant Eyes: A Literary-Cultural Approach to the Parables in Luke*. Grand Rapids: Eerdmans, 1983.

Berlo, David. *The Process of Communication*. New York: Holt, Rinehart and Winston, 1960.

Blauw, Johannes. *The Missionary Nature of the Church*. New York: McGraw-Hill, 1962.

Bridgman, Percy W. *The Logic of Modern Physics*. New York: Macmillan, 1932.

Bright, Jane O., and William Bright. "Semantic Structures in Northwestern California and the Sapir-Whorf Hypothesis." In *Cognitive Anthropology*, edited by Stephen A. Tyler, 66–78. Prospect Heights, Ill.: Waveland, 1987.

Brown, George McAfee. *Theology in a New Key: Responding to Liberation Themes.* Philadelphia: Westminster, 1981.

Bruce, F. F. *The Epistle to the Hebrews.* Grand Rapids: Eerdmans, 1964.

Brunner, Emil. "The Necessity for Dogmatics." In *The Necessity of Systematic Theology*, 2d ed., edited by John Jefferson Davis, 75–84. Grand Rapids: Baker, 1978.

Bultmann, Rudolf. *Jesus Christ and Mythology.* London: SCM, 1960.

Buswell, James O., III. "Contextualization: Theory, Tradition, and Method." In *Theology and Mission*, edited by David J. Hesselgrave, 87–111. Grand Rapids: Baker, 1978.

Caird, G. B. *The Language and Imagery of the Bible.* London: Duckworth, 1980.

Carson, D. A. *Biblical Interpretation and the Church: The Problem of Contextualization.* Nashville: Thomas Nelson, 1985.

Casagrande, Joseph B., and Kenneth L. Hale. "Semantic Relationships in Papago Folk Definitions." In *Studies in Southwestern Ethnolinguistics*, edited by D. Hymes, 85–105. Berlin and New York: Mouton, 1967.

Chase, Stuart. *The Tyranny of Words.* New York: Harcourt, Brace, 1938.

Coe, Shoki. "Contextualizing Theology." In *Mission Trends No. 3*, edited by G. H. Anderson and T. F. Stransky, 19–24. Grand Rapids: Eerdmans; New York: Paulist, 1976.

Conn, Harvie. "Contextualization: A New Dimension for Cross-Cultural Hermeneutics." *Evangelical Missions Quarterly* 14 (1978):39–46.

————. *Eternal Word and Changing Worlds: Theology, Anthropology, and Mission in Trialogue.* Grand Rapids: Zondervan, Academie Books, 1984.

Cotterell, F. Peter. "The Nicodemus Conversation: A Fresh Appraisal." *Expository Times* 96 (May 1985):237–42.

Davis, John Jefferson. "Contextualization and the Nature of Theology." In *The Necessity of Systematic Theology*, 2d ed., edited by John Jefferson Davis, 169–90. Grand Rapids: Baker, 1980.

Demarest, Bruce, and Gordon R. Lewis. *Integrative Theology.* Vol. 1. Grand Rapids: Zondervan, 1987.

Elwood, Douglas J. "Asian Christian Theology in the Making." In *Asian Christian Theology: Emerging Themes*, edited by Douglas J. Elwood, 23–39. Rev. ed. Philadelphia: Westminster, 1980.

————. *What Asian Christians Are Thinking: A Theological Source Book.* Quezon City: New Day, 1978.

England, John C., ed. *Living Theology in Asia Today*. Maryknoll, N.Y.: Orbis, 1982.

Fabun, Don. *Communications: The Transfer of Meaning*. Belmont, Calif.: Glencoe, 1968.

Feld, Helmut. *Der Hebräerbrief*. Darmstadt: Wissenschaftliche Buchgesellschaft, 1985.

Ferm, Deane William. *Third World Liberation Theologies: An Introductory Survey*. Maryknoll, N.Y.: Orbis, 1986.

Fleming, Bruce C. E. *Contextualization of Theology: An Evangelical Assessment*. Pasadena, Calif.: William Carey Library, 1980.

Flessemann-van Leer, Ellen, ed. *The Bible: Its Authority and Interpretation in the Ecumenical Movement*. Geneva: World Council of Churches, 1980.

Flew, Antony. "Theology and Falsification." In *New Essays in Philosophical Theology*, edited by Antony Flew and Alasdair Macintyre, 96–99. London: SCM, 1955.

Geisler, Norman L. "Some Philosophical Perspectives on Missionary Dialogue." In *Theology and Mission*, edited by David J. Hesselgrave, 241–57. Grand Rapids: Baker, 1978.

Geyer, Alan. "Toward a Convivial Theology." *Christian Century* (April 23, 1969):542.

Gibb, H. A. R., and Johannes H. Kramers. *Shorter Encyclopedia of Islam*. Ithaca, N.Y.: Cornell University Press, 1965.

Gross, Edward N. *Is Charles Kraft an Evangelical? A Critique of "Christianity in Culture"*. Collingswood, N.J.: Christian Beacon, 1985.

Gulick, John. *The Middle East: An Anthropological Perspective*. Pacific Palisades, Calif.: Goodyear, 1976.

Gutiérrez, Gustavo. *A Theology of Liberation*. Translated and edited by Caridad Inda and John Eagleson. New York: Orbis, 1973.

Hastings, Adrian. *African Christianity*. New York: Seabury, 1976.

Haye, Sophie de la. *Byang Kato: Ambassador for Christ*. Achimota, Ghana: African Christian, 1986.

Henry, Carl F. H. "Revelation, Special." In *Baker's Dictionary of Theology*, edited by Everett F. Harrison, 458–59. Grand Rapids: Baker, 1960.

Hesselgrave, David J. *Communicating Christ Cross-Culturally: An Introduction to Missionary Communication*. Grand Rapids: Zondervan, 1978.

———. "A Legacy of Enmity." *Moody Monthly* 88 (October 1986): 72–75.

Hick, John. "The Outcome: Dialogue Into Truth." In *Truth and Dialogue in World Religions: Conflicting Truth Claims*, edited by John Hick, 140–55. Philadelphia: Westminster, 1974.

————. *Truth and Dialogue: The Relationship between World Religions.* London: Sheldon, 1974.

Hiebert, Paul G. "Critical Contextualization." In *The Best in Theology,* vol. 2, edited by J. I. Packer and Paul Fromer, 396–99. Carol Stream, Ill.: Christianity Today, n.d.

Hills, Edward F. *The King James Version Defended.* Des Moines: Christian Research, 1956.

Holl, Karl. "Die Missionsmethode der alten und die der mittelalterlichen Kirche." In *Kirchengeschichte als Missionsgeschichte,* vol. 1, *Die Alte Kirche,* edited by H. Frohnes and U. Knorr, 3–17. Munich: Kaiser, 1974.

Holtom, Daniel C. *Modern Japan and Shinto Nationalism.* Chicago: University of Chicago Press, 1943.

Hughes, Thomas Patrick. *Dictionary of Islam.* New Delhi: Oriental, 1976.

Inch, Morris A. *Doing Theology across Cultures.* Grand Rapids: Baker, 1982.

————. *Making the Good News Relevant: Keeping the Gospel Distinctive in Any Culture.* Nashville: Thomas Nelson, 1986.

Irwin, Nathan D. "On What Authority—The Quran or the Bible?" *Trinity World Forum* 5, 1 (1979):6–8.

Jewett, Paul K. "Neo-orthodoxy." In *Baker's Dictionary of Theology,* edited by Everett F. Harrison, 375–79. Grand Rapids: Baker, 1960.

Jordon, Clarence. *The Cotton Patch Version of Matthew and John.* New York: Association, 1973.

Kahl, Hans-Dietrich. "Die ersten Jahrhunderte des missionsgeschichtlichen Mittelalters. Bausteine für eine Phänomenologie bis ca. 1050." In *Kirchengeschichte als Missionsgeschichte,* vol. 2a, *Die Kirche des frühen Mittelalters,* ed. Knut Schäferdiek, 11–76. Munich: Kaiser, 1978.

Kantor, Marvin, and Richard S. White, trans. *The Vita of Constantine and the Vita of Methodius.* Ann Arbor: University of Michigan, 1976.

Käsemann, Ernst. *Der Ruf der Freiheit.* Tübingen: J. C. B. Mohr, 1972.

Kato, Byang H. "The Gospel, Cultural Context, and Religious Syncretism." In *Let the Earth Hear His Voice,* edited by J. D. Douglas, 1216–23. Minneapolis: World Wide, 1975.

————. *Theological Pitfalls in Africa.* Kisumu, Kenya: Evangel, 1975.

King, Robert G. *Fundamentals of Communication.* New York: Macmillan, 1979.

Korzybski, Alfred. *Science and Sanity.* Lancaster, Pa.: The Science Press, 1933.

Koyama, Kosuke. "Thailand: Points of Theological Friction." In *Asian Voices in Christian Theology,* edited by Gerald H. Anderson, 65–86. Maryknoll, N.Y.: Orbis, 1976.

————. *Waterbuffalo Theology.* Maryknoll, N.Y.: Orbis, 1974.

Kraft, Charles H. *Christianity in Culture: A Study in Dynamic Biblical Theologizing in Cross-Cultural Perspective.* Maryknoll, N.Y.: Orbis, 1979.

———. *Communication Theory for Christian Witness.* Nashville: Abingdon, 1983.

———. "Interpreting in Cultural Context." *Journal of the Evangelical Theological Society* 21, 4 (December 1978):357–67.

Langer, Susanne K. *Philosophy in a New Key.* New York: New American Library of World Literature, Mentor Books, 1948.

Larkin, William J., Jr. *Culture and Biblical Hermeneutics: Interpreting and Applying the Authoritative Word in a Relativistic Age.* Grand Rapids: Baker, 1988.

Lehman, Arno. *Es begann in Tranquebar.* Berlin: Evangelische Verlagsanstalt, 1955.

Lewis, C. S. *The Abolition of Man.* New York: Macmillan, 1947.

Lightner, Robert. *Neo-liberalism.* Chicago: Regular Baptist, 1959.

Longacre, Robert. *An Anatomy of Speech Notions.* Lisse, Netherlands: Peter de Ridder, 1977.

Litpay, Lothar. "Christianity and Other Religions." *Communio Viatorum* 22 (Spring/summer 1979): 59–72.

Luther, Martin. *A Commentary on St. Paul's Epistle to the Galatians.* 2d ed. Translated by Theodore Graebner. Grand Rapids: Zondervan, 1939.

Luzbetak, Louis J. *The Church and Cultures.* Techny, Ill.: Divine Word, 1970.

McGavran, Donald A. *The Clash Between Christianity and Cultures.* Washington, D.C.: Canon, 1974.

McIlwain, Trevor. *Building on Firm Foundations.* Sanford, Fla.: New Tribes Mission, 1987.

Malinowski, B. "The Problem of Meaning in Primitive Languages." In *The Meaning of Meaning,* edited by Charles K. Ogden and Ivor A. Richards, 450–51. London: Kegan Paul, Trench, Trubney, 1923.

Matheny, Tim. *Reaching the Arabs: A Felt Need Approach.* Pasadena, Calif.: William Carey Library, 1981.

Mbiti, John M. *African Cultural Revolution and the Christian Faith.* Nigeria: Challenge Publications.

———. *African Religions and Philosophy.* New York: Praeger, 1969; Garden City, N.Y.: Doubleday, Anchor Books, 1970.

———. *Biblical Christianity in Africa.* Achimota, Ghana: African Christian.

———. *Concepts of God in Africa.* New York: Praeger, 1970.

———. *New Testament Eschatology in an African Background.* London: Oxford University Press, 1971.

————. *The Spirits*. Achimota, Ghana: African Christian; Garden City, N.Y.: Doubleday, Anchor Books, 1970.

Metz, Johann Baptist. "Christentum in Politik-jenseits Bürgerlicher Religion." In *Jenseits Bürgerlicher Religion*, 94–112. Munich: Kaiser, 1980.

————. "Kirche und Welt im Lichte einer 'Politischen Theologie.' " In *Zur Theologie der Welt*, edited by Johann Baptist Metz, 99–117. Mainz: Grünewald, 1973.

————. "Politische Theologie des Subjekts als Theologische Kritik der Bürgerlichen Religion." In *Glaube in Geschichte und Gesellschaft*, edited by Johann Baptist Metz, 29–42. Mainz: Grünewald, 1980.

————. *Zur Theologie der Welt*. Mainz: Grünewald, 1973.

Michel, Otto. *Der Brief an die Hebräer*. Gottingen: Vandenhoeck and Ruprecht, 1975.

Míguez-Bonino, José. *Christians and Marxists. The Mutual Challenge to Revolution*. Grand Rapids: Eerdmans, 1976.

————. *Doing Theology in a Revolutionary Situation*. Philadelphia: Fortress, 1975.

————. "For Life and against Death: A Theology That Takes Sides." In *Theologians in Transition*, edited by James Wall, 169–76. New York: Crossroad, 1981.

Moltmann, Jürgen. "Einführung in die 'Theologie der Hoffnung.' " In *Das Experiment der Hoffnung*, edited by Jürgen Moltmann, 64–81. Munich: Kaiser, 1974.

————. *Politische Theologie—Politische Ethik*. Munich: Kaiser, 1984.

————. *A Theology of Hope*. New York: Harper and Row, 1967.

Müller, Karl. *200 Jahre Brüdermission*. Vol. 1. Herrnhut: Verlag der Missionsbuchhandlung, 1931.

Nicholls, Bruce J. *Contextualization: A Theology of Gospel and Culture*. Downers Grove: Inter-Varsity, 1979.

————. "Crucial Questions and a Theology of Gospel and Culture." *Theological News* 10 (1978).

————. "What Is Contextualization of Theology?" *Theological News* (October 1973):

Nida, Eugene A. *Customs and Culture: Anthropology for Christian Missions*. New York: Harper and Row, 1954.

————. *Message and Mission: The Communication of the Christian Faith*. New York: Harper and Row, 1969.

————. *Towards a Science of Translating: With Special Reference to Principles and Procedures Involved in Bible Translating*. Leiden: E. J. Brill, 1964.

Nida, Eugene A., and William D. Reyburn. *Meaning Across Cultures*. American Society of Missiology Series No. 4. Maryknoll, N.Y.: Orbis, 1981.

Nida, Eugene A., et al. *Style and Discourse*. Cape Town, South Africa: The Bible Society, 1983.

Niles, Daniel T. *Buddhism and the Claims of Christ*. Richmond: John Knox, 1967.

"Neo-orthodoxy." In *Corpus Dictionary of Western Churches*, edited by T. C. O'Brien, 531–32. Washington: Corpus Publications, 1970.

Ogden, Charles K., and Ivor A. Richards (with supplementary essays by B. Malinowski and F. G. Crookshank). *The Meaning of Meaning*. 8th ed. New York: Harcourt, Brace, 1946.

Oxnam, Bromley G. *A Testament of Faith*. Boston: Little, Brown, 1958.

Padilla, C. René. "Hermeneutics and Culture—A Theological Perspective." In *Gospel and Culture*, edited by John R. W. Stott and Robert T. Coote, 83–131. Pasadena, Calif.: William Carey Library, 1979.

Pan, James. "Contextualization: A Methodological Enquiry With Examples From The History of Theology." *South East Asia Journal of Theology* 21/22 (1980/81): 51–53.

Parshall, Phil. *New Paths in Muslim Evangelism: Evangelical Approaches to Contextualization*. Grand Rapids: Baker, 1980.

Peters, George W. *A Biblical Theology of Missions*. Chicago: Moody, 1972.

———. "Issues Confronting Evangelical Missions." In *Evangelical Missions Tomorrow*, edited by W. T. Coggins and E. L. Frizen, 156–71. Pasadena, Calif.: William Carey Library, 1977.

Pickering, Wilber N. *The Identity of the New Testament Text*. Nashville: Thomas Nelson, 1977.

Pobee, John S. *Toward an African Theology*. Nashville: Abingdon, 1978.

Prabhavananda, Swami, and Frederick Manchester. *The Upanishads: Breath of the Eternal*. New York: The New American Library, 1957.

"A Preliminary Inquiry by Buddhists and Christians on the Religious Dimensions in Humanity's Relations to Nature." In *Dialogue with People of Living Faiths and Ideologies*, 84–92. Geneva: World Council of Churches, 1978.

Rahner, Karl, and Herbert Vorgrimler. *Kleines Konzilskompendium*. Freiburg: Herder, 1967.

Ramm, Bernard. "Liberalism." In *Baker's Dictionary of Theology*, edited by Everett F. Harrison, 322–23. Grand Rapids: Baker, 1960.

Redfield, Robert. *The Primitive World and Its Transformation*. Ithaca, N.Y.: Cornell University Press, 1957.

Richards, Ivor A. *Practical Criticism*. New York: Harcourt, Brace, 1935.

———. *The Philosophy of Rhetoric*. London: Oxford University Press, 1935.

Rissi, Mathias. *Die Theologie des Hebraerbriefs*. Tübingen: J. B. C. Mohr, 1987.

Richardson, Don. *Peace Child*. Glendale, Calif.: Regal, 1974.

Ro, Bong Rin, and Ruth Eshenauer, eds. *The Bible and Theology in Asian*

Contexts: An Evangelical Perspective on Asian Theology. Taichung, Taiwan: Asia Theological Association, 1984.

———. "Theological Trends in Asia: Asian Theology." *Asian Theological News* 13 (October/December 1987):2–3, 15–17.

Robinson, Charles, trans. *Anskar: Apostle of the North.* From Rimbert's *Vita Anskarii.* London: SPG, 1921.

Rogers, Jack B., and Donald K. McKim. *The Authority and Interpretation of the Bible: An Historical Approach.* San Francisco: Harper and Row, 1979.

Rommen, Edward. *Namenschristentum.* Bad Liebenzell: Verlag der Liebenzeller Mission, 1985.

Samartha, Stanley J. "Dialogue Between Men of Living Faiths, the Ajaltoun Memorandum." In *Dialogue Between Men of Living Faiths,* edited by Stanley J. Samartha, 114. Geneva: World Council of Churches, 1971.

Sapir, Edward. "Communication." In *The Psychology of Language, Thought, and Instruction: Readings,* edited by J. P. De Cecco, 75–78. New York: Holt, Rinehart and Winston, 1967.

———. *Language.* New York: Harcourt, Brace and World, 1921.

Shannon, C. E., and W. Weaver. *The Mathematical Theory of Communication.* Urbana, Ill.: University of Illinois Press, 1964.

Sharpe, Eric J. *Fifty Key Words: Comparative Religion.* Richmond: John Knox, 1971.

Shaw, R. Daniel. *Transculturation. The Cultural Factor in Transculturation. The Cultural Factor in Translation and Other Communication Tasks.* Pasadena, Calif.: William Carey Library, 1988.

Smith, Wilfred Cantwell. *Towards a World Theology: Faith and the Comparative History of Religion.* Philadelphia: Westminster, 1981.

Soden, Hans von. "Die Christliche Mission in Altertum und Gegenwart." In *Kirchengeschichte als Missionsgeschichte,* vol. 1, *Die Alte Kirche,* 22–31. Munich: Kaiser, 1974.

Spradley, James P. "Foundations of Cultural Knowledge." In *Culture and Cognition: Rules, Maps and Plans,* edited by James P. Spradley, 3–38. Prospect Heights, Ill.: Waveland, 1987.

———. *Participant Observation.* New York: Holt, Rinehart and Winston, 1980.

Stott, John R. W. and Robert T. Coote, eds. *Down to Earth: Studies in Christianity and Culture.* Grand Rapids: Eerdmans, 1980.

Sumithra, Sunand, and Bruce J. Nicholls. "Critique of Theology in Indian Cultures." In *The Bible and Theology in Asian Contexts: An Evangelical Perspective on Asian Theology,* edited by Bong Rin Ro and Ruth Eshenauer, 196–97. Taichung, Taiwan: Asia Theological Association, 1984.

Szczesny, Gerhard. *The Future of Unbelief.* New York: G. Braziller, 1961.

Taber, Charles. "Hermeneutics and Culture: An Anthropological Perspective."

In *Gospel and Culture*, edited by John R. W. Stott and Robert T. Coote, 129–30. Pasadena, Calif.: William Carey Library, 1979.

Theological Education Fund (TEF) Staff. *Ministry in Context: The Third Mandate Programme of the Theological Education Fund (1970–77)*. Bromley, Kent, England: Theological Education Fund, 1972.

Thiselton, Anthony C. *The Two Horizons: New Testament Hermeneutics and Philosophical Description With Special Reference to Heidegger, Bultmann, Gadamer, and Wittgenstein*. Grand Rapids: Eerdmans, 1980.

Thomas, M. M. *The Acknowledged Christ of the Indian Renaissance*. Bangalore: Christian Institute for the Study of Religion and Society, 1970.

————. "India: Toward an Indigenous Christian Theology." In *Asian Voices in Christian Theology*, edited by Gerald H. Anderson, 11–35. Maryknoll, N.Y.: Orbis, 1976.

————. *Man and the Universe of Faiths*. Madras: Christian Literature Society, 1975.

————. *Secular Theologies of India and the Secular Meaning of Christ*. Bangalore: Christian Institute for the Study of Religion and Society, 1976.

————. "Theological Insights for a Secular Anthropology." In *Asian Christian Theology: Emerging Themes*, edited by Douglas J. Elwood, 289–98. Rev. ed. Philadelphia: Westminster, 1980.

Thundy, Zacharias P. *Religions in Dialogue: East and West Meet*. Edited by Kuncheria Pathil and Frank Podgorski. Lanham, Md.: University Press of America, 1985.

Tienou, Tite. "The Church in African Theology: Description and Analysis of Hermeneutical Presuppositions." In *Biblical Interpretation and the Church: Text and Context*, edited by D. A. Carson, 151–65. Exeter: Paternoster, 1984.

Torres, Sergio. "Opening Address." In *African Theology en Route*, edited by Kofi Appiah-Kubi and Sergio Torres, 3–9. Maryknoll, N.Y.: Orbis, 1979.

Triebel, Johannes. *Bekehrung*. Erlangen: Verlage der lutherischen Mission, 1976.

Troeltsch, Ernst. *Die Absolutheit des Christentums*. Munich: Kaiser, 1969.

Warfield, B. B. "The Idea of Systematic Theology." In *The Necessity of Systematic Theology*, 2d ed., edited by John Jefferson Davis, 127–67. Grand Rapids: Baker, 1978.

————. *The Inspiration and Authority of the Bible*. London: Marshall, Morgan and Scott, 1951.

Watt, W. Montgomery. *Islamic Revelation in the Modern World*. Edinburgh: University Press, 1969.

Weber, Hans-Reudi. *The Communication of the Gospel to Illiterates: Based on a Missionary Experience in Indonesia*. London: SCM, 1957.

Werner, Oswald, and Gladys Levis-Pilz. "Memory and Context: Toward a Theory of Context in Ethnoscience." In *Language and Logic in Personality and Society,* edited by Harwood Fisher, 55–92. New York: Columbia University Press, 1985.

Werner, Oswald, and G. Mark Schoepfle. *Systematic Fieldwork,* vol. 1, *Foundations of Ethnography and Interviewing.* Beverly Hills, Calif.: Sage, 1987.

Whorf, Benjamin Lee. *Language, Thought and Reality. Selected Writings of Benjamin Lee Whorf.* Edited by John B. Carroll. Cambridge, Mass: M.I.T. Press, 1956.

Yoder, Percy B. *Toward Understanding the Bible.* Newton, Kans.: Faith and Life, 1978.

Zwemer, Samuel. *The Heirs of the Prophets.* Chicago: Moody, 1946.

Index of Subjects

AACC. *See* All-Africa Council of Churches

Abraham: in Indian context, 233; theology of hope, 44

Absolutes: language and, 181–82, 184, 187, 188, 189–91; theological system, 155

Abstraction: Chinese and, 224; language and, 207; levels of, 66; in semantics, 184; symbols and, 188, 190. *See also* Concrete relational thinking

Accommodation, cross-cultural: Asian issue, 83; limits to, 125; New Testament, 8–11; Old Testament, 5–6; lack of, 224

Accommodation theologies: African, 98, 107–11; Asian, 72; Middle Eastern, 123–26

Actual time, African concept of, 101

Adaptation, cross-cultural: in contextualization, 149. *See also* Accomodation, cross-cultural

Adventus, Moltmann concept of, 45, 45 n

Africa: Christianity superficial in, 99; church growth, 96; concrete relational thought, 206, 208; Kato proposal for, 110–11

African theology: described, 96–97; Kato assessment of, 106–12; Mbiti theology, 98–106

Agbeti, J. K., 98

Ajaltoun (Lebanon) Consultation. *See* "Dialogue Between Men of Living Faiths"

All-Africa Council of Churches (AACC), 108

Allah, 135–36

Allman, Daniel von, 54, 65

Alves, Rubem, 87

Anderson, Rufus, 32

Andrews, Charles F., 76

Anfechtung, Thai contextualization of, 84, 176

Anglo-American church: contextualization in, 50–51; effect of war on, 48

Animistic worldview, 83, 220

Ansgar, Bishop of Hamburg, 20, 21–22

Apatheia (Thai dispassionate worldview), 81

Apologetical theology, 213

Apologetics: contextualization continuum, 148; early church, 16–19; liberal